MAGISTRATES' COMPANION TO THE COMPETENCES

2nd Edition

By JANET CARTER
LL.B (Hons), Barrister, DPMS, MCIPD

First published April 2000
2nd edition published May 2001

Lawtexts,
PO Box 289,
Leeds LS6 3YD

ISBN 0-9540636-0-0

CONTENTS

(N.B. Competence 11 (liquor licensing) is not included, as a comprehensive training pack has been prepared and circulated to all courts by the Justices' Clerks' Society.)

Dedicated to the memory of my mum, dad and aunt Mary

ACKNOWLEDGEMENTS

For their advice and input I thank Mark Adamson, Gordon Airy, Mohammed Rashid Ali, J.P., Ruth Allan (Youth Justice Board), Sallie Davies, J.P., Lesley Gunawan, Brian Holland, David Jennings, Travis Johnson, J.P., Ann Robinson, Jodie Sheppard and Ian Webster.

For their patience, support and encouragement I thank my husband Neil and our sons, John and Andrew.

PREFACE

Magistrates have enormous powers which fundamentally affect people's lives every day. A choice of one option rather than another and the way that something is said or done in court, can make a real difference to the individual concerned and to the community we live in. Every magistrate has a role in the retiring room to suggest options and penalty combinations based on their own views and initiative, rather than on the representations made by the advocates in court. Every chairman has the opportunity to build a rapport, create an impression and make an impact. Fair and imaginative decisions and delivery need sound basic knowledge and awareness which is drawn together from a variety of sources into this one book.

It is a comprehensive textbook for magistrates about the powers and procedures of the adult court, the youth court and the family court. It can be used in a variety of ways to deal with different individual needs.

For the new magistrate, or new panel member, it encompasses all the 'need to know' information. For the experienced magistrate, mentor and appraiser, it provides an update of law and practice in order to remain abreast of the many changes and developments over recent years, along with the benefit of numerous examples and practical discussion. The new sentencing guidelines and options are explained in detail together with the impact of the Human Rights Act and recent case law and guidance which has resolved many of the issues raised in the first edition.

For the magistrate who is preparing for appraisal, the information is set out under each competence heading as listed in the personal development log and enables easy, 'dip-in' access to any selected areas, with the option of a self-test quiz to test out personal knowledge.

Throughout the text I have used the masculine gender purely to avoid tedious reference to both genders – please assume the feminine as equally applicable. I have stated the law to the best of my understanding as at the 26th March 2001.

It sets out to be a Companion – factual where necessary, conversational where appropriate, and friendly and supportive throughout.

Janet Carter,
Leeds,
March 2001.

CHAPTER 1
COMPETENCE 1
The framework within which magistrates operate

INTRODUCTION

This chapter sets out the context of the magistrates' court in relation to the higher courts, together with an outline of the main players and court users. It also includes a summary of the Human Rights Act 1998 which impacts on many aspects of the magistrates' court and its functions.

The structure of the judicial system

Most appraisal schemes simply seek an outline knowledge of the court structure which is in any event subject to the review of The Right Honourable Lord Justice Auld. The report will be published during 2001, but it is unlikely to produce overnight transformation. The diagram below shows the hierarchy of the courts and the appeal route.

1.1 The High Court

1.1.1 The House of Lords is the ultimate domestic appeal court and deals with appeals on points of law which involve matters of public importance.

1.1.2 The Court of Appeal is made up of two divisions – the Civil Division and the Criminal Division. The hearing is not a rehearing with all the evidence, but merely a review of the lower court's decision. However fresh evidence may be admitted if it is in the interests of justice to do so.

1.1.3 The High Court is made up of three divisions – Chancery, Family and Queen's Bench Division. The Queen's Bench Division is the largest of the three and its work includes dealing with criminal appeals originating primarily from the magistrates' court. Such appeals relate to interpretation of the law on a question set down by the magistrates or prosecutor or by way of judicial review. Trials in the High Court are heard either in London or in one of the 26 provincial trial centres.

The decisions of the above courts are binding on the magistrates' court, provided that they are compatible with the Human Rights Act.

COMPETENCE 1

1.1 The structure of the Judicial System

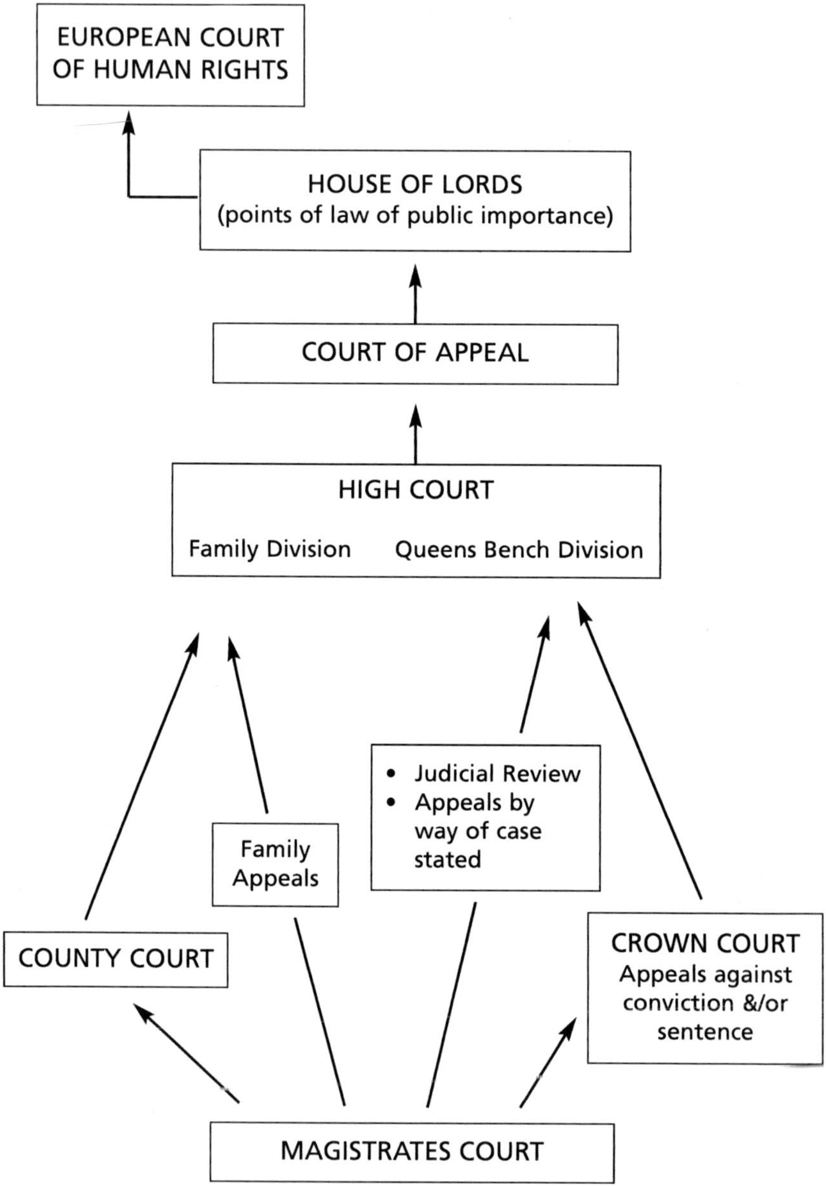

1.2 The Civil Division/County Court

Civil matters include family cases, probate disputes and personal injury claims and appeal is to the Civil Division of the Court of Appeal.

Whilst the magistrates' court has some civil jurisdiction, predominantly, family law cases and licensing, the bulk of civil matters are dealt with in the County Court or the High Court.

Victims in magistrates' courts' cases may well pursue the civil aspect of their case in the County Court e.g. compensation claims arising from traffic accidents, disputed compensation claims arising from criminal charges.

1.3 The Criminal Division/Crown Court

Appeal on criminal matters is to the Criminal Division of the Court of Appeal which is presided over by the Lord Chief Justice.

Criminal work is dealt with by the magistrates' court and the crown court. In fact the crown court only deals with about 5% of criminal cases and juries only decide about 1% of criminal cases (Elliot and Quinn, 1998).

Between one and four magistrates sit on appeals to the crown court, depending upon the type of case, along with the circuit judge or recorder. The decision is that of the majority on the bench and the magistrates carry equal weight to the professional judge, unless a casting vote is required. The judge or recorder presides and his rulings on legal matters bind the magistrates.

1.4 The Magistrates' Courts - Summary Justice

The country is divided geographically into commissions which are then subdivided into petty sessional areas, with benches of lay magistrates. There are about 31,000 lay magistrates, hearing over one million criminal cases a year – 95% of all criminal cases. Additionally there are approximately 182 district judges (magistrates' courts), formerly known as stipendiary magistrates.

1.5 Appeals from magistrates' courts

1.5.1 Criminal appeals to the crown court against conviction/sentence

The appeal is based on fact only e.g. whether the defendant intended to steal the property or not. Dealing with an appeal involves rehearing the case. The parties are not confined to the evidence given in the magistrates' court.

crown court will give reasoning for any different decision and the magistrates involved in the original case are entitled to see the reasons.

Example:

Custodial sentence is too severe for this defendant who has never served a custodial penalty before and has taken positive steps to deal with his drug addiction – reduced from 4 months imprisonment to 28 days enabling immediate release to re-commence drug rehabilitation programme.

1.5.2 Civil appeals

Appeals concerning family proceedings go to the Family Division of the High Court. Appeals on licensing matters are heard by the crown court.

1.5.3 Appeal to High Court by way of case stated

This type of appeal relates to a question of law or jurisdiction (as opposed to fact). The proceedings are questioned on the ground that it is wrong in law or in excess of jurisdiction, by requesting the court to state a case for the opinion of the High Court. Never be influenced by solicitors who 'threaten appeal'. There is no discredit in a decision being appealed provided that you have taken the advice of the legal adviser and have announced and recorded good reasons for your decision.

The appeal is heard by 2 or 3 judges of the Queen's Bench Division of the Divisional Court in respect of criminal matters, who simply hear counsel from each side. The court may confirm, reverse or vary the decision; give the magistrates their opinion of the relevant point of law; or make such other order as it sees fit, which may include ordering a rehearing before a different bench.

1.5.4 Appeal to High Court by way of application for judicial review

The review is limited to considering whether the magistrates' court has failed to exercise its jurisdiction properly or whether it has come to some error of law which appears on the face of the record. It is not focused on the decision, but on the decision-making process.

The decision may be quashed and remitted back to the magistrates with a direction to reconsider it and reach a decision in accordance with the findings of the High Court or damages and remedies may be ordered by the High Court. Application must be made within 3 months of the date when grounds for the application first arose.

Judicial review is not an appeal as such but a challenge to the decision making process and leave must be obtained from a High Court judge that there is an arguable case.

1.5.5 Appeal from the High Court

On a criminal matter, the High Court must first certify that a point of law of general public importance is involved in the decision and leave must be given for the appeal to the Court of Appeal. Leave is not usually required for an appeal on a civil matter.

1.5.6 Petition to the European Commission of Human Rights

The European Commission ceased to exist in October 1999. There is now only a single full-time European Court of Human Rights (see 1.7).

1.6 The European Court of Justice and EC law (*distinguish from the European Court of Human Rights!*)

This court sits in Luxembourg and deals with disputes arising from European Union legislation. The European Union is derived from the previous European Economic Union (EEC) and basically deals with economic and social policy which aims to reduce barriers for the free movement of resources. As one of the 15 members of the Union, the English courts must apply EC law even if it conflicts with English Law. In fact EC law is very rarely quoted or argued in the magistrates' court.

1.7 The European Convention on Human Rights and the Human Rights Act 1998

1.7.1 The European Convention

In the aftermath of World War II, the Council of Europe, established by the governments of Western Europe, drew up a set of universal human rights which were proclaimed in the European Convention of Human Rights and Fundamental Freedoms in November 1950. The Convention was drafted mainly by British lawyers and sought to ensure that the war atrocities would never be repeated and that basic rights and freedoms would be guaranteed.

The objective of the Convention was 'the protection of individual Human Rights, and the maintenance and promotion of the ideals and values of a democratic society. These values are pluralism (*members of minority groups are able to maintain independent traditions*), tolerance and broadmindedness.'

The European Convention on Human Rights came into force in international law in 1953. Originally it permitted states to take actions against one another before the European Court of Human Rights. In 1966 the United Kingdom recognised the right of individual petition with respect to its own citizens.

The final step of incorporation of much of the Convention into our domestic law lies in the Human Rights Act 1998, implemented in October 2000. This entitles individuals to argue Convention rights in the UK courts and places responsibility on all public authorities, including the courts, to apply Convention rights.

1.7.2 Human Rights Act 1998 (a summary)

1. The Act does not create any new offences.
2. It simply creates a 'new way of thinking,' which emphasises freedom, fairness and flexibility.
3. It does this by incorporating most of the Convention rights, set out in Articles and Protocols into our domestic law and stating that we must take account of Convention case law and interpret our own domestic legislation and case law compatibly if at all possible.
4. Some Articles give ABSOLUTE RIGHTS which we must interpret 'absolutely' with the Convention and its case law. We have no room for manoeuvre, e.g. prohibition of slavery (Article 4), no punishment without clear definition of what the legal situation is (Article 7).
5. Some Articles give LIMITED RIGHTS which apply unless the specific limitations apply, e.g. Article 5 - right to liberty except in limited circumstances e.g. after conviction, if necessary to prevent offending or absconding.
6. Some Articles give QUALIFIED RIGHTS which carry qualifications as to whether the rights apply or not in a particular situation. These are the rights which are argued most commonly in the magistrates' courts because they are engaged whenever the court seeks to interfere with someone's private life and activities. This, of course, is a situation which arises with most types of bail condition and sentence – most of them do actually impact on how, where and with whom, the defendant chooses to spend his time.
   The qualified rights are the right to private and family life; thought, conscience and religion; expression, assembly and association. Once a qualified right is engaged 'the 3 questions' must be considered. Taking an example of a bail condition of night-time curfew. This clearly interferes with the right to private and family life (Article 8).

   (1) Is the interference, legal, clear and accessible? *Yes, the Bail Act allows the court to impose such a bail condition if the relevant statutory*

exception applies and any member of the public can obtain and read the Bail Act if they so wish.

(2) Does the interference pursue a legitimate aim? *Yes, the usual aims of bail conditions (and sentences) are 'to prevent crime and disorder' or 'protect the rights, freedoms or morals of others'.*

(3) Is the interference proportionate i.e. not a 'sledgehammer to crack a nut'? *Yes, if it is a serious offence, committed during night-time hours and there is a real risk of repetition. No, if it is a minor offence, committed during daylight hours.*

The reality if that advocates accept that the interference (i.e. the court order), is legal and pursues a legitimate aim and these 2 questions are usually 'taken as read'. The argument lies as to whether any interference with rights and freedoms is actually proportionate to the crime and the circumstances. It is therefore an important part of any decision-making process to check whether the outcome e.g. restrictive bail condition or sentence, is proportionate and include this consideration in the reasons. The final question before making any court order must therefore be, 'Is the interference/i.e. the order, proportionate?'

7. Reasons must be given for all decisions in order to show compliance with Article 6 which gives the 'right to a fair trial'. The Article requires a 'fair ... hearing' by 'an independent and impartial tribunal' and very significantly, also requires, judgements to be 'pronounced publicly' (except in limited circumstances). It is important to announce that the court considers that the order is proportionate as this effectively states that rights and freedoms have been properly considered.
8. All public authorities must act compatibly with the Convention. This includes the court and most of the agencies which the court comes into contact with e.g. police, local authorities.

Further detail and a suggested structured approach to dealing with Human Rights Act issues is given in appendix 1, along with relevant commentary throughout the text.

The Criminal Justice System

1.8 The respective roles of the Home Office and the Lord Chancellor's Department

The Home Office is responsible for policy and legislation regarding the police, probation service, prisons, national security, immigration, elections and civil rights.

The Lord Chancellor's Department is responsible for the administration of the court system, the appointment of judges and magistrates, legal aid and contributes to the work on law reform. The Lord Chancellor is the head of the domestic judiciary and is qualified to sit as a judge in the House of Lords.

1.9 The role of the police, prison and probation service

The police are responsible for the detection, apprehension and institution of criminal proceedings.

The prison service is responsible for the accommodation of defendants who are remanded in custody or sentenced to custodial sentences.

The new National Probation Service (April 2001), now described as a 'law enforcement agency', is responsible for assisting courts in making sentencing decisions and providing for the supervision and rehabilitation of offenders. The overriding aims of the service are to protect the public, reduce re-offending and provide for the proper punishment of offenders. (See also 1.30).

1.10 The Crown Prosecution Service (CPS)

Subject to a few exceptions, the Crown Prosecution Service is responsible for conducting all police prosecutions. The service is independent of the police and has been in existence since 1986. The CPS lawyers review each file, decide whether or not to prosecute and if so, appear in court to present the prosecution case. Each of the 31 areas is headed by a Chief Crown Prosecutor and the service as a whole is headed by the Director of Public Prosecutions (see also 2.19 for fuller discussion).

1.11 Other prosecuting agencies and court users

There are numerous prosecuting agencies which prosecute a variety of matters including the following:

- British Transport Police – e.g. trespass on the railway lines, urinating in public areas around railway stations
- Vehicle Inspectorate – e.g. overloaded vehicles
- Trading Standards Department – e.g. breach of Trade Descriptions Act
- Environment Agency – e.g. water pollution, no fishing licence
- Department of Transport – e.g. no vehicle excise licence, fail to notify change of ownership
- RSPCA – e.g. cruelty to animals
- H.M. Customs and Excise – e.g. fail to pay duty
- Post Office – e.g. theft of postal packages by postmen.

1.12 The legal profession and paralegal service providers

The legal profession is made up of solicitors, barristers, legal executives. There are around 70,000 solicitors and a number specialise in representing defendants in the magistrates' court. Barristers appear occasionally in the magistrates' court upon the instructions of a solicitor as they cannot be approached directly by the defendant. Additionally there is a growing number of paralegal support staff who may pursue a one year diploma programme which will move them into a fee earning role. In 1999, provision was made for the prosecution of straightforward guilty plea criminal cases by lay presenters, rather than by solicitors/barristers.

1.13 The variety of legislation under which matters are brought before the court

Most criminal prosecutions in the magistrates' court are brought under the following statutes which each carry definitions of the various offences and penalties:

- Theft Act 1968 – theft, robbery, burglary, handling stolen goods, taking a motor vehicle without consent, going equipped for theft, deception
- Public Order Act 1986 – violent disorder, affray, causing harassment, alarm or distress, threatening behaviour
- Road Traffic Acts – dangerous driving, speeding, no insurance
- Offences against the Person Act 1861 – assault occasioning actual bodily harm, wounding
- Misuse of Drugs Act 1971 – possession and supply of illegal drugs e.g. ecstasy, heroin, cannabis
- Criminal Damage Act 1971 – criminal damage and arson.

The statutory law is further developed and interpreted through rules, regulations and case law. Cases are also brought before the court under local bye-laws.

Civil Cases in the magistrates' courts

1.14 Community safety legislation

In recognition of the different problems in different localities, local communities must now create a crime reduction strategy. New orders are also available to control behaviour which is considered by the court to be 'anti-social'; to control the movements of registered sex offenders and to enable curfews to be enforced on children under the age of 10 (see 2.4 for fuller discussion).

1.15 General licensing

Most of the court's liquor licensing functions are performed by the licensing committee which is appointed by the bench at the Annual General Meeting in October. It consists of between 5 and 20 magistrates. The committee's duties include the following:

- To grant, renew, revoke, transfer and remove licences of licensed premises – e.g. public houses, licensed restaurants, off-licensed shops, licensed clubs.
- Consent to the alteration of licensed premises.
- Grant of occasional permissions.
- Fix or vary the general licensing hours for the district.

The licensee must be considered by the committee to be a 'fit and proper person' and the premises must be suitable.

A lay bench deals on a regular basis with the following matters:

- To grant protection orders (temporary authorisations) prior to full transfer.
- Interim authorities (initially valid for 28 days).
- Occasional licences for supply of liquor in unlicensed premises for particular events.
- Extensions of licensing hours for special events.
- Registered club licences (premises, contents and profits belong to members).

(See 2.6 for fuller discussion of licensing matters dealt with by a lay bench).

The other licensing committee is the betting and gaming committee which is also appointed by the bench at the Annual General Meeting in October. It consists of between 5 and 15 magistrates and deals with the following matters:

- Applications to grant, renew or cancel bookmakers' permits, betting office licences and agency permits.
- Gaming licences (applicant must first obtain certificate of consent from the Gaming Board of Great Britain).
- Bingo club licences.
- Gaming machine registration certificates (by 'qualifying' clubs– maximum of three gaming machines – maximum stake of 50p).
- Registration certificates for members' clubs for gaming (gaming must be the principal purpose of the club).

1.16 The role of local authorities

The local authority plays an active part in the work of the court and includes the following:

- Bringing care and supervision proceedings in respect of children in the family court and Emergency Protection Order applications to any magistrate.
- Enforcement of council tax.
- Enforcement of relevant legislation e.g. Food and Environment Protection Act 1985, local parking offences, noise pollution, etc.

1.17 Other agencies and court users

Examples of the various prosecuting agencies are listed at 1.11. The expression 'court users' also encompasses the Crown Prosecution Service, defence advocates, the Probation Service, Youth Offending Team, the police and prisoner escort services.

Local area and community competences 1.18 to 1.25

There are various sources of information which will assist in drawing up a back-cloth for the cases which come before the court in terms of 'who are we dealing with?' and 'where do they come from?'

The next National Census will be in 2001. Unfortunately the information carried in the last census, 1991, is likely to be very much out of date, but details can be obtained from the local library.

Further information can be obtained from the local authority, in particular the Community Safety Strategy document (see 2.4). This statutory document has a 3-year life and in most strategies there will be an introduction as to the make up of the community which will provide useful information for magistrates.

1.18 Crime statistics

Crime statistics published in January 2001, based on offences notified to the police for the 12 months ending September 2000 reveal the following facts:

- 5.2 million notified offences, with an overall fall of 0.2%.
- Robberies rose by 20.8% (much of which is blamed on robberies of mobile phones from and by teenagers).
- Violent crime rose by 6.8%.

- Drug offences, particularly possession of cannabis down by 11%.
- Burglary down by 8%.
- Theft of and from motor vehicles down by 6%.
- 8 out of 10 of the most rural forces recorded drops in overall offending.

The most helpful local resource is the Chief Constable's Annual Report which gives information about the local police divisions, recorded crime statistics, arrests, traffic management, public order input, community policing and resources.

Bench membership, committees, etc.

1.27 Magistrates' Courts Committee (MCC)

The magistrates' courts are managed by 42 magistrates' courts committees. They are financed by the local authority with a grant of 80% from central funds. The slice of the central cake is cash limited and is based upon various formulae which includes the performance related aspect of case completion.

Membership is determined by a selection panel which is made up representatives from each bench if the committee is made up of 2 or more petty sessions areas. Candidates must be active magistrates. Nomination is by a magistrate and seconded by 3 other magistrates. Membership is for a period of up to 3 years with the right to be re-selected up to a maximum service of 9 years. The committee consists of no more than 12 members including any co-opted members (except Inner London). A statutory code of conduct applies to committee members and selection panels.

The general powers and duties of the committee include the following:

- Responsible for the 'efficient and effective' administration of the magistrates' courts for their area.
- Make and administer schemes providing for training courses for magistrates.
- Appoint a justices' chief executive and justices' clerk(s).
- Produce strategic plans and annual reports to the Lord Chancellor's Department.
- Abide by directions to keep magistrates informed as to the activities of the committee and ascertain views on particular matters.

Sub-committees usually cover specific functions e.g. buildings, court facilities, finance and information technology, training.

1.28 Local Advisory Committee

Magistrates are appointed by the Lord Chancellor on behalf of the Crown, on the recommendation of the Lord Chancellor's Advisory Committees or by the Chancellor of the Duchy of Lancaster (Greater Manchester, Merseyside and Lancashire).

Members of the local advisory committee are appointed by the Lord Chancellor. This follows an interview and a recommendation from the advisory committee appointments panel. The panel normally consists of the advisory committee chairman, or his nominee and any two members of the committee, one of whom must be a non-magistrate.

The committee size is not stipulated, but should ensure that there are sufficient members to provide panels of a minimum of two for first stage interviews and three for second stage interviews. So far as practicable, one member of the panel should be a non-magistrate i.e. about 1/3 of the committee membership should be non-magistrates. There is no expectation that every member should see every candidate.

The term of office is for nine years and should only be extended in exceptional circumstances.

The duties of the committee include the following:

- Determine the number of magistrates to be recommended each year.
- Recruit and recommend magistrates.
- Aim for a balanced bench to reflect the local community in terms of gender, ethnic origin, geographical spread, occupation and political affiliation.
- Consider the case for appointment of a district judge and make recommendations.
- Ensure that magistrates fulfil their undertaking to sit and undertake training.
- Consider and where appropriate make recommendations about the conduct and competence of magistrates

(Lord Chancellors Directions for Advisory Committees on Justices of the Peace 1998).

Directions have recently been given to advisory committees that the Lord Chancellor has relaxed the requirement to achieve average sittings of about 35 half days per annum (not to be confused with the 26 half days minimum).

1.29 Specialist panels

The two obligatory specialist panels are the youth panel and the family panel which each service the relevant courts. Members are appointed at the

October Annual General Meeting and serve for three years. Whilst it is possible to serve on both panels, this may be onerous as the work is specialised and both youth and family law is in a state of constant change. Specialised training is required and appraisal is conducted on the specialised competences (see competences 7 and 9). Panel members must meet at least twice a year. The number of panel members is fixed to ensure that:

- Magistrates are available to sit, with a man and a woman on each bench so far as practicable and
- Magistrates achieve at least 18 sittings in the adult court and about 13 sittings on a panel in order to maintain continuity of experience in both courts.

The Lord Chancellor has indicated that 70 half day sittings is a reasonable maximum for those sitting solely in adult court. However, a maximum of 100 sittings per annum is acceptable for those sitting on specialist panels.

Many courts also choose to have a specialist fine enforcement panel. Specific competences in relation to enforcement (competence 12) are particularly relevant to panel members but should arguably be demonstrated by the full bench.

1.30 Probation Liaison Committee

Statutory probation liaison committees ceased to exist on 1st April 2001, when the probation service structure altered fundamentally. Instead of 54 separate and independent probation services, each governed by a probation committee, there is now a single unified service, the National Probation Service (NPS) for England and Wales with a National Director, who reports to the Home Secretary. The NPS is administered by 42 local boards, which tie in with the police areas and a London service. The boards do not carry any automatic membership of magistrates, unlike the previous probation committees.

Discretionary liaison arrangements are expected to continue in a format to suit local requirements in order to provide a vehicle for information and feedback between the court and the probation service.

1.31 Bench Training and Development Committee (BTDC)

The committee is either elected or selected at the Annual General meeting. The choice of election or selection is a matter for each bench. There are between 3 and 12 members – again, a matter of choice provided that the number is a multiple of 3 to enable 1/3 to retire each year. The maximum period of membership is 6 years.

The role of the committee is to:

- Compile annually a list of approved chairmen – by September 2002, 'approved' chairmen effectively should be described as 'appraised as competent within the past 3 years'.
- Determine the necessary number of chairmen – based on the maximum average sittings of the chairmen on the approved list and ensuring a sufficiency of chairmanship sittings to ensure experience is sustained.
- Removal of a chairman from the approved list – whether following an unsatisfactory appraisal or advisory committee notification.
- Devise and keep under review a scheme of appraisal.
- Devise and keep under review a scheme for the mentoring of new magistrates.
- Select, appoint, train and monitor appraisers and mentors – in practical terms there is an important liaison role to meet on a regular basis at least with a representative of each team, if not the full team.
- Select magistrates to undertake chairmanship training against agreed criteria – at least, this should be subject a satisfactory appraisal on the basic competences.
- Receive appraisal reports to determine whether magistrates meet the competence requirements.
- Convey identified training needs as required to the MCC and the Training Manager.

1.32 The role of the Liaison Judge

Each magistrates' court is allocated a liaison judge. This is an excellent relationship to enable queries or concerns to be answered and resolved between the magistrates' court and the crown court. The intention is also that the liaison judge can become involved in training presentations and facilitating visits to the crown court. This helps to develop a clear understanding of the type of cases which should be committed and what actually happens in committals for sentence, plea and directions hearings, committals for trial and bail appeal cases in chambers.

Bench practices and culture

1.33 Sitting patterns

The Lord Chancellor expects magistrates to sit in court on at least 26 half days per year but hopes that most magistrates will be able to sit for at least 35 half days. His view is that adult only magistrates should sit for a maximum of 70 half day sittings and panel members for a maximum of 100 half day sittings.

Sitting patterns vary on each bench, and are organised in various ways which include computerised annual/quarterly/monthly rotas by some and weekly liaison with the listing office by others. The benches for various courts may be determined on an annual basis or may be determined on the day. Some benches will expect magistrates to be available for full days and list cases accordingly; others operate on jig-saws of half day availability.

Since the introduction of MNTI there is a need for greater flexibility in changing bench make-up at relatively short notice. Mentors must be listed to sit with their new magistrates and on a wider basis there is a need to list appraisers with their appraisees. These arrangements obviously compound the usual day-to-day difficulties of unforeseen absences; ensuring a male/female mix in the panel courts if at all possible; preserving tied bench matters for sentence and avoiding the situation of magistrates sitting on trials where they have recent previous knowledge of the defendant.

1.34 Bench policies and procedures

An important feature of lay justice is the element of 'local justice.' Different areas have different problems to deal with e.g. areas which are ethnically sensitive, football hooliganism, and even urinating in city centre taxi rank areas! Such problems have to be catered for, possibly by discussion with other local agencies so that the court can play an effective co-operative role when court proceedings are necessary. This may well result in local policy and procedures e.g. annual meetings with ethnic minority community leaders; local fine tariff guidelines for urinating in a public place.

Bench procedures, as opposed to policies, are likely to be formulated by the justices' clerk. They are usually conveyed as training information in order to deal with local situations and with changes in the law (which often arise at very short notice!). Policies on the other hand are matters for discussion between the clerk, the bench chairmen and possibly the full bench at the half yearly bench meeting or at the Annual General Meeting. Many benches now have regular newsletters as well as the correspondence which frequently goes out to the full bench.

1.35 Approaches to training, mentoring and appraisal

The training function is now held predominantly by the bench training and development committee (BTDC see 1.31) who will refer needs to the magistrates' court's committee who effectively hold the purse strings, possibly through a training sub-committee.

The training requirements are now governed by the relevant competences which are set out in the personal development log held by each magistrate.

Most courts are now offering training courses which mirror aspects of the log. The log enables the magistrate to tick off the relevant areas as and when confident to do so. This activity may well be shared with the mentor during the early sittings in order to record progress. Thereafter, it enables the appraiser to quickly identify areas which should be referred on to the BTDC for training consideration, if aspects are not ticked off.

A new magistrate should normally have between 8 and 11 mentored sittings in the first 2 years, followed by an appraisal. All magistrates should be appraised at a minimum of once every 3 years on all relevant competences e.g. a youth panel chairman could be appraised on one sitting in the youth court on all basic competences, adult chairmanship, youth and youth chairmanship competences, based upon observation and some questions.

See appendix 2 for an example of an appraisal form for basic competences, together with the standard of knowledge and/or features for observation in respect of each competence. Note that, whilst the competences are consistent across the country, the standards and paperwork vary, and various models exist.

Most BTDCs have now created 'job descriptions' for mentors and appraisers based on the models provided by the judicial studies board and these will provide local criteria for selection and the extent of responsibilities.

1.36 Magistrates Association activities

The aims of the Association are:

- To establish policy which will best serve the lay magistracy through addressing issues which affect magisterial practice and consulting members on such issues as they arise;
- Communicating policy decisions to members;
- Representing members' views and safeguarding their interests;
- Providing opportunities for education and training;
- Offering information, advice and support to individual members as appropriate;
- Encouraging the development of a sense of common purpose.

The publication 'The Magistrate' is published to members. Membership is not obligatory and the sentencing guidelines published by the Magistrates Association may be purchased by any member of the public.

The 'Magistrate in the Community' (MIC) project involves magistrates going out to community groups and giving presentations, and welcoming visitors to the courts in order to increase awareness of the magistracy and the role of the magistrates' court.

1.37 Informal activities

Most benches have a formal or informal social committee who arrange get-togethers which will be advertised on the notice-board. As with any working relationship there is much to be gained from meeting together away from the workplace; gaining a new perspective; sharing experiences together and getting to know colleagues as individuals as well as magistrates. Any 'magistrate-event' must always be checked out so that judicial dignity is preserved and there can be no perceptions of bias by linking in, for instance with local solicitors, on the basis of 'what would the public think if they observed the event taking place?'

CHAPTER 2
COMPETENCE 2
Basic law and procedure

INTRODUCTION

This chapter covers the main knowledge-based competence for adult court and principally describes the criminal process from start to finish – from laying the information through to the bail process, trial and sentence.

It also covers the licensing matters which may be heard before any lay bench, and the wider community picture.

Demonstrating knowledge of the prosecution process

How criminal prosecutions are initiated

2.1 Laying of an information

The laying of an information is followed either by the issue of a summons or warrant. An 'information' is exactly what it says – information describing the offence, the statutory authority, the name and address of the party charged and the party laying the information. It need not be in writing and it is a regular occurrence for a prosecutor to lay an oral information in court with an alternative charge to the original.

2.2 Issuing of a summons

Once the information has been laid, the magistrate or justices clerk must go through the judicial exercise of deciding whether to issue a summons or warrant. Is the offence known to law? Is it a summary offence or an indictable offence? When a summary offence is being considered, was it allegedly committed within the commission area and is the relevant date within the past 6 months? If not, a summons cannot be issued! No signature required – hand back the information!

The summons itself is effectively a directive to attend or at least respond to the court in answer to the allegation on a specific date and time.

2.3 Issuing of a warrant

When a warrant is sought the information must be in writing and must be substantiated on oath. When issuing a warrant in respect of an offence, the issuing magistrate must be satisfied that the offence is either indictable or imprisonable or that the defendant does not have a fixed address. A summons should always be considered first, particularly for minor offences, as a warrant at this stage is essentially authorising arrest without conviction. The second consideration should be for a warrant with bail. A warrant without bail should only be granted when there is information to suggest that the defendant would not attend court following a bail warrant.

Warrants are issued in a wide range of other circumstances e.g. following a failure to surrender to bail, search warrants, utility warrants, fine default warrants and these are discussed in the relevant parts of the text.

2.4 Community Safety

Community safety hinges on crime prevention rather than crime processing and statutory responsibilities now exist. Local authorities and police forces are under a duty to co-operate in the formulation and implementation of crime reduction strategies for the local authority area. Other agencies are also involved. The purpose is to reduce crime in local communities and this is achieved through local crime audits, local consultation, determination of priorities and responsibilities for necessary actions. The local community strategy must be published and reviewed every three years. It is an interesting and helpful document for magistrates to read and may be obtained from the local authority.

The partnerships do have legislative armoury particularly in the form of new orders namely Anti-Social Behaviour Orders, Sex Offender Orders and local child curfews, as described below:

2.4.1 Anti-Social Behaviour Order (ASBO)

Purpose 'to allow people to live their lives free from fear and intimidation'

- Application by police or local authority in consultation with each other.
- Order against individual (minimum age of 10) or several people.
- Civil order i.e. proved on balance of probabilities but with criminal sanctions.
- Behaviour has caused or likely to cause harassment, alarm or distress to one or more persons e.g. noise nuisance and disturbances.
- Prohibition against doing anything described in the order e.g. to keep away from specified area.
- Statutory defence that the behaviour was reasonable.
- Breach - summarily (6 months/£5000) or on indictment (fine/5 years).

🕑 Minimum = 2 years Maximum = 'until further order.'

2.4.2 Sex Offender Order (SOO)

To deal with the risks of certain types of sex offender particularly following release from custody

- Application by police.
- Civil order with criminal sanctions.
- Defendant is a sex offender.
- Defendant has acted in a way which gives reasonable cause to believe an order is necessary to protect public from serious harm.
- Defendant becomes subject to registration with local police (if not already).
- May prohibit from doing anything prescribed by order e.g. keep away from named school(s).
- Breach – summarily (6 months/£5000) or on indictment(fine/5years).
- ⌚ Minimum = 5 years. Maximum = until further order.

2.4.3 Child Curfew Orders

To address the problem that 'unsupervised children gathered in public places can cause real alarm and misery in local communities and can encourage one another into anti-social and criminal habits.'

- Power to make local child curfew scheme vested in local authority in consultation with relevant chief constable(s) and other bodies as appropriate.
- Home Secretary must confirm the scheme.
- Ban on children of specified ages under 10 being in specified public areas during curfew.
- Specified hours of curfew between 9pm and 6 am (may vary for different age groups).
- Curfew inoperative if child is with parent or responsible person aged 18 or over.
- Curfew notices to be posted conspicuously.
- Constable may take child home <u>or</u> to suitable accommodation if he believes the child would suffer significant harm.
- Constable must notify local authority for investigation within 48 hours.
- Proceedings may follow to safeguard the welfare of the child.
- ⌚ Ban may last up to 90 days.

2.5 TV Licences

The information is currently laid by 'TV Licensing' and a summons is issued along with a statement which is essentially a record of the interview between the user and the TV Licence officer. It states that a licence could not be produced and usually contains an admission of use and the date of last use. The summons advises that the case may proceed in the defendant's absence; that costs will be applied for in the specified sum and a response form is enclosed to record mitigation and means.

As with any prosecution, there is an element of discretion and very often the users will be given the opportunity to obtain a licence after the visit within a period of time in order to avoid prosecution. The Cash Easy Entry system enables users to purchase a licence by periodical payments. As soon as the first instalment is paid, the user is licensed. When default occurs the licence will cease and prosecution may follow.

Licensing by the lay bench

The extent of knowledge required by individual magistrates will depend upon whether it is normal practice for their full bench to deal with licensing matters or whether they are reserved only for licensing committee members.

2.6. General licences

Whilst the vast majority of licences are dealt with by either the licensing committee or the betting and gaming committee (see 1.15), a number of licences are dealt with by lay justices on a regular basis. Information as to purpose and relevant procedures follows.

2.6.1 Protection Orders

- Purpose:

To enable licensed premises to continue in business if the current licensee is no longer in control of the premises. It provides a temporary authorisation for someone else to exercise the licensee's rights and remains in force until the conclusion of the second Transfer sessions after the order is made. By this time the expectation is that a full Transfer will be applied for.

- Criteria:

The applicant must satisfy the magistrates that he is a 'fit and proper' person and intends to apply, and could be granted, a transfer at a licensing session. The police will make representations and previous convictions may be put before the court which may cause concern e.g. recent offence of violence. The court would also need to be satisfied that the applicant had some relevant experience or held the British Institute of Inn-keeping National Licensee's Certificate. The bench may well ask relatively inexperienced applicants to quote the relevant normal permitted hours and describe who should not be served in order to assess whether they are 'fit and proper.'

- Normal Permitted hours:

  ➢ 'On' licence
  Weekdays (other than Christmas and Good Friday) 11.00 a.m. to 11.00 p.m.
  Sundays (other than Christmas Day) and Good Friday 12 noon to 10.30 p.m.
  Christmas Day 12 noon to 3.00 p.m. and 7.00 p.m. to 10.30 p.m.
  Drinking up time = 20 minutes/30 minutes if ancillary to a meal.

  ➢ 'Off' licence
  Weekdays 8.00 a.m. to 11.00 p.m.
  Sundays 10.00 a.m. to 10.30 p.m.
  Good Friday 8.00 a.m. to 10.30 p.m.
  Christmas Day 12 noon to 3.00 p.m. and 7.00 p.m. to 10.30 p.m.

Must not serve children under 18, people who are drunk and police officers in uniform.

2.6.2 Interim authorities

- Purpose:

To enable the licensee to be replaced but the applicant need not intend to apply for a transfer of the licence (unlike a protection order). The holder is subject to licensing laws as if he were the holder of the licence itself.

- Criteria:

  ➢ Applicant must be a fit and proper person
  ➢ Authority is valid for 28 days but if an application is made during that time, it will continue in force until transfer application is determined
  ➢ A maximum of two interim authorities may be granted before the licence is transferred
  ➢ A justices clerk is able to make an administrative grant in limited circumstances.

2.6.3 Occasional Licences

- Purpose:

To provide alcohol in unlicensed premises for a particular event by a licensee who will provide the liquor and the staff.

- Criteria:
    - ➢ There must be an 'occasion'.
    - ➢ When the hours extend beyond the normal permitted hours it will also be necessary to show that the event is 'special' e.g. a wedding in a village hall.
    - ➢ The licensee must satisfy the bench that the event will be properly run either by the applicant himself or by experienced staff.
    - ➢ The function must not pose a threat to public order. The police may well have representations to make about numbers involved, timing and the effect on the neighbourhood.
    - ➢ The premises must be suitable and licensed for such occasions.
    - ➢ The maximum period for an Occasional Licence is 3 weeks e.g. trade fairs.

2.6.4 Special Order of Exemption (Extensions)

- Purpose:

Extension of normal permitted hours for a specified occasion.

- Criteria:
    - ➢ The occasion must be 'special' in a local or national sense e.g. silver wedding anniversary, Bank Holidays; not simply a weekly dance at a hotel or a weekly football match.
    - ➢ The event must not pose a threat to public order - is the time justified and reasonable? e.g. inconvenience to local residents may require an earlier ending to noisy revelries.
    - ➢ Personal application may be required if appropriate.

2.6.5 Club Registration Certificates

- Purpose:

To enable the supply (rather than sale) of alcohol to members of a club. Although alcohol appears to be 'purchased', it is in fact a distribution of the club's assets and a justices' licence as such is not required. The police, fire service or local authority may object to the grant or renewal of such licences.

- Principal criteria:
    - ➢ The club must be conducted in good faith as a club e.g. consider any tied arrangements for liquor source, diverting profit from the club itself, sales to non-members.

- Rules for membership provide for 2 days waiting time between nomination or application and admission to membership i.e. the public cannot simply walk in, sign membership and be served with a drink.
- There must be at least 25 members.
- An elective committee must control the intoxicating liquor.
- Intoxicating liquor must only be supplied to members or guests in accordance with the club rules.
- The club premises are suitable for the use to which they are to be put.
- The club is not conducted in a disorderly or illegal fashion.
- Certificate valid for 1 year initially followed by 10 year grants.

Back to the criminal process ...

SEQUENCE OF EVENTS

2.7 Prosecution outlining of facts

Before the prosecution begins, all witnesses must be cleared from the court to wait outside the court until called to give their evidence, so that each witness is heard to be giving their own independent recollection.

The prosecution case in a criminal matter must be proved beyond reasonable doubt and the initial outline will give the basis on which the proof will be given. At this stage the prosecutor will describe what is alleged to have happened and how it is intended to prove the various elements of the offence.

It is recommended that the magistrates refrain from taking detailed notes at this point so that there is no appearance of the case being decided upon representations rather than on actual evidence. Obviously it is helpful to get a feel for the case and in particular to identify any potential line of defence which is disclosed in interview e.g. mistaken identity, self-defence. This will highlight the evidence which must be noted carefully.

2.8 Prosecution case

Undisputed evidence may simply be read from statements.

> Example:
>
> A statement from the owner of a stolen motor car that he was the owner and that nobody else had any right to remove the car from the car park. A description of the car with details of where and

when he parked it and when he returned to find that it had gone. Simply read out by the prosecutor. No dispute, but the facts are material to the case.

Witnesses must be called if the evidence is not agreed and the evidence must be given on oath or by solemn affirmation. The court usher will endeavour to establish the nature of the appropriate holy book before the witness is called.

The administration of the oath is lawful provided that the oath appears to be, and is, binding on the witness's conscience. The ceremony itself is immaterial for the purpose of perjury provided that the oath has been accepted without objection. When a witness does object to taking the oath, he must be allowed to affirm and this must be regarded as equally binding.

Normally witnesses will attend voluntarily and will be paid appropriate expenses. Occasionally it is necessary for a summons or warrant to be issued in order to secure attendance. In such circumstances the issuing magistrate must be satisfied that the witness would not attend voluntarily.

The witness may normally be led through undisputed matters, but thereafter must give his own version of events from his own experience. The prosecutor will question first 'in chief', followed by cross-examination by the defence. The prosecutor may then re-examine and finally the magistrates may ask any clarifying questions.

2.9 No case to answer

Once the prosecution case is complete, the court may dismiss the case either on the invitation of the defence or on its own initiative. The criteria for dismissal at this stage are:

- No evidence to prove an essential element in the alleged offence e.g. no actual bodily harm is proved in a s.47 assault, or
- The evidence given by the prosecution witnesses has been so discredited by cross-examination or is so manifestly unreliable that no reasonable tribunal could safely convict on it e.g. widely different versions of events.

The prosecution should be given the opportunity to respond before the decision is made to dismiss on this basis.

2.10 Defence case

The defendant is under no obligation to give evidence and he may choose to remain silent. However, he must be warned that if he does choose not to give evidence then the court may draw an 'inference from his silence' i.e. may understandably come to the conclusion that he has something to hide.

The failure to give evidence cannot be the only factor to justify a conviction, and it is very important to stress in reasons the other supporting evidence. The silence may properly contribute to the totality of evidence which proves beyond reasonable doubt that the defendant is guilty.

The same inference applies if the defendant chooses not to answer questions during the course of his evidence and again the court must give an appropriate warning.

The defendant will normally give evidence first, followed by his witnesses.

2.11 Verdict

Trial - Structured decision making

The decision-making following a trial will normally be conducted in the retiring room and the following process is based upon the structure recommended by the Judicial Studies Board, which provides a clear framework for recording and announcing reasons.

Verdict reasons - example

Charge of criminal damage.

A. What needs to be proved and by whom?

1) What are the elements of the offence charged?

There are 2 elements to the criminal damage charge - (i) that damage was caused by the defendant and (ii) that this was either intentional or reckless.

2) What is the burden of proof and where does it fall?

The prosecutor must prove the offence beyond reasonable doubt.

B. The evidence

3) Identify what facts are agreed.

It is agreed that the defendant caused damage to window valued at £50.

4) Identify what facts are disputed.

It is disputed that it was an intentional kick or reckless kick and it is said instead that it was caused by an accidental fall.

5) Exclude any evidence which is not admissible.

We exclude the hearsay evidence given by one of the witnesses that her friend heard the defendant bragging about the incident.

6) What is found to be fact with reasons? Preferred evidence.

We find that the damage was caused by an intentional kick. The 2 prosecution witnesses give consistent eye-witness evidence of a deliberate 'kung-fu' kick' and we find them to be reliable witnesses. The defendant gave a confused and improbable version of events that he tripped and fell backwards and damaged the window purely with his body weight. No other witnesses were called by the defendant.

C. Any aspects of law including inferences from the silence of the accused.

We note that the defendant failed to account for glass splinters inside his shoe when interviewed in the presence of his solicitor (see 2.10) and he did not reply to the prosecutor's question "You did kick the window, didn't you?" The question was repeated after a warning about the implication of his silence was given by the clerk and again he failed to answer. (see 2.10). We add this to the clear evidence given by the prosecution witnesses.

We have heard argument that there was a breach of Article 6(2) because the presumption of innocence was not afforded to the defendant. It is said that a presumption of guilt has been made instead simply because he chose to remain silent at the police station and he chose not to answer a question in court today. We find that there has been no breach of this right. He was represented at the police station and he was given advice today about the domestic law inference. Furthermore we have not based our decision solely upon the silence as there is other compelling evidence from the prosecution witnesses.

D. Is the case proved?

Has the burden of proof been discharged in respect of all elements of the offence?

We find that the prosecution have proved beyond reasonable doubt that the criminal damage was caused by the defendant intentionally.

Reasons should not normally take up more than half a side to a side of A4 paper unless there are separate issues surrounding numerous witnesses or arguments in law to be determined. It is important to recognise that the

Practice Direction 2000 states that 'it shall be the legal adviser's responsibility to assist the court, where appropriate, as to the formulation of reasons and the recording of those reasons'. Furthermore, the legal adviser has the responsibility to advise on 'the appropriate decision making structure to be applied in any given case', 'whether or not the justices have requested that advice'. Use the clerk!

2.12 Mitigation and other information and submissions

Previous convictions

Immediately after verdict is announced, the prosecutor supplies details of any previous convictions. Care must be taken when considering the previous convictions to identify whether previous offences bear some similarity e.g. dishonesty <u>or</u> violence, and also whether they are stale. Whilst the provisions of the Rehabilitation of Offenders Act 1974 do not apply to criminal proceedings it is recommended that the spirit of those provisions should normally be applied. Previous convictions form one of the most common aggravating features. It is important to identify whether all, or only some, are actually cited in court for comment, and then whether all, or only some, actually do make a difference to the sentence, and if so, they must be referred to specifically in reasons.

Rehabilitation periods.

Offences punished by:

6 months – 30 months custody/detention	= 10 years
Up to 6 months custody/detention	= 7 years
Community orders and fines	= 5 years

The periods must be entirely clear of offending, otherwise the clock begins again.

Mitigation

Perusal of the record will be followed by mitigation which is given either by the defendant himself (prompted by the chairman) or by his solicitor. This will include information about the offender which may affect suitability for particular sentences, home background, employment, financial situation, health and his attitude towards offending.

The court may feel that further information is required and the services of the probation service may be called upon at this stage. The nature of the involvement will depend upon the information required and the sentence(s) which the court has in mind.

Pre-sentence report (PSR)

A pre-sentence report must always be considered if the court intends to impose a custodial sentence unless the court considers this to be 'unnecessary.' The Court of Appeal has given guidance that it should be the 'inevitable practice' that a pre-sentence report should be obtained if the court is contemplating a prison sentence for a defendant for the first time, other than for a 'very short period indeed' (R v. Gillette 1999). There is also recent guidance on when a report may be 'unnecessary'; 'if the PSR would tell the court nothing the defendant's advocate cannot tell it, and if making every possible assumption in the defendant's favour still makes a custodial sentence inevitable' (R v. Armsaramah 2000).

Pre-sentence reports are usually required when an assessment as to suitability for a particular order is necessary e.g. for a drug treatment and testing order, and for most of the accredited programmes. The probation officer in court will advise whether a full report is recommended or whether the sentence can be explored by a specific sentence report on a short stand down enquiry.

The purpose of a pre–sentence report is to provide information to the sentencing court about the offender and the offences committed and to assist the court to decide on a suitable sentence. It must be in writing and copies must be provided to the court, the defence, the defendant, CPS and some other specified prosecutors. It must provide a systematic assessment and include the following sections and information:

- Offence analysis – nature and circumstances of offence; assessment of culpability and level of premeditation; assessment of impact on any victim from CPS papers or from a victim statement; indication of whether or not any positive action has been taken to make reparation or address offending behaviour since the offence was committed.

- Offender assessment – status in relation to literacy/numeracy; accommodation; employment; special circumstances; evaluate any patterns of offending; details of any substance misuse; relevant personal background.

- Assessment of the risk of harm to the public, self-harm and the likelihood of re-offending.

- Conclusion – evaluates the offender's motivation and ability to change; states whether offender is suitable for a community sentence; makes a clear and realistic proposal designed to protect the public and reduce offending, including custody where this is necessary; if probation -

outline of supervision plan; if curfew - suitability of address and effect on other occupants; if custody – any anticipated effects on offender.

(National Standards for Supervision of Offenders in the Community 2000).

Much debate has taken place over the years about what the court should say when adjourning for a pre-sentence report. The most important point is that the court should be guarded about binding a future bench. An adjournment 'for a pre-sentence report to consider suitability for community service' effectively leaves the next bench with no other option if the defendant is suitable. Case law is very clear that once the expectation of a particular penalty is created, the next bench certainly cannot impose custody. Their hands are tied. Similarly, an adjournment within the magistrates' court carries the expectation that the defendant will finally be sentenced by the magistrates' court and the powers will therefore be limited to a maximum of 6 months imprisonment for a single offence.

The test is basically 'are we able to define what the report should cover?' If the answer is 'no', there is more to explore in court and it may well be that powers are insufficient and the case should be committed for sentence. If the answer is 'yes', consider whether that enquiry can be covered by a specific sentence report by way of stand-down, e.g. to consider suitability for community service.

If adjourning for a pre-sentence report, ensure that there is a rider to enable the next bench to commit to prison or indeed to crown court if appropriate. On a lesser note, it is almost always helpful to specifically seek means information, if only for compensation and costs – so much easier than awaiting instructions after the principal sentence is determined on the report.

Specific sentence report (SSR)

The purpose of a specific sentence report is to provide information about the offender and offence so as to assist the sentencing court to determine the offender's suitability for a specific sentence. It is written, but may well be presented orally to the court. It is used to speed up the provision of information to the court to allow sentencing without delay on the day, following a short stand-down of the case. National Standards are clear that the officer may recommend a full PSR if he believes that further investigation is required. The national target is to reach 20% of community penalties being imposed following a SSR rather than PSR. Some courts are already exceeding this figure.

During the course of an SSR enquiry, the new National Probation Service may also consider the likelihood of re-offending on a scoring system, and may suggest that an accredited programme should be explored by an adjournment for a pre-sentence report. Information as to suitability for the specific sentence will also be given. This is a major move into the objective of offence prevention by using accredited programmes which have been proved to reduce offending.

2.13 Sentence decisions

This is arguably the most important knowledge competence area and is covered under the following headings:

- Structured approach to sentencing.
- Sentencing reasons specimen pro forma.
- Sentencing powers.
- Sentencing mentally disordered offenders.
- Ancillary orders.
- Traffic penalties.

Structured approach to sentencing

Having gathered all of the information it is necessary to process it in a structured manner. The '4 O' approach is recommended. This provides a dual function of providing a useful and simple agenda for discussion and also provides a useful checklist for reasons.

1. Offence
2. Offender
3. Objective
4. Options

1. Offence

- What is the sentencing guideline entry point? e.g. community penalty.
- What is the nature and extent of criminal intent? A pre-meditated offence is more serious than a spontaneous offence.
- What is the nature and extent of any injury or damage to the victim? Personal injury is more serious than financial damage.
- What are the aggravating features?
  - ➢ Matters specific to the offence as listed in the guidelines e.g. high value, unprovoked.
  - ➢ Relevant previous convictions.
  - ➢ Was offence committed on bail? (<u>must</u> increase).
  - ➢ Is the offence racially aggravated? (<u>must</u> increase).
  - ➢ Any failures to respond to previous sentences? (<u>may</u> increase).

- What are the mitigating features?
  - Matters specific to the offence as listed in the guidelines. e.g. low value, provocation.

What is the level of seriousness at this stage? e.g. custody

2. Offender

- Positive good character e.g. no relevant previous convictions, solid employment record, faithful discharge of family duties.
- Credit for guilty plea. In determining sentence on an offender who has pleaded guilty, the court must take into account the stage in the proceedings when the intention to plead guilty was indicated and also the circumstances in which this indication was given. If a less severe penalty is therefore imposed, the court must state the reason in open court (s. 48 Criminal Justice and Public Order Act 1994).
  The sentencing guidelines state that 'A timely guilty plea may attract a sentencing discount of up to a third but the precise amount of discount will depend on the facts of each case'. Case law is clear that there should be some credit, however small, even if the defendant was caught red-handed or if the plea is entered at the last moment before a trial begins (the witnesses are spared the trauma of actually giving evidence). One third is a guideline, not a tramline.
- Co-operation with the police is highly relevant. Giving the correct name and address is a start! Failure to do so, and obstructing the police surely cannot be overlooked in the final sentence.
- Hard evidence of genuine remorse e.g. apology to the victim. This is a step ahead of the solicitor simply conveying his client's remorse in court.
- If the offence is fuelled by drink or drugs – a genuine self-motivated determination to address the addiction. Again, this is rather more than a general expression of future intention.
- Youth/immaturity would often justify a less rigorous penalty than for an adult. (R v Howells 1998).

What is the level of seriousness at this stage?
Check – Are magistrates courts powers sufficient? If not, it may be appropriate to return to court and indicate that the court is minded to commit to the crown court for sentence and seek representations.

3. Objectives

- Punishment
- Protection of the public
- Rehabilitation
- Deterrence to others

What is the court aiming to do? Which options would cover this objective?

4. Options

- What is the most suitable option to satisfy both the level of seriousness and the objective?
- Do we need a PSR or can we proceed by a stand-down for an SSR?
- The victim's views (if known) may affect the court's selection of penalty. Would custody cause or add to the distress of the victim? The view may well tip the balance e.g. grandmother was victim of robbery by grandson but wished him to return to live with her and provide practical support to her following his period on remand in custody – a community order was upheld following appeal by prosecution (R v. Hayes 1999).
  However, the evidence of effect must be presented as formal written statements duly served on the defendant for investigation and comment. Pure opinion of the victim or his family on the appropriate level of sentence should not be taken into account e.g. letter from victim's husband as to effect of robbery on his wife (R v Perks 2000).
- How much/how long? If custody, the period should be no longer than necessary to meet the penal purpose which the court had in mind.
- If custody is less than 12 months, 'would an even shorter period be equally effective in protecting the public and deterring the criminal?' (R v Ollerenshaw 1999).
- Remember compensation, costs and ancillary orders!

Check – is the sentence commensurate with seriousness?
Are the magistrates' powers sufficient?

Be ready to give reasons for each stage of the process – purely and simply, what did you take into account at each stage in language that the defendant (and a judge) will understand? Not a House of Lords judgement – just a few meaningful sentences. The 'pro-forma' below is slightly adapted from the example provided in the sentencing guidelines and will give any defendant the basis for why he has, or has not been sentenced in accordance with the sentencing guidelines which can be obtained by any member of the public.

Sentencing reasons specimen pro-forma

1. We are dealing with an offence of ...

2. We have used the sentencing guidelines in this case.

3. EITHER

We do not find any aggravating or mitigating features.

OR
We have taken into account the following aggravating features of the offence which make it more serious:

- *Your previous record, ... namely the offences of ... /as cited*
- *It was committed on bail*
- *It was racially aggravated*
- *You have failed to respond to other penalties, namely ...*

And *(specific features)...*

4. And the following mitigating features of the offence :

5. And your personal circumstances:

- *Including your net weekly income of ...*
- *And (specific features) ...*

6. We have taken into account the fact that you pleaded guilty at an early stage/ but not until .... and we have reduced the sentence accordingly.

7. As a result we have decided that a fair and proportionate sentence is:

8. (If relevant) We have decided not to award compensation because:

Most penalties arguably engage the right to private and family life (and sometimes other qualified rights as well) under the Human Rights Act. The principal issue is to consider carefully whether the infringement is 'proportionate' as required by the Act e.g. the number of community service hours for this particular offence/offender. By including this aspect into the checklist, it is clearly demonstrated, particularly to the defence solicitor(!) that the right has been considered. Its translation to the lay defendant lies in the word 'fair'!

Cases dealt with in absence of defendant - reasons

1. We have dealt with this matter/these matters in the absence of the defendant(s) because we are satisfied that statements were served by first-class post/personally at least 10 days ago and we believe that the defendant(s) is/are aware of the case(s) and has/have chosen not to respond to the court.

2. We have used the sentencing guidelines in this case.

3. EITHER
We do not find any aggravating or mitigating features
OR
We find the following aggravating and/or mitigating features ...

4. We have calculated the amount of the fine by using the average net income figure for Xshire of ... (and we have deducted the average rent/mortgage and council tax figures of ...)

Although the above reasons may well only be announced after the first case or the last case of a lengthy 'paper list' e.g. TV licences, it is important that any members of the public can hear how the penalty has been arrived at and the files can be interpreted easily if a defendant telephones the court to ask how on earth the court reached such a decision.

Example.

- 'Why was it dealt with in my absence?'
'Because the summons and statements were sent first class and they were not returned and the court felt that you were well aware of the case to be put to the court, and chose not to attend. The address was ...'
'I moved from there months ago'.
= re-opening advice.
- 'I'm guilty but why was I fined £110?'
'The guideline fine is for half of your net weekly income. The court had no information from you and used the average net income for Xshire which is £220'.
'I receive benefits of £41.
= fine rectification advice.

Neither example requires an appeal, simply because the reasons are on the face of the file!

Finally, to emphasise that the Practice Direction requires the legal adviser to advise on the appropriate structured decision making approach (whether requested or not) and it is the legal adviser's responsibility to assist the court, where appropriate, in the formulation of reasons and the recording of those reasons.

Sentencing powers

Sentencing powers are built on a hierarchy of seriousness with an increasing restriction on liberty as set out in the diagram.

COMPETENCE 2

2. 13 Sentence Decisions

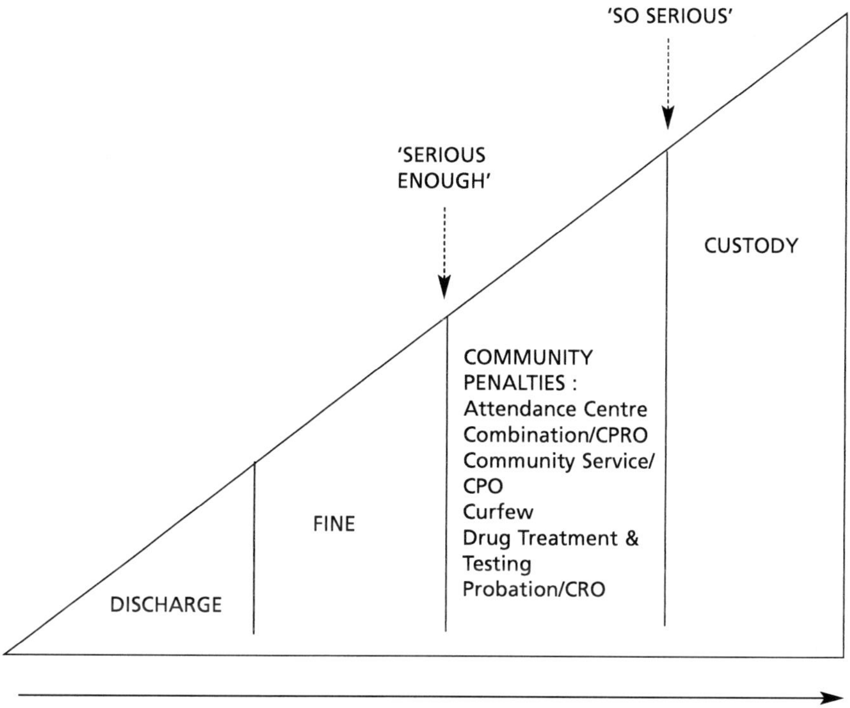

RESTRICTIONS ON LIBERTY INCREASES

> New names!
> CPRO (instead of combination order) = Community punishment and rehabilitation order.
> CPO (instead of community service order) = Community punishment order.
> CRO (instead of probation order) = Community rehabilitation order.

2.13.1 Absolute discharge

The court must be of the opinion that 'it is inexpedient to inflict punishment' e.g. extremely strong mitigation such as a fireman driving through a red traffic light to an emergency or offences of a purely technical nature.

2.13.2 Conditional discharge

The criteria are the same as for an absolute discharge, but the court feels that the condition of committing no further offences must be attached e.g. discharged for a period of 12 months on the condition that no further offences are committed. If a further offence is committed within the specified period then the court may sentence for the original offence in addition to the new matter. It is an order which does not anticipate any further offending and so reaches the conclusion that punishment is 'inexpedient,' which in itself carries a message on the previous convictions as to its low level of seriousness. This option must be distinguished from the notion of requiring 'something to hang over', because further offending is expected. In such circumstances, a greater punishment may be more appropriate to the level of seriousness e.g. a fine or community penalty, possibly with a binding over order.

- Defendant must be present so that the order may be explained.
- ◷ Minimum period – none. Maximum – 3 years.

2.13.3 Fines

- Minimum – none.
- Maximum – depends upon the amount fixed by law for the particular offence. The maximum fines are described as 'levels 1 to 5' rather than fixing specific amounts in every piece of legislation. This enables the various levels to be adjusted from time to time. As at March 2001, the levels are as follows:

  Level 1 = £200
  Level 2 = £500
  Level 3 = £1,000 e.g. drunk and disorderly.
  Level 4 = £2,500 e.g. criminal damage.
  Level 5 = £5,000 e.g. 'no insurance.'

A very small number of offences carry higher maxima e.g. some health and safety offences.

Fines are fixed after considering 5 aspects which are each considered below:

(i) Sentencing guideline band.
(ii) Net income.
(iii) Aggravating/mitigating features.
(iv) Credit for guilty plea.
(v) Outgoings and limitation of 12 month repayment period.

(i) Sentencing guideline band

All offences which have an entry point of 'fine' in the sentencing guidelines are given an entry band as follows:

A = 50% of net income e.g. drunk and disorderly.
B = 100% of net income e.g. no insurance.
C = 150% of net income e.g. criminal damage.

This ensures a starting point figure which is individual to each defendant – no wide ranges – an actual figure.

(ii) Net income

Debate has followed the introduction of the guidelines as to what actually constitutes the 'net income'. Whilst it is no doubt agreed that income tax and national insurance should be properly deducted before arriving at the net income, there are other aspects.

Arguably, family allowance should be ignored as this is specifically allocated to the children. By ignoring the allowance, it ensures that the larger family has a higher protected income, bearing in mind that a net income of say, £200 will be the starting point fine, whether the defendant is a single person or a defendant with a family to support.

A more complex aspect is the comparison between a defendant in receipt of benefits with no rent/mortgage or council tax to pay out of that income, as compared to a waged defendant who has roof costs and council tax to pay out of his income. Some benches have therefore taken the view that roof costs and council tax should be deducted from a waged income so that the 'net figure' is then fairly equated with that of the defendant on benefits i.e. both are fined from 'the money left to actually live on'. A defendant paying board – deduction of $1/2$ as his notional roof cost contribution.

When a case is dealt with in the absence of the defendant and any information as to his means, it is important for the court to have access to the local average net income and also the average rent/mortgage and council tax figures. These are readily accessible using the latest New Earnings survey/ Regional Trends and local authority figures.

In West Yorkshire the relevant figures in 2000 give £270pw net income across both genders as an average from the various petty sessions divisions, with an average rent/mortgage of £45pw and council tax of £5 (rounded down). This creates a fine in absence of £220 (£270 less rent/council tax) for a band B offence, i.e. 100%.

(iii) Aggravating/mitigating circumstances

Using a structured approach, the aggravating and mitigating features of the offence must be considered, followed by offender mitigation, when considering quantum. If any of these factors come into play, then they should be announced in the reasons as explanation for deviation from the guideline figures. In many situations, particularly traffic document offences dealt with in the absence of the defendant, there will be no information before the court apart from the fact that documents were not held, and in those circumstances it will be difficult to justify an increase or decrease.

It cannot be emphasised enough that deviation may well be perfectly appropriate, provided there is a clear reason which a reasonable person could understand.

Examples:

Aggravating features.

- Drunk and disorderly.

Abusive language to fellow passengers on a public bus. Had to be ejected by the driver; police assistance had to be sought, and the bus was delayed. Protracted incident with inconvenience and discomfort to others. Fine increased.

- Mitigating features.

No insurance.
Genuine misunderstanding that friend's insurance covered the defendant. Isolated incident. Fine reduced.

(iv) Credit for guilty plea

Up to 1/3 should normally be deducted for a timely guilty plea, e.g. a net income of £60 for a band B offence would carry an entry point fine of £40.

The previous guideline band figures were all helpfully divisible by 3, for ease of credit deduction. Of course this is rather more difficult when the net income is, say £122.43p!

An easy reference fines calculator is available at appendix 3 which is based on rounding down all income figures to figures divisible by 3 and then giving the entry point of 1/3 credit. Remember this is a starting point only and can quite properly go up and down. It is worth emphasising that any offence which carries substantial aggravating or mitigating features should vary from the entry point and reasons must be given for that variation by way of explanation (see below).

(v) Outgoings and limitation of the 12 month rule

Case law is clear that fines should normally be payable within 12 months maximum. This guidance requires the court to take outgoings into account in order to assess just how much per week/month, a defendant can actually afford to pay, if the fine cannot be paid immediately. If the appropriate instalment rate is £4 per week, then effectively the maximum fine is £4 x 50 weeks = £200. This final aspect of fixing the fine can result in re-visiting the guideline fines for a multiple offender so that the total fine falls within the guideline period.

The order to pay

- The whole amount is due now. Can it be paid now?
- If not, how much can be paid now? At least try and obtain the first instalment.
- What is a fair and realistic instalment rate? This should have been considered when checking the 12 month capability. A period to coincide with income is helpful e.g. weekly/monthly, but consider the hidden costs of lengthy weekly orders and possibly consider a fortnightly payment. However this is irrelevant if the court operates a free card payment system.
- When can the payment practically be received – when is pay day? Is payment to be brought in or sent?
- State the date (and the day of the week) for payment(s) to be made.
- Warn the defendant that missed payments render the whole amount due and default may result in imprisonment.

A careful, reasoned assessment and a careful explanation and warning can reduce the number of defaulters on the fine default list and the cost of pursuing payments. It is well worth the extra minute or two whilst the defendant is there in court. Fine default provisions are discussed at chapter 12.

2.13.4 Compensation

- Maximum = £5000.
- Compensation takes precedence over a fine or costs if means are limited.

- Whilst a formal application is unnecessary, any amount relating to damage must either be agreed or proved. A court assessment may be accepted if evidence cannot reasonably be obtained. Any challenges should be pursued in the civil court.
- Home Office guidelines exist for personal injuries and are set out in the sentencing guidelines e.g. £125 for a black eye.
- The Criminal Injuries Compensation Board do not make awards in a sum less than £1000 and it is therefore important for the court to explore the possibility of compensation for personal injuries.
- Injury includes 'terror and distress' e.g. victim in the house when a window was smashed. Seek representations before determining the extent of the penalty e.g. provocation may reduce seriousness.
- Applies to damage but note limitations in respect of motor accidents unless the vehicle is stolen or if the defendant is uninsured. The Motor Insurance Bureau do not pay the first £300 (October 2000) in such circumstances and the court should therefore consider ordering the defendant to pay the victim if the 'bad driving' element is proved along with the 'no insurance'. Additionally, the court should consider an award for loss of 'no claims' bonus and insurance excess payments by the victim – schedules will be required.
- Reasons must be given if compensation is not granted in full e.g. insufficient evidence of loss, insufficient means to pay in full.

🕒 Maximum payment period dependant upon means = 2 years or exceptionally 3 years.

COMMUNITY PENALTIES – OFFENCE IS 'SERIOUS ENOUGH'

The following offences are examples of offences which carry an entry point of community penalty:

Possession of class A drugs; common assault; going equipped for theft; theft; vehicle interference.

2.13.5 Attendance Centre Order

- Imprisonable, 'serious enough' offences only.
- Under 21 year olds (under 25 limit for fine defaulters only).
- A reasonably accessible centre.
- Regimes vary e.g. physical activities, woodwork, First Aid, victim awareness etc. and magistrates are generally welcome to arrange visits to their local centre.

🕒 Minimum = 12 hours. Maximum = 36 hours (3 hours per occasion).

2.13.6 Community service order/Community punishment order

- Imprisonable,' serious enough' offences only.
- Carry out unpaid work.
- Restricts personal freedom, produces something useful for local community and as reparation for the harm done.
- Defendant must be suitable and provision must be available.
- Must keep in touch with the officer, notify change of address and perform work as directed.
- Order may be reviewed on the application of the defendant or officer.
- Consent is not required.
- ⏱ Minimum = 40 hours (5 hours+ per week). Maximum = 240 hours (21 hours per week) within 12 months. Up to 10% of hours for completing associated basic literacy/qualifications.

2.13.7 Probation order/ Community rehabilitation order

- 'Serious enough' offence.
- Aims – rehabilitation, or protecting the public from harm, or preventing further offences.
- Supervision plan to be drawn up within 15 days of making the order and include individual and/or group supervision and be related to tangible outcomes.
- Defendant must keep out of trouble, keep in touch with the probation officer and notify any change of address.
- Nationally accredited programmes are available, based on research that they can reduce re-offending rates e.g. substance misuse, sex offenders, drink/drive offenders, enhanced thinking skills programmes.
- At least 12 appointments should be made within the first 12 weeks, including a home visit. 6 appointments in the second 12 weeks and thereafter, monthly.
- Order may be reviewed on the application of the defendant or officer.
- ⏱ Minimum = 6 months. Maximum = 3 years.

2.13.8 Combination Order/ Community punishment and rehabilitation order

- Imprisonable, 'serious enough' offences only.
- Reserved for offences which are at the 'top end' of the community band as the restriction on liberty is so high.
- ⏱ Probation element = 12 months to 3 years. Community service element = 40 hours to 100 hours.

2.13.9 Curfew Order

- 'Serious enough' offence.
- Specified place or places e.g. 2 addresses may be used.
- Information required about the place(s) and the attitude of other occupants who are likely to be affected before imposition.
- Approved person responsible for monitoring defendant's whereabouts e.g. security company contract.
- Is not confined to defendants who commit offences at night! It is simply a restriction on liberty to punish and/or prevent further offending.
- Additional (and usual) requirement may be made for electronic monitoring i.e. tagging. The equipment is usually installed within 24 hours unless the offender does not have a telephone when a 'limited use' (tagging and 999 calls) telephone will be fitted within 5 days.
- May combine with other community penalties for single offence but there are practical difficulties if multiple orders are breached.
- ⏱ Minimum = 2 hours per day. Maximum = 12 hours per day up to 6 months maximum.

2.13.10 Drug Treatment and Testing Order

- 'Serious enough' offence.
- Facility must be available. This is a high cost order and is budget-limited – real evidence of motivation is important.
- Defendant is dependent on or has propensity to misuse drugs.
- Requires and may be susceptible to treatment.
- Local criteria will usually seek a link between offending and drug-taking.
- Treatment requirement – by specified person, at specified institution at specified intervals if non-resident.
- Testing requirement – to specify the minimum number of occasions on which samples are required in each month.
- Supervision by a probation officer for the treatment and testing period and he will be informed of the test results.
- Order will be periodically reviewed by court at least monthly. If good progress is made, may amend for reviews without a formal hearing.
- Consent essential – may revoke and re-sentence if consent is withdrawn.
- ⏱ Minimum = 6 months. Maximum = 3 years.

2.13.11 Community orders: enforcement, amendment, revocation

Breach action may be taken after one unacceptable failure, where appropriate. For offenders on community sentences the supervisor must warn the offender using a 'yellow card' warning letter and give only one warning in any 12 month period of supervision before commencing breach action (National Standards 2000). This is likely to be enhanced into statutory requirement in the near future – one recorded warning and then court action (s.53 CJCSA 2000).

The outcomes for failure without reasonable excuse to comply with the requirements of the relevant order are as follows:

- No action – a warning from the court as to other possible outcomes of breach may well have the desired effect, together with a clear explanation of the obligations of the order and if at all possible, details as to the next appointment
- Fine not exceeding £1000 (Guideline entry point is band B)
- Community service order (CSO) for up to 60 hours (max aggregate 240 hours CSO)
- Attendance centre order for breach of probation order only
- Loss of benefits – pilot areas only(s.64 Child Support Pensions and Social Security Act 2000)
- Revoke and re-sentence - custody may be imposed if there has been wilful and persistent refusal to comply
- (When in effect, s.53 Criminal Justice and Court Services Act 2000, creates a presumption of imprisonment in respect of specified orders, unless exceptional circumstances apply).

The court must take into consideration the extent to which the offender has complied with the order in determining the breach penalty.

An application may be made for amendment/ revocation by the defendant or supervisor if circumstances change e.g. revocation of CSO due to ill health. An alternative penalty is imposed which reflects any work already done on the CSO.

In 1996, 10% of probation orders and 20% of community service orders were brought before the court on breach. By 2000, with more stringent guidance, a total of 40% of probation orders and 50% of community service orders were brought before the court on breach.

OFFENCE IS 'SO SERIOUS'

The following offences are examples of 'custody' entry points in the sentencing guidelines:

Assault on a police officer; harassment causing fear of violence; indecent assault; possession of a bladed instrument; drive whilst disqualified.

Note that more serious offences are designated as an entry point of committal to crown court e.g. dwelling burglary, and clearly custody is envisaged.

2.13.12 Custody

(i) Criteria:

- Offence(s) is/are 'so serious' *or*
- Violent/sexual offence and only a custodial sentence would be adequate to protect public from serious harm *or*
- Wilful and persistent refusal to comply with community order.

(ii) Requirements:

- Reasons must be announced e.g. " We believe that this offence of assault is so serious because it was unprovoked, it caused serious injury to a vulnerable victim and you have failed to respond to a probation order made last year for a similar offence."
- Practical effects must be explained i.e. remission of a half of the sentence subject to good behaviour; account to be taken of the period in custody on remand and the power to order a return to custody if a further offence is committed during the balance of the sentence.
- Pre-sentence report required unless considered 'unnecessary' e.g. a recent report is available, defendant has previously served custodial sentences and has already served the period on remand in custody.
- Legal aid must be considered – defendant must either fail to apply or be refused following advice from the court.
- ⏲ Minimum = 5 days imprisonment (7 days for fine defaulters) / 21 days detention for offenders aged 18 to 21.
- ⏲ Maximum = 6 months (or statute maximum if less) for single offence/12 months for 2+ either-way offences.

(iv) General relevant factors in borderline cases:

- Previous good character.
- Positive good character e.g. solid employment record, faithful discharge of family duties.
- Physical or mental disability.
- Never served a previous sentence of imprisonment.
- Extent of responsibility taken – early guilty plea; hard evidence of genuine remorse.
- If fuelled by drink/drugs – practical steps demonstrate a genuine, self-motivated determination to address addiction.
- Youth and immaturity.

One day's detention

Distinguish this option from 'imprisonment'! It is available for imprisonable offences and enables the court to detain within the precincts of the court or at any police station until 8pm as a primary sentence or in default of paying a fine (including the 18 to 21 age group). Custody criteria do not apply. Nevertheless it is a restriction on liberty and if a lengthy period is considered, it may be appropriate to allow consultation with the duty solicitor. Examples of its use are: detention in the courtroom 'until the court rises' for fineable offences where there are very limited means or an inability to pay; 'deemed already served' in respect of defendants/defaulters who have already spent a night in the cells; 6 hours detention for defendants who are arrested for failing to attend court (the likelihood of compliance with any court order may well be very low); as a method of wiping out outstanding costs/back duty which cannot be remitted.

2.13.13 Suspended sentence of imprisonment

- Imprisonment is appropriate.
- Suspension can be justified by the exceptional circumstances of the case – not simply youth, good character or early guilty plea but e.g. offender is sole carer of dependants; stolen money has been repaid; significant provocation. A defendant who is aware of his serious medical condition at the time of committing a familiar offence cannot successfully argue for 'exceptional circumstances (R v. Wickens 2000)
- Commission of a further offence during the period – may activate fully, or substitute a lesser term, or commence a further suspension period or make no order.

⏱ Minimum = 1 year from the date of the order. Maximum = 2 years.

2.13.14 Committal for sentence

The following offences are examples of 'committal to crown court' entry points in the magistrates' guidelines:

Affray; s.47 assault; burglary of dwelling; supply of class A/B drugs; dangerous driving; racially aggravated harassment; theft in breach of trust; violent disorder; s.20 wounding.

Effectively the guideline is stating that the offence is likely to merit more than 6 months imprisonment and would therefore be beyond the powers of the magistrates' court.

It is important to be particularly vigilant about the limitation of sentencing powers so that cases are properly committed to crown court for sentence if appropriate. In most cases this can be identified after the prosecution outline e.g. serious domestic burglary. Discussion should always take place on the bench as to appropriate venue where the entry point is committal. The defence must be allowed to address the court following the bench's indication that it is minded to commit to crown court. Occasionally there may be sufficient mitigation to bring the case down to magistrates' powers, but it is important to add a rider to any adjournment for pre-sentence reports that the next bench may commit the case to the crown court. If the rider is not added, the court has effectively given the indication that the maximum penalty will be 6 months imprisonment and even the crown court cannot go on to increase after that indication has been given.

The National Mode of Trial guidelines and sentencing guidelines provide helpful indicators of aggravating features for specific offences which assist in the determination of whether a case lies outside the magistrates' powers.

Example:

> Dangerous driving – aggravating features.
>
> (i) Alcohol or drugs contributing to dangerousness (ii) Grossly excessive speed (iii) Prolonged course of dangerous driving (iv) Degree of injury or damage sustained (v) Other related offences.

There is also a wealth of case law which provides assistance.

Case law examples:

- Domestic burglary

Both defendants of good character, pleaded guilty, gained access to an unoccupied house but were apprehended before any property was taken – 12 months imposed by the Court of Appeal. This case suggests that the starting point for any home burglary must surely be committal to crown court. (R v. Fogarty & Mahoney 1991).

- Concerned in the supply of class A drugs (e.g. ecstasy, heroin)

Defendant referred one customer to her boyfriend who supplied small quantity of ecstasy tablets in another part of the nightclub – 12 months. Again, this case seems to provide very clear guidance that any involvement in supply of class A drugs should be committed to crown court. (R v. Patel 1998).

- Theft in breach of trust

Defendant employed as a postman stole postal packets containing a total of £100 – 12 months. (R v. Poulter 1985).

- Protection from Harassment

Conduct causing fear of violence (s.4) was also in breach of an existing restraining order made under the Act. Consider the history, seriousness, effect on the victim, the victim's views, guilty plea and remorse – 15 months. (R v. Liddle 1999).

- Racially aggravated offences

Court of Appeal guidance was given in the case of R v. Saunders 1999 that the court should consider the following features:
- Nature of hostility demonstrated by language and/or use of weapon
- Whether location was public or private
- The number of demonstrators for and against
- Whether remarks were made in a crowded area e.g. in a mosque, or in an empty room.
- In the case concerned, a racially aggravated assault, it was said that up to 2 years should be added if the offence was racially aggravated, even if it was initially non-custodial. Effectively, this guidance will take most racially aggravated cases out of the magistrates' jurisdiction.

SENTENCES ON MENTALLY DISORDERED DEFENDANTS

1. Probation order + treatment requirement

- Evidence of approved medical practitioner that condition requires and may be susceptible to treatment.
- Satisfied that arrangements have already been made – hence some inevitable delays.
- Specify place and treatment as resident/non-resident patient or 'under direction of duly qualified medical practitioner.'
- Defendant must express willingness to comply.
- Maximum = full period of probation order.

2. Hospital or guardianship order

Same criteria apply to both:

- Imprisonable offence.
- Consider all circumstances and other available options.
- Evidence of 2 registered medical practitioners as to mental condition and recommendation is made.

- Arrangements already made for reception into hospital within 28 days of order or
- Local social services authority or specified person willing to receive offender into guardianship i.e. care and protection rather than treatment.
- Hospital order is reviewable and discharge is at discretion of hospital managers but if limitations are appropriate then commit to crown court for a restriction order. Guardianship order is indeterminate but subject to regular reviews.

ANCILLARY ORDERS

1. Binding over

- Order to 'keep the peace' and/or 'to be of good behaviour ... and in particular not to assault/molest/interfere with ... or repeat the following behaviour, namely ... (JCS and MA guidance 2000). In order to ensure clarity and certainty under the Human Rights Act, it is important to specify the behaviour which will be punished on breach.
- Court has grounds for believing that there is a possibility of a future breach of the peace.
- Order to enter into a recognisance in terms chosen by the court as to duration and amount e.g. 'bind over to keep the peace for 6 months in the sum of £50', all or part of which is forfeited if the bind over is breached. (Means information is therefore required.)
- Refusal to enter into the recognisance may result in imprisonment up to 6 months (defendants over 21 only) or earlier agreement to enter the recognisance, but proportionality suggests that only a few hours of detention is likely to be appropriate for the type of behaviour usually complained of.
- This is a highly valuable, deterrent order and should arguably be considered on the court's own initiative whenever dealing with offences of threats and violence, as an additional penalty.

◷ No maximum or minimum periods.

(See 5.27.5. for procedure).

2. Compensation

See 2.13.4 above. Compensation may be an order in its own right or ancillary to another penalty. Always consider – is there a victim? If so, always consider – may compensation be awarded?

3. Exclusion Order (licensed premises)

- Prohibits defendant from entering specified premises without licensee's consent.
- Violent offence or threatened violence on licensed premises.
- Breach penalty = level 3 fine/1 month imprisonment.
- Minimum = 3 months. Maximum = 2 years.

4. Forfeiture

- Property has been used by offender to commit offence.
- No 3rd party rights.
- Depends upon relevant statute.

e.g. Misuse of Drugs Act 1971 – any tangible property e.g. drugs, scales, if satisfied that it relates to the offence. Prevention of Crime Act 1953 – offensive weapon may be forfeited.
Obscene Publications Act 1964 – 'shall' order forfeiture of any seized articles.

5. Football banning order

- Order may be made following a conviction or on complaint by the police.
- Prohibits subject from entering a football ground to attend a 'regulated match' and requires him to report to a police station to ensure that he does not travel to a regulated match played abroad.
- Offender convicted of a 'relevant offence' e.g. vandalism in the ground, threats of violence on journey to match.
- Reasonable grounds to believe that banning order will help prevent violence or disorder at or in connection with any regulated football matches. Reasons must be given if order is not made.
- Subject must report to a police station specified within 5 days (unless in custody) and surrender passport when regulated matches are played outside the UK unless there are reasons for not doing so e.g. pre-booked holiday.
- Breach penalty = 6 months/£5,000.
- Note that minimum period is for 3 years – consider 'proportionality' of order for minor offence.
- Criminal order following conviction: Min = 3 years. Max = 5 years. (6 years to 10 years if custodial sentence imposed). Civil order: Min = 2 years. Max = 3 years.

6. Prosecution costs

- Court to determine 'just and reasonable' amount.
- Normal maximum repayment period – 12 months.
- Amount must be specified in the order.

- May include costs of carrying out investigations.
- Full details to be notified to defendant e.g. on the summons itself if guilty plea by letter.
- Representations may be made.
- Enforceable as a fine.

7. Restraining order

- Offender is convicted of an offence contrary to the Protection from Harassment Act 1997 – causing harassment (s.2) or conduct causing fear of violence (s.4).
- Order to protect victim from further harassment or fear of violence.
- Definition may be similar to a bail condition and may contain specific exclusions and restrictions. (Check proportionality of the restriction as the right to private and family life and freedom of association are likely to be engaged.)
- The order should identify the protected parties e.g. 'prohibit from conduct which amounts to harassment of X and Y', rather than simply must not 'contact or communicate with hostel staff' (R v Mann 2000).
- Breach = 6 months/£5,000 or 5 years/fine at crown court. If in conjunction with new offence, consider committal to crown court for sentence (R v Liddle 1999).
- ⌚ No maximum or minimum order; 'until further order' may be appropriate.

8. Sex Offender registration (obligatory)

- Convicted of relevant offence e.g. intercourse with a girl under 13, intercourse with girl aged 13-16/ offender is over 20, possessing indecent photographs.
- Register with local police within 14 days.
- Disclose name, address, date of birth and notify police of any change of address of 14 days or more.
- Failure to comply = fine / 6 months imprisonment.
- ⌚ Maximum period = 5 years if non-custodial penalty/7 years if custody imposed or until sentenced at crown court.

Ancillary orders of restitution, deprivation, confiscation and recommendation for deportation are available but rare – consult the clerk!

TRAFFIC PENALTIES

1. Endorsement and penalty points

Endorsement is obligatory for specified offences e.g. no insurance, failing to comply with a red traffic light. The only exception is when special reasons apply (see (9) below). Every endorsable offence carries penalty points, whether fixed e.g. 3 penalty points for a defective tyre or discretionary e.g. 3-9 for driving without due care and attention.

Where there are a number of offences committed on the same occasion the court must normally impose penalty points on the most serious offence only.

Example:

1.1.2001	Fail to stop	points range 5 to 10	(none allocated)
1.1.2001	Fail to report	points range 5 to 10	(10)

= 2 similar offences arising out of the same incident and circumstances,

but only one set of points allocated to the offence judged by the bench to be the most serious on the facts e.g. 10 points for the failure to report – as it was a deliberate decision taken over 24 hours rather than the panic of 'failing to stop' at the time of the accident.

However, the court may determine that separate points should be allocated 'if it thinks fit' and reasons must be given.

Example:

7.7.2001	Driving otherwise than in accordance with licence = 3
7.7.2001	Speeding = 3
7.7.2001	Defective tyre =3

Same occasion but separate penalty points awarded because the offences are so dissimilar – a document offence, a driving offence and a defect offence – different actions and mental culpability for each type and the reason is given.

2. Disqualification

(a) Obligatory

A minimum period of 12 months disqualification applies to the following offences unless special reasons apply:

(i) Driving or attempting to drive whilst unfit through drink/drugs.

(ii) Driving or attempting to drive with excess alcohol.

(iii) Failing to provide a specimen without reasonable excuse.
Dangerous driving.
Aggravated taking without consent (even the passenger!).

In respect of offences (i)(ii)(iii) the period of 12 months is increased to 3 years if the offender has already been convicted within the past 10 years. It is increased to 2 years if the offender has been disqualified for 56 days or more on 2 or more occasions in the 3 years preceding the offence. This may sound complicated but the legal adviser will draw this to your attention as necessary, but it is well worth being broadly aware how the minimum periods can increase.

Since 1.1.2000 the disqualification period for the alcohol-related offences may however be reduced if the offender satisfactorily completes a specified approved course. The reduced period is not less than 3 months and cannot exceed 1/4 of the unreduced period e.g. a 12 month ban may be reduced to 9 months. The course fee is income-related and is payable by the defendant to the course organiser. Consent is required on the day of sentence. This enables the court to announce the reduced period and appropriate warnings can be given that the course fee must be paid <u>and</u> the course must be satisfactorily completed at least 2 calendar months prior to the end of the disqualification if the reduced period is to be effective.

(b) Discretionary

A discretionary disqualification may be imposed for any endorsable offence, and also taking a motor vehicle without consent (although not endorsable).

Example:

> The sentencing guidelines suggest that a discretionary disqualification of up to 56 days is imposed for the offence of exceeding a 70mph limit by 31-40 mph, i.e. over 100 mph.

Any previous points will remain on the licence for 3 years for the purpose of totting (see below). It is now permissible to consider a discretionary disqualification in parallel with the possibility of imposing points and reaching a totting situation (Jones v. Chief Constable of West Mercia 2000). However, the nature of the record must be carefully considered before imposing a short disqualification for the current offence. The other option is to impose penalty points which would take the offender into a 6 month minimum totting disqualification. The totality must be considered and a 14 day ban for excessive speeding may not reflect the fact that it is the 3rd motoring offence within a short period and a 6 month totting ban may then be more proportionate.

(c) Totting

When 12 penalty points are accumulated in the 3 year period, the court must disqualify for a minimum of 6 months unless 'exceptional hardship' is proved. The minimum of 6 months is increased to 12 months if there has been 1 other disqualification of 56 days or more within the 3 year period, and to 2 years if there has been 2 such disqualifications.

It is desirable to hear sworn evidence as to the exceptional hardship. The court may decide either not to disqualify at all or may reduce the period if satisfied that there is 'exceptional hardship.'

It will usually be necessary for the defendant to produce written evidence that he requires a driving licence to continue his employment e.g. contract, letter from employer, along with details of his financial situation and the financial effect of becoming unemployed. Similarly evidence should be sought to prove that any onerous family transport responsibilities must inevitably fall upon the defendant. Alternative employment arrangements and alternative modes of transport should be explored. It is relevant that the hardship may well fall upon the defendant's family or employees.

A totting disqualification is the only type of disqualification which 'wipes the slate clean' and points are removed. It is therefore worth recognising that a short totting ban of say 7 days will leave the defendant without any points on his licence. However, the same reason cannot be put forward for 'exceptional hardship' if a further offence is committed during the 3 year period and it may well be that a 'delayed' ban would justifiably be for more than the 6 month minimum as the points would obviously be higher.

(d) Interim disqualification

Disqualification may be ordered on an interim basis when a defendant is committed to the crown court for sentence; remitted to another magistrates court; subjected to deferment of sentence or adjourned following conviction e.g. for pre-sentence reports.

The disqualification will lapse if the defendant is not sentenced before the expiry of 6 months. The final disqualification will take into account the interim period e.g. an obligatory 12 month disqualification will effectively be back-dated to the commencement of the interim ban. This is a useful power which ensures that the public are protected immediately, albeit there are further issues to pursue before final sentence.

(e) Disqualification until test is passed

The court *must* disqualify an offender until he passes an extended driving test if he is convicted of dangerous driving. The court *may* disqualify until an ordinary test is passed in any case involving obligatory endorsement if there is concern about the safety of other road users e.g. lengthy ban arising from a serious careless driving case. The offender is then effectively reduced to provisional driver status and must display 'L' plates and carry a qualified passenger. Failure to do so constitutes an offence of driving whilst disqualified.

(f) Revocation of licence by DVLA, Swansea

A new driver who has passed his test within the past 2 years and acquires 6 penalty points will be subject to revocation of his full licence by Swansea. Effectively he will revert to provisional licence status. Whilst this is not an order of the court, account should be taken of the implication. In a recent case, the sentencing court awarded 6 points and declared that it would not disqualify as the defendant lived in a rural area and required a full licence. The Court of Appeal substituted 5 points as it was considered that the sentencing court had effectively disqualified him, by rendering him liable to revocation and the requirement to drive with a qualified passenger at all times (Re: Damien Edwards 2000).

3. Special reasons

Endorsement and disqualification may be avoided if the court is satisfied that a special reason exists. The reason must satisfy 4 criteria:

Mitigating or extenuating circumstance.
Not a legal defence e.g. that defendant was not 'driving' the car.
Directly connected to offence e.g. emergency situation, laced drinks, rather than relating to the offender e.g. hardship to individual if disqualified.
Factor which the court ought properly to take into consideration e.g. whether the defendant acted responsibly and reasonably.

The court must then consider whether to exercise its discretion. This will depend upon various factors e.g. in what manner was the vehicle driven, the reason for the car being driven, danger to others.

There are numerous cases involving special reasons and the clerk's advice should always be sought before making a determination in this complex area.

Example:

A frequent special reason put forward is 'shortness of distance driven.' Recent guidance has been given that the court must look not only at what the defendant had actually achieved but at what he intended – in the case concerned he fully intended to drive home and special reasons were not made out (CPS v. Dean Humphries 2000).

THE RULES OF EVIDENCE

2.14 Sequence and purpose of questions

2.14.1 Evidence in chief

These questions are asked by the party calling the witness i.e. prosecution or defence. The purpose is to assist the witness to put forward his version of events of what he saw or did. Questions cannot usually be put which suggest the answer. These are called leading questions and permission will be given by the other advocate 'to lead' only on the undisputed facts e.g. the date and time of the incident. Other leading questions can only be allowed in unusual and technical circumstances which the clerk will advise upon if the circumstances should arise.

Example:

"Is it correct that on the 1st May you saw the person with the tattoo on his arm strike the victim in his face with a clenched fist?"

This would not be allowed. Instead the question would have to be opened up to the witness in stages:

Where were you at 6pm on the 1st May?
What did you see?
You say that you saw men shouting at each other and one of them struck the other; can you describe the man who struck the blow?
Was there anything about the man that was particularly distinctive?
Would you describe how the blow was struck?

Questions which disparage the witness's credibility are also usually disallowed e.g. Is it correct that you have several convictions for making false statements, deception and perverting the course of justice?

2.14.2 Cross-examination

These are questions by the 'opposing' advocate and the purpose is to probe the version of events and check out the accuracy and truthfulness. Differences between the original statement and the evidence given in court will often form the basis of cross-examination. The witness does not have the benefit of the statement when giving evidence, although he is allowed to refresh his memory before coming into court.

Leading questions can be asked in cross-examination. These will usually take the form of statements which describe a particular (preferred) scenario, followed by the question "Isn't that what really happened?".

It is essential that any disputed matters are put in cross-examination if they are to form part of the case. This enables the witness to agree or disagree. When a defendant is unrepresented it is helpful to delegate the task of assisting the defendant to the court clerk. The clerk may then assist the defendant in framing his questions and also ensure that the nub of the defence is properly put in cross-examination e.g. that the criminal damage was caused purely by an accidental stumble.

2.14.3 Re-examination

This provides the opportunity for clarification of issues which have arisen during cross-examination e.g. an admission by the defendant in cross-examination that he was possibly a 'little drunk' at the time can be re-examined to explore the actual effects of the alcohol. It is not possible to introduce any new matters at this stage. It simply enables an advocate to assist his client to answer fully any facts which were not part of the instructions before trial. Again, leading questions cannot be used.

Finally, the magistrates may ask questions to clarify matters which have already been referred to in evidence. It is important that the bench do not enter into the arena and begin raising new issues which should have been put by prosecution or defence to establish guilt or innocence. It may assist to check that any question from the bench begins with the statement which is to be clarified i.e. You said that ... and we would like to know ...

In theory the court may ask such questions at any stage, but there is much to be said for leaving the advocates so far as possible to present the case as they feel most appropriate initially. Frequent interjections can distract the advocate and confuse the witness as to the role of the court – one cross-examination at a time is sufficient for a nervous witness to deal with.

2.15 Tests of evidence/burdens of proof

The burden of establishing proof will always rest with one party.

In criminal cases the burden lies on the prosecution to satisfy the court that the case is properly proved. The defence may therefore choose to say nothing at all. The standard of proof is 'beyond reasonable doubt.' This does not mean proof 'beyond a shadow of doubt'. Where there is a remote possibility in favour of the defendant, can it be answered by the sentence 'of course it is possible but not in the least probable'? If so, then the case is proved beyond reasonable doubt.

Where the defendant bears a burden of proof, either through statute or common law, the standard is the same as for civil cases – 'on the balance of probabilities.' The tribunal must consider 'we think it more probable than not'.

Example:

No insurance allegation.

> Prosecution must prove beyond reasonable doubt that defendant was driving without insurance. Defendant pleads 'Not Guilty' and the burden then shifts by statute to the defendant to prove on the balance of probabilities that he was covered.
>
> Evidence might include a bank statement showing monthly payments to the insurance company together with sworn evidence that the original certificate has been lost and the company have since gone out of business and a duplicate cannot therefore be obtained. Is it 'more probable than not', that he was covered?'

2.16 Hearsay evidence

In criminal proceedings a witness cannot usually give evidence as to the truth of a statement made by someone else e.g. "the shop assistant said that the thief had a tattoo." The court cannot have any regard to the existence of a tattoo. The person who made the statement is not available in court for cross-examination and she may well have been mistaken about her observation. In civil proceedings evidence is not excluded on the ground that it is hearsay. There are some exceptions in criminal proceedings, notably statements by witnesses who are in fear of the defendant. The starting point for a fair trial is that the defendant should be able to call witnesses and cross-examine them, and the court must therefore make full enquiry before hearsay is allowed e.g. Have statements been disclosed?

What is the basis for suggesting that the witness is in fear of his life to attend court?

2.17 Differences in civil/criminal cases

Criminal proceedings

Proof is 'beyond reasonable doubt'.
'Prosecutor or informant' brings the case to court.
Defendant 'defends'.

Civil proceedings

Proof is on the 'balance of probabilities'.
'Applicant or complainant' brings the case to court.
Respondent 'responds'.

WHO DOES WHAT

2.18 The role of the police

The primary function of today's police is:

To uphold the law fairly and firmly
To prevent crime
To pursue and bring to justice those who break the law
To protect, help and reassure the community

The police are responsible for the investigation of the vast majority of criminal offences; the arrest and interview of the suspect; the charging or reporting of the suspected offender and the submission of the initial file.

Police powers are contained within five Codes of Practice which include powers to arrest without warrant; to stop and search and to conduct road checks. Breach of the powers may result in disciplinary proceedings and inadmissibility of the relevant evidence.

An information laid by the police cannot be laid in the name of the police force but must be laid either by the Chief Constable or some other person authorised by him e.g. the local Inspector by name and he will appear on the court register as informant.

2.19 The role of the Crown Prosecution Service

The Crown Prosecution Service conducts the conduct of all cases commenced by the police, with a few exceptions. The Service is independent of the police. The 2000 Code for Crown Prosecutors highlights the duty to review all files presented by the police. It sets out two stages in the decision to prosecute.

The first stage is the evidential test which requires 'enough evidence to provide a realistic prospect of conviction.' The objective test is whether a properly directed bench or jury is more likely than not to convict. The second stage is the public interest test. The Code gives examples of common factors where a prosecution is less likely to be needed. Examples include where the court is likely to impose a nominal penalty; where the prosecution is likely to have a very bad effect on the victim's health; where the defendant is elderly or suffering from significant ill health or where the defendant has put right the loss or harm caused. The Code states that any offence which is motivated by discrimination is likely to require prosecution.

Example:

Offences of driving without due care and no insurance.

> Under the previous guidelines the expectation in many areas was that a fine would be ordered on the insurance matter alone, which would normally be payable over the full 12 months (i.e. entry point of £540). There was little point in pursuing the driving without due care as the full 12 months repayment period had already been 'used up' on the insurance matter. A 2nd offence would usually attract 'no separate penalty' and there was little point in pursuing proof and evidence.
>
> With the new guidelines, it is now more likely that fines can be allocated to each offence as fine levels are generally much lower for the offence of no insurance. There is the additional consideration of being able to award separate penalty points, disqualification and, importantly, the ability to add compensation up to £300 to the victim as the 'fault' is on record (see 2.13.4). This change in sentencing practice may well change the view of CPS in deciding which offences to proceed with.

2.20 The role of e.g. Health & Safety, Environmental Health Agencies

Local authorities and nationalised industries may prosecute their own cases e.g. relating to dangerous workshop machinery; dirty restaurants and kitchens; false descriptions on garments. These are specialised areas of work and it is entirely appropriate for the bench to ask questions in order to understand the nature of the problem created. Magistrates are not expected to be experts and such proceedings must inevitably involve substantial explanation and description of circumstances.

Where offences are contrary to the customs and excise legislation it is specifically provided that such cases are prosecuted by HM Customs and Excise and this right applies even if the defendant is charged at a police station. Similarly the Serious Fraud Office has the responsibility of prosecuting serious and complex frauds.

2.21 The prosecutor in court

Following a guilty plea the prosecutor outlines the facts to the court, produces any previous convictions and makes any claims for compensation and costs. In a trial situation the prosecutor will usually speak to the prosecution witnesses as they arrive and may bring them into court to explain procedures before the case begins. He will then outline the case, call his own witnesses, cross-examine the defence witnesses and make any submissions on law.

The prosecutor in court may not be the prosecutor who has 'conduct of the file' for the purpose of review and this can create difficulties if the court wishes to make progress on an application to adjourn. Enquiries may well be ongoing to establish whether the two tests described above are satisfied and the prosecutor may feel that it is inappropriate for him to take a view in court.

By the same token it may be possible to make progress on decisions in court after discussion with the defence solicitor e.g. production of medical certificates or confirmation that the defendant is already serving a substantial sentence of imprisonment which may render prosecution to be against the public interest. Obviously such discussions can be conducted more openly if the bench retire. The outcome may well be a withdrawal or reduction of charge.

2.22 The defence lawyer in court

The defence solicitor will essentially take instructions; advise on plea; assist in making an application for legal aid if appropriate; interview witnesses and conduct the case in court. Occasionally counsel are instructed by solicitors to conduct proceedings in the magistrates' court.

The professional duties of a solicitor are contained within the Guide to the Professional Conduct of Solicitors which is published by the Law Society. The duties include the following:

- Must promote and protect fearlessly and by all proper and lawful means the client's best interests
- Must not deceive or mislead the court

- Must not rehearse, practise or coach witnesses in relation to their evidence
- Must not accept instructions to act for 2 or more clients where there is a conflict or a significant risk of conflict between the clients e.g. blaming each other.

In general there is no duty upon a solicitor to enquire in every case as to whether his client is telling the truth.

Article 6 of the Human Rights Act gives every defendant the right to defend himself in person or through legal assistance of his own choosing (if paying personally) or if he has insufficient means then legal assistance is to be given free if the 'interest of justice' so require.

Convention case law is clear that lawyer/client communications must be private and confidential; must not be subject to restrictions e.g. in the hearing of the interviewing police officer and must not be unreasonably delayed for a defendant in police custody. Defendants on bail might usefully be urged to make an appointment at their solicitor's office to give instructions before the hearing. Where there have been previous delays in this respect, the court might consider attaching a condition of bail to make and keep an appointment with his solicitor before the next hearing.

2.23 The role of witnesses

Much work has been done over recent years to encourage members of the public to come forward and act as witnesses by the creation of witness support facilities within the court. It is well recognised that being a witness may well feel to be a thankless burden. Lots of questions, possible lack of total recollection, cross-examination, waiting around to give a statement to the police, waiting around at court and perhaps, worst of all, facing a defendant across the courtroom. The defendant may be found guilty and the sentence may weigh as a responsibility on the witness. The defendant may be acquitted and the witness may feel that he has been branded as a liar by the court.

It is a nerve-wracking experience and every support and encouragement must be given if justice is to prevail. It may well be appropriate to allow all witnesses to give their evidence sitting down. They are not on trial. They are simply being asked to tell the court what they have seen or heard. Similarly it may be helpful and courteous to allow a comfort break from time to time. This applies particularly to non-professional witnesses who may not be used to speaking for lengthy periods in public and even more so if the witness is also the victim. It would be quite wrong for emotional weariness to overtake the strength to tell the truth in the face of professional cross-examination.

It is easy to remember to thank witnesses for their attendance after giving evidence, but it should also be done when the witnesses attend but are not called – they still had the sleepless night! Calling them into court informally may be a little embarrassing, but at least they have been recognised and properly acknowledged.

CASE MANAGEMENT

Scheduling and timetabling

2.24 Statutory time limits

Time limits apply to various aspects of the criminal process. The most important are set out below:

1. The general rule is that an information must be laid within 6 months from the date of a summary offence e.g. speeding. There is no time limit for indictable matters e.g. theft.

2. The maximum period for which someone may be detained without charge or appearance before a court is 36 hours.

3. A defendant who is charged with an offence and kept in custody must be brought before the magistrates court as soon as practicable after being charged and in any event not later than the first sitting of the court after being charged.

4. A defendant who is charged and bailed must be bailed to a date which is not later than the first sitting of the court after charge or a later date if the appearance cannot be so accommodated. The normal period for court appearance is within 48 hours of charge if the local court is sitting on a daily basis.

5. The maximum period for the first two remands in custody is 8 days. Thereafter the maximum period is 21 days after conviction and 28 days before conviction.

6. The maximum period of remand in custody in respect of indictable offences is 70 days between first appearance and commencement of the committal or trial. The maximum period of remand in custody in respect of offences which are triable summarily is 56 days. Application may be made to 'extend the custody time limits' in specified circumstances, provided that the prosecution have acted with all due diligence and expedition, and application must be made to the court.

7. Where a defendant has allegedly breached his bail conditions he must be brought before the court as soon as reasonably practicable and in any event within 24 hours after his arrest.

There are also nationally agreed pre-trial guidelines e.g. 'not guilty' plea to summary trial within 8 weeks if the defendant is on bail.

2.25 The court diary

As court processes have become more complex it has become necessary to 'book' cases into the daily court space. The principal aim is to ensure that court rooms are used effectively and that parties do not have to wait any longer than necessary for their case to be listed. Similarly it is important that parties are not kept waiting for lengthy periods for their case to be called on the day.

The main variable in the court diary is the listing of a trial. It is virtually impossible to predict accurately how long the case will take. At the pre-trial review hearing an estimate will be given based upon the issues involved and the number of witnesses to be called. However, on the day of the trial it is often the case that the defendant will finally admit the matter and the court time set aside may well be wasted.

A further variable is of course the number of detected crimes on any one day. The outcome may well be a very large list at the first available court. It may also have an effect on custody remand cases where lengthy bail applications cannot be planned into the diary with any accuracy.

The positive feature of the diary is that local predictions can in fact be made in many cases and time slots are allocated on an 'average time' basis e.g. 20 minutes for a pre-sentence report matter,10 minutes for a 'guilty plea' on bail, 2 minutes per parking offence summons.

The reality is that, with the flexibility and patience of the principal resource of the magistrates, courtrooms are generally used effectively and court lists are almost invariably completed every day.

2.26 The case in court for the first time

A case may arrive in court for the first time either by summons or by charge. The charge cases will appear either on bail or in custody. The first appearance for criminal bail cases is a date which is not later than the first sitting of the court after the person is charged with the offence unless it cannot be accommodated until a later date.

In order to make progress within the tight time-scale, arrangements exist for the early preparation of adequate Advance Disclosure and for the CPS prosecutor to review files at the police station or Criminal Justice Support Unit. Files are then designated either as 'Early First Hearing' files or 'Early Administrative Hearing' files. Basically the admitted offences will normally be listed as first hearings before a bench and the remainder will be listed for an administrative hearing, with the prospect of fixing a trial or adjourning on for further information and review, possibly with directions.

2.27 Uncontested road traffic matters

Most summary traffic matters are dealt with by way of summons. The majority of defendants choose not to attend and either enter a guilty plea by post based upon the prosecution facts which are sent to them, or alternatively the case can be proved without their response if full statements are sent to them at least 10 days before the hearing. In the latter scenario it is open to the defendant to ask for the case to be re-opened if he did not receive the summons and statements e.g. he was on holiday or had moved from the address given to the officer at the time. The court will obtain a print-out of the driver's record from DVLC Swansea in readiness for the case to proceed – with or without a licence in court.

INITIAL DECISIONS

2.28 Adjournments and their effects

Adjourning a case to another day carries various implications which include the following:

- Justice is delayed.
- Defendant and victim have to wait longer for an outcome and this may cause stress and prolonged misery.
- The impact of any sentence becomes distanced from the crime and its effect may be reduced.
- Court space and magistrates' time is wasted if the case was 'booked in' as a lengthy matter.
- The recollection of the defendant and any witnesses becomes more hazy as time goes by.
- The court budget is enhanced by completed cases and effective use of court room space rather than by adjourned cases and early finishes.

The court should therefore be cautious in granting adjournments, even if they are agreed by prosecution and defence. Questions should be asked to ensure that the case cannot fairly progress any further for good reason.

- What is the reason for the adjournment? e.g. witness has not attended.
- What was the anticipated action today? e.g. trial.
- How may previous listings have there been? e.g. 7 in total and 2nd for trial.
- What steps have been taken to prepare for, or to resolve the difficulty? e.g. witness has not yet attended at the defence solicitor's office to provide a witness statement in spite of several letters over a period of weeks.
- Can the difficulty be resolved today/differently? e.g. telephone the witness; deal with the trial as a part-heard matter and either issue a witness summons if criteria apply or proceed in absence of the witness today.

(The criteria for the grant of a witness summons are that the witness is likely to be able to produce material evidence and that the person will not voluntarily attend as a witness. Enquiry may therefore properly be made as to the nature of the evidence. What is it? Are any other witnesses providing the same evidence? To what extent (if any) is it material to the case?)

The average time from offence to completion in the magistrates' court for defendants in indictable cases was 111 days in June 2000.

2.29 Remand Provisions

2.29.1 The general right to bail

There is a general right to bail for all unconvicted defendants, and convicted defendants if the case is adjourned for reports, with one exception. This arises where the defendant is charged with murder/attempt, rape/attempt or manslaughter if he has previously been convicted (and imprisoned in the case of manslaughter) of one of the five offences. In this very rare scenario, there must be exceptional circumstances found for the grant of bail – note that the previous total prohibition on bail in these circumstances has now gone.

Apart from this single provision any unconvicted person shall be granted unconditional bail unless one or more of the statutory exceptions to bail apply. Convention case law states that the court must consider the presumption of innocence and the respect for individual liberty and refuse bail only where there are 'relevant' and 'sufficient' reasons and in all cases. Reasons must be given.

2.29.2 Statutory exceptions to bail

Specific statutory exceptions must be found and reasons must be given for finding them if unconditional bail is not granted. The exceptions which apply to imprisonable offences are based upon the court's belief that there are reasons (*set out in italics*) to believe that the defendant will:

- Fail to surrender to court because ... *previous failures to answer bail; lack of community ties; strength of evidence; the nature and gravity of the offence and probable sentence.*

Fear of absconding cannot be gauged <u>solely</u> on the basis of the severity of the sentence risked as it flies in the face of a presumption of innocence and an additional reason would be required e.g. along with the strength of evidence.

- Commit offences on bail because ... *of previous offences committed on bail.*

The previous offences must be comparable in nature and seriousness to justify this reasoning and the danger of committing further offences must be plausible.

- Interfere with witnesses or obstruct the course of justice because ... *of behaviour/proximity towards witnesses.*

General references to a mere possibility of interference is not enough. There must be a real and ongoing risk. The risk may substantially reduce or disappear after statements have been made.

- Requires custody for his own protection/welfare because ... *of evidence of self-injury.*

- Already serving a sentence in custody ... *imposed on ...*

- Not practical to obtain sufficient information to make a bail decision because of ... *recent arrest on ...*

Such a remand must be for the shortest possible period in order to obtain the information e.g. overnight to check out bail address or locate hostel vacancy.

- Arrested in breach of bail granted in the proceedings ... *breach admitted or found proved.*

- Impractical to complete report enquiries because ... *no likelihood of co-operation whilst on bail.*

In Leeds city, approximately 1/3 of defendants failed to comply with instructions for preparation of a pre-sentence report in 1999. It is well worth warning a defendant that failure to comply with the condition may result in the report being prepared on remand in custody instead.

- Charged with an indictable/either way offence whilst already on bail ... *namely .... whilst on bail for ... to ...*

Again, this is inappropriate in isolation as it is making a presumption that the defendant actually committed a further offence on bail – he is simply charged and may be innocent.

2.29.3 Unconditional bail

If there are no exceptions found, the court must grant unconditional bail. Even an apparently non-punitive condition such as residence cannot be imposed simply because it will ensure that there is a mailing address for the defendant. There must be valid reasons to believe that the defendant will fail to surrender in order to justify such a condition. Furthermore, some defendants simply do not have a permanent address. Unconditional bail carries one obligation – to attend court on the appointed date and time. Failure to attend court (or a police station) on bail is an offence in its own right, which carries imprisonment. Failure to attend may also result in a warrant being issued for arrest and possibly a remand in custody until the case is dealt with.

2.29.4 Conditional bail

Various conditions may be considered in order to address the exceptions (risks) found and so avoid a remand in custody. Potential conditions must always be considered before moving on to a remand in custody. Always remember that the defendant has a right to unconditional bail, and the second stage is a right to conditional bail, rather than custody. What exception has been found (with reasons for it) and can the particular risk be covered adequately by a condition or not?

(i) Fail to surrender exception:

- To live and sleep at ......

Make sure that the address is available and the householder is aware. Placing a curfew on this condition is not appropriate unless there is evidence of night-time offending as well. A belief that a defendant may leave the area simply requires a stable, genuine, 'living at' address. A curfew would be a disproportionate restriction.

- To report to ... police station between ... and .. on ...

Consider the purpose of reporting, the realities of apprehension if a day is missed and the best use of police manpower. Is daily or weekly reporting really necessary in the particular case? A single reporting condition shortly before the next hearing can usefully generate an arrest for a date set down for progress to be made. The police are likely to prioritise arrest if the bail form is marked that the date is fixed for a trial!

- To reside at a hostel approved by the Anytown Probation Service and to abide by the rules of the hostel and to reside initially at the ... hostel.

The initial residence aspect allows the probation service to have flexibility to move the defendant without having to come to court to vary the location if this should become necessary subsequently.

The purpose of a Home Office approved hostel (101 hostels in January 2001), is to provide an enhanced level of supervision with the aim of protecting the public by reducing the likelihood of offending. There is 24-hour cover with at least 2 members of staff on duty at any one time. The normal curfew is 11pm to 7am. All bailees are subject to ongoing assessment and support. The bail hostel is an expensive, specialised resource rather than a 'bed for the remand period' – if that is all that your defendant needs, please do not tie the officer's hands to a hostel – leave the suggestions of accommodation open.

- To provide a surety in the sum of ...

The court must consider the financial resources which are actually available, the character of the proposed surety and the residence and relationship proximity. Is it realistic that this person lives near enough and is influential enough on the defendant to ensure his attendance? It is no longer necessary to find that the defendant may leave the United Kingdom. A warning must be given that the whole sum may be forfeited dependent upon the culpability of the surety if the defendant fails to attend.

- To provide a security namely ... cash, passport.

An additional rider might be considered 'and not to make any application for a duplicate passport or any other foreign travel documentation'.

(ii) Would commit further offences/charged with further offence whilst on bail exceptions:

- To live and sleep at .... and to remain indoors at that address between ... and ..

Curfews should only be imposed where there is evidence to support a genuine concern that further offending will be generated during the curfew period.

- Not to enter ... area where crime committed, areas frequented by the witnesses.

Be careful with definitions of areas and the reality of enforcement. Shoplifters may be realistically kept out of named shops, or specific parades of shops but it is usually unrealistic, unnecessary and disproportionate to bar them from whole areas of cities where they are likely to travel in their day-to-day life.

(iii) Would interfere with witnesses/obstruct the course of justice exceptions:

- Not to contact directly or indirectly ....named witnesses.

Where this is a serious concern it may be worthwhile to stress that arrest may follow upon breach and that a separate offence of obstructing/perverting the course of justice may well be considered which in itself would carry imprisonment. If the contact has been by e-mail – include it specifically; through a 3rd party – include him by name in the definition 'and any other 3rd party'. In domestic cases, it may be worth reminding the defendant that the condition is there to protect him as well, and if the other party wishes to communicate, they should both come to court for it to be varied or deleted rather than breaking the condition.

- Not to enter ... area where crime committed, areas frequented by witnesses.

This condition can afford some peace of mind to witnesses, whether they are store detectives following a shoplifting charge; victims of burglaries in a particular neighbourhood; licensees of public houses where a disturbance has occurred or victims of domestic violence who simply wish to proceed with their daily life to local shops, pub and school. Keep the restriction proportionate to the crime and the risk, and seek representations on your suggested definition e.g. defendant may have existing contact arrangements with his children.

The bench may attach a condition requiring the defendant to attend for interview with his solicitor before the next hearing. This condition is simply to ensure progress and provide the court with a justification for referral to the duty solicitor if there has been no effort to seek advice during the adjournment.

2.29.5 Implications of Human Rights Act

Most conditions will engage the Human Rights Act, and care must be taken particularly with Article 8, the right to private and family life (the right to do as we please) and Article 11, freedom of assembly and association (the right to go where and with whom we want to). Both Articles contain qualified rights. The 3 questions must therefore be asked in order to ensure that the condition (restriction) is:

1. Based on law which is clear and accessible i.e. the Bail Act.
2. Pursues a legitimate aim e.g. to prevent disorder or crime; to protect the rights, freedoms and morals of others.
3. Is proportionate i.e. is no more than is necessary to deal with the situation.

The other important Article is Article 7, 'no punishment without law' (no punishment unless we know exactly how and when we are breaking the law) as this requires certainty of restriction e.g. 'not to interfere with prosecution witnesses' – who are they? 'not to enter the city centre' – where are the city limits? Neither condition complies with Article 7 unless it can be argued that the defendant 'just happens to know!'.

2.29.6 Custody

When the bench find exceptions but cannot safely attach conditions to deal with the risks, then the defendant must be remanded into custody. At this stage it is worth checking that the court has sufficient information on which to make a full bail decision. A further statutory exception to bail is that 'the court does not have sufficient information on which to make a decision'. When this is the case e.g. address to be checked out, then the remand must be for the shortest possible period e.g. overnight. A remand in custody before conviction is a serious infringement of liberty and it is wrong to rely on a 'stronger application next week' if the decision simply rests upon information which can be obtained overnight.

The exceptions and reasons must be announced and recorded .The initial maximum period of remand is 8 clear days to prison/detention or 3 days to police cells.

A remand to police cells is for the purpose of enquiring into other offences and the defendant must be brought back before the court as soon as that need ceases. In the meantime he must have his detention periodically reviewed under police detention rules.

The period of remand may be extended to 28 days after the 2nd remand in custody. This period is subject to the requirements that the defendant is before the court; that representations are sought from both parties and that care is taken to set a realistic early date for the next stage of the proceedings e.g. for committal.

2.29.7 A structured approach to bail

A bail decision is critical. The ultimate decision of a remand in custody is available and this is very often based on slim information about a defendant who is not convicted. The decision-making process is entirely about ensuring good behaviour during the bail period and attending court. It is not about guilt or innocence. The 'ABC' approach is suggested as a structured approach for the decision and for the reasons.

A. Adjournment (or not!)

Should the case be adjourned? The advocates will be aware of the basis for the adjournment and if they have no objection, they will understandably tend to focus their attention on the bail representations. However, the court must first consider carefully whether the case should be adjourned at all. Could it proceed today? This is particularly relevant when the defendant appears in custody on a warrant, having failed to attend an Early First Hearing. It is likely that the police file will be available along with the court work and the expectation should be for the case to go ahead.

The first question is 'why can't the case proceed?' rather than 'shall we grant bail?' The second question is 'what is the shortest adjournment for progress to be made?' rather than 'what date are we adjourning to?'

In any pronouncement, the word adjourn should normally be followed by 'because' ..., 'so that' ... and this aspect is part of the decision-making process.

B. Bail

- Offence

What is alleged by the prosecutor? What is conceded (if anything) by the defence? Is the evidence strong and if so, what is the probable sentence?

(This may be relevant to failure to surrender!) Is there a reliance on the prosecution witnesses and are they vulnerable? Remember that the issue of guilt or innocence is not an issue for a bail decision. The only concern is whether the facts of the offence suggest that there could be further offending, interference with witnesses, or – with strong evidence, it may affect the expectation of attending court if a custodial sentence is probable.

- Offender

Does the defendant have a stable address? Does he have family or employment commitments? Are there any previous convictions? Is the previous bail record good or bad? What are the explanations/circumstances of any recent failures to attend? Was the defendant on bail at the time of the alleged offence?

- Options (non-custodial)

If there are no concerns (exceptions) found, then unconditional bail must be granted.
Where there are exceptions with reasons, can they be allayed by relevant conditions?
Define any conditions carefully so that both the defendant and the arresting officer have the same understanding of what they mean?
Check that any conditions are proportionate in relation to qualified rights engaged.
Consider specific/exceptional reasons for granting bail in respect of murder, manslaughter or rape.

C. Custody

If exceptions and reasons are found and conditions cannot safely be attached to allay concerns, then custody becomes inevitable. (Check with clerk that selected exceptions apply if the offence is non-imprisonable.)

Check that the bench have sufficient information on which to make a bail decision. If not, consider overnight remand using exception 'insufficient information' and identify exactly what information is required e.g. address to be checked out.

Exceptions and reasons must be announced. In compiling the pronouncement for conditional bail or refusal of bail, simply focus on the exceptions put forward, any other exceptions considered and the reasons to justify them.

2.29.8 Failure to surrender to bail

It is an offence to fail to surrender to bail (police or court bail) in criminal proceedings, without reasonable excuse. The offence carries a maximum of 3 months imprisonment/level 5 fine in the magistrates' court and on committal to crown court, carries 12 months/fine.

Procedure

Following a failure to surrender to court bail, the offender should be invited to give his explanation. The prosecutor will then consider whether proceedings are appropriate and if he so concludes, he will invite the justices to put the charge through their legal adviser. This procedure ensures compliance with Article 6 and avoids the court being compromised if they do not accept the initial explanation (JCS 01/2001). It is important to be vigilant that the charge is considered by the prosecutor. Whenever the defendant appears in the dock on warrant following a failure to attend on court bail – enquire! This is potentially a very important conviction for future benches in considering the extent of bail risk.

Sentencing

The guideline fine for the offence is band B. However the penalty of 1 day's detention is often appropriate if the accepted mitigation is a genuine 'mix up' of dates with voluntary surrender, particularly if it has already been served by a salutary night in the cells. A surrender early during the day may merit a few hours of detention before release.

It is extremely important though to distinguish the circumstances which may call for a custodial sentence e.g. lengthy period prior to arrest and evidence of intention to escape justice. In such circumstances an adjournment along with the principal offence may be appropriate so that a substantial consecutive prison sentence may be considered. Alternatively it may be sufficiently serious to justify a custodial sentence even if the defendant is acquitted of the substantive charge e.g. 7 months imposed by the Court of Appeal even though defendant was acquitted of the fraud charge and had eventually surrendered (R v. Christopher Clarke 2000).

Note that it is also an offence to fail to surrender as 'soon as reasonably practicable', even if there is reasonable cause for failing to surrender on the original date!

2.29.9 Other points relevant to bail

1. Specific reasons must be given if bail is granted in respect of murder, manslaughter and rape e.g. satisfied that the general public are not

endangered by the release and the witness is sufficiently protected by the bail conditions.

2. A defendant has the right to make 2 applications which may be based on any argument. Thereafter the court may decline to hear arguments as to fact or law which it has heard previously. The question must be asked 'What is the change of circumstances and how does it relate to the exceptions found?'

3. The prosecutor may ask for bail to be reconsidered based upon information which was not available to the court or to the police when the original bail decision was made e.g. a new witness comes forward and the strength of evidence increases substantially.

4. Applications may be made to the court to vary conditions of police and court bail at any time e.g. to change address/time of reporting. Always ask for a brief outline of the offence and the details of the surrounding conditions. A variation of a single condition in isolation may sound uncontroversial until it is placed in context e.g. the return home to live with mother may place the defendant back into the proximity of vulnerable witnesses.

5. Breach of bail conditions must be put to the defendant and resolved within 24 hours of the arrest. The case cannot be adjourned. There is no penalty, except that the whole question of bail is properly re-opened if the court is 'of the opinion' that the defendant has broken or is likely to break the condition. Formal evidence is not required.

6. The prosecution may appeal if the court grants bail in respect of TWOC offences and offences carrying 5 years or more, providing that bail was opposed. Appeal lies to a judge of the crown court and oral notice must be given before the defendant is released and written notice must be given within 2 hours. It will usually be necessary to retire for a short time after the oral notice has been given so that the prosecutor can formulate the written notice of appeal. The judge will then hear the case within 48 hours.

2.30 Plea before venue/mode of trial

2.30.1 Types of offences

Offences which are **'indictable only'** must be 'sent' to the crown court e.g. murder, manslaughter, rape, robbery and since January 2001, this will normally take place at the first hearing. The second bail application is therefore heard at the crown court. Related offences may also be 'sent' under this fast-track procedure.

Offences which are **'summary only'** must be dealt with by the magistrates' court (unless committed to crown court at the same time as indictable matters) e.g. speeding, drunk and disorderly.
The remainder of matters may be dealt with either by the magistrates or by the crown court and are referred to as **'either-way'** matters e.g. theft, handling stolen goods, burglary.

2.30.2 Guilty plea on 'either-way' offences

The defendant is asked in court whether he wishes to indicate his plea or not. The court must explain that if he indicates that he would plead guilty then he may be committed for sentence to the crown court if the court believes that greater punishment is required after hearing the case.

Following an indication of a guilty plea the prosecution facts will normally be read out. Occasionally it may be conceded at the outline stage that the case should properly be committed for sentence e.g. domestic burglary involving forced entry, ransacking and high value theft. It is important to determine whether the magistrates' powers are going to be sufficient before determining sentence or adjourning for pre-sentence reports.

It is very easy for the defence to make a suggestion for a serious case to be adjourned for pre-sentence reports immediately after the prosecution facts are given. Be careful. At this stage it is very important to make a decision as to seriousness.

If the case is worth more than 9 months imprisonment (i.e. 6 months with credit a guilty plea) then the bench should indicate instead that it is minded to commit the case for sentence and allow the defence the opportunity to make representations. The representations may well produce sufficient mitigation to reduce the level of seriousness, but if they do not, then the case should be committed for sentence.

2.30.3 'Not guilty' plea on either-way offences

When the defendant indicates that he would plead 'not guilty' or chooses not to indicate any plea, then the mode of trial must be determined. Prosecution and defence may make representations as to venue based upon the outline facts, the relative seriousness of the offence and any legal or factual complexity. The bench will then make its decision as to venue.

It may be helpful to refer to the Mode of Trial guidelines in order to identify aggravating features. At this stage it must be assumed that the prosecution version of events is correct e.g. stolen goods are valued at over £10,000 even if this is disputed.

When the bench determines that summary trial is appropriate, the defendant (or any one of them) may nevertheless elect trial by jury. Alternatively, he may choose to be tried in the magistrates' court but must be warned that if found guilty, the case could be sent to the crown court for sentence.

Basically, the defendant may always elect to be tried by a judge and jury. Sometimes the court will insist!

When trial by jury is sought or directed, the matter is then prepared for committal for trial. An adjournment may well be necessary in order to prepare the written statements for the committal.

The defence solicitor will then decide whether or not the statements disclose a 'prima facie' case i.e. a case to answer. If a 'prima facie' case is conceded, the statements are simply handed to the court and the defendant is remanded to a plea and directions hearing date at the crown court. He is warned that he must ask within 14 days for specific witnesses to attend if he intends to cross-examine them. If the defence consider that the statements do not disclose sufficient evidence, then they must be read out to the bench, who must make the determination as to whether there is a case to answer or not. If not, the case is discharged in the magistrates' court.

See 2.13.14 for examples of cases which should properly be committed to the crown court.

ROLES IN CASE MANAGEMENT

2.31 Police, CPS, Probation, other court officers and users

Each agency plays an important part in ensuring that cases are dealt with efficiently and effectively. The introduction of the 'Narey' provisions for early first hearings and early administrative hearings is an example of agencies liaising closely and working towards mutually positive outcomes. Defendants are charged and bailed within a very short period and in the interim the police file is prepared; the CPS will review; the court will list and the probation service will obtain any relevant information for potential stand down enquiries on the day of plea and sentence. Every agency is answerable for its results and contribution both through its own professional hierarchy and also through the local court user group.

2.32 The court clerk

The court clerk's contribution to case progress lies in the following:

- Delegated powers used particularly in administrative hearings to identify issues, make directions and timetable actions
- Advice to the bench as to national and locally agreed time limits and strategies to reduce delay
- Recording of the bench's reasons for adjournments together with any directions e.g. officer in the case or his superior officer to attend and explain reason for delay if committal cannot proceed on next occasion.

The new Practice Direction 2000 refers to 'the legal adviser' rather than 'the court clerk' which reflects a growing reference to the new title.

2.33 The court office

Administrative officers are usually responsible for the court diary (2.25) and will deal as effectively as possible with the numerous daily modifications to the diary.

2.34 The bench itself

The most important management inevitably comes from the bench itself. The suggested questions for any adjournment application are set out at 2.28. There are a few 'DON'Ts':

1. Do not simply say 'this case <u>must</u> proceed next time.'

   With efficient management every case should surely proceed further at every listing. There is a real danger in creating a distinction of those cases which have arrived at 'final warning' stage. By the same token, there may well be a very good reason for adjournment and the 'must proceed' argument then becomes counter-productive to justice.

   Instead say exactly what the bench wish to happen next time, e.g. 'for medical evidence to be obtained by the defence and served on the prosecution at least x days before the next hearing, and for the charge to be put and plea entered.' All parties know exactly what is required of them and the court is able to list the matter for plea and also focus specifically on any application for further adjournment.

2. Do not cut down the adjournment period to an unrealistic period.

   It is tempting to grant a 'border-line' application but then reduce the period sought in order to avoid any further delay. The reality is that this in itself can create further problems. The short adjournment 'for a week' may overload a busy court diary if the first available space is 3 weeks later and inevitably some cases are then rushed or adjourned with little enquiry by the end of the day.

Similarly, some adjournment periods simply cannot be reduced in time. The obtaining of certain evidence may well require initial consent from the Legal Aid Board before enquiries can even begin. Police officers' shifts are unlikely to coincide with the CPS reviewing officer's day in the office and meaningful discussion may take some days to arrange. The outcome is another listing and another adjournment – possibly for the sake of an extra week or so.

2.35 The lay magistrate sitting alone

The following powers may be exercised by a single magistrate:

- Deal with a bail application
- Extend bail or to impose or vary conditions of bail
- Withdraw or dismiss an information
- Discharge an accused where no evidence is offered
- Make an order for payment of defence costs out of central funds
- Request a pre-sentence report and indicate seriousness
- Request a medical report and remand accused
- Remit offender to another court for sentence
- Appoint earlier time for attendance on police bail
- Extend custody time limit or overall time limit
- Order convicted accused to produce driving licence
- Direction prohibiting publication of matters
- Give, vary or revoke directions for conduct of trial including timetable, attendance of parties, service of documents and manner in which evidence is to be given
- Give, vary or revoke orders for separate or joint trials.

The importance of case management

2.36 The principle of 'justice delayed'

The maxim is that 'Justice delayed is justice denied.' The effects of adjournment as set out at 2.28 are largely negative. This is well understood and much publicity and discussion has centred around speeding up justice. The outcome is that cases are generally being dealt with more quickly and this is generally to everyone's advantage.

However, it is worth considering the other side of the coin that there is a danger of speed and statistic overtaking the more important aspect of justice. Some adjournments are completely valid. Sometimes advocates do need more time to determine the appropriate plea and if pressed for progress they will advise their client to enter 'no plea' or plead 'not guilty' plea and elect trial by jury in order to preserve their position. A short adjournment may have allowed time to interview witnesses, pursue forensic evidence, view videos and thereafter enter a guilty plea in the magistrates' court.

Similarly the court probation officer will sometimes suggest that a full written pre-sentence report may be more helpful to the court than a specific sentence report on the day. A probation order is legally and practically capable of following on from a stand down enquiry and in many courts this is now the norm. However, the probation officer may consider it to be useful for a more detailed enquiry and home visit in order to assess the suitability of the defendant, the extent of existing support from other sources and the potential objectives for any order. Again, a rushed decision may result in an unnecessary order which the defendant is incapable of committing himself to in any event.

A final example is the requirement for compensation claims to be agreed or proved. Very often, details simply have not been obtained for early hearings and it is tempting to 'leave them for the civil court'. Often the defence solicitor simply wants sight of the detail and he will then advise his client to accept the claim. Often, there is an acceptance of a lower figure and the means situation limits the sum payable to the agreed amount in any event. Compensation is the right of the victim and he too would prefer to avoid the delay and inconvenience of starting a fresh action.

2.37 Efficiency and effectiveness in handling cases

Efficiency and effectiveness is seen most clearly within the courts' budget formula which includes statistics relating to the length of time taken for cases to be processed and the early closure of accounts. The monthly completion rate for summons cases and charges therefore features as a target in the business plans of most courts. Early case completion translates into a positive contribution towards the share of the national budget for each court. Through the collection of other statistics it is possible to work out the average cost per case in each court.

2.38 Enforcement of disposals

By far the greatest enforcement process applies to money orders – fines, compensation, costs, and back duty.

As stated above, the court is required to keep statistics as to effectiveness and this includes monthly calculation as to the average days of account arrears and the monthly proportion of accounts closed. Money order enforcement procedures are covered in detail in chapter 12.

The enforcement of community orders is governed by National Standards. Breach action may be taken after one unacceptable failure. Where breach action is not taken, there is a formal warning using a 'yellow card' warning letter and only one warning may be given in any 12 month period. Breach options for community orders are considered at 2.13.

PROCEDURES FOR APPLICATION OUT OF COURT

Information and warrants for search

2.39 Search warrant - Police application

Whilst search warrants play a vital part in many major criminal investigations, it should always be remembered that the court is giving the police the right to break into someone's house possibly in the early hours of the morning. The decision should be taken with great care. Although the list of enquiries appears to be lengthy, they are brief checks and brief questions which may occasionally prevent the possibility of lifetime trauma for innocent people. A warrant may be considered for anywhere in England or Wales. It is a discretionary decision and the application is dealt with in private. Notes should always be taken.

Legal requirements

- Serious arrestable offence committed.
- Material on the premises which is likely to be of substantial value to the investigation.
- Material is likely to be relevant and is not excluded/special category.
    - Entry will not be granted without a warrant, or
      Purpose of search may be frustrated or seriously prejudiced unless a constable arriving at the premises can secure immediate entry, or
      Not practicable to communicate with any person entitled to grant entry/access to the premises.

Checking the applicant and the application

- Check officer's warrant card/identity.
- Check that application has been authorised by an inspector, or other senior officer if urgent.

- Check that the legal basis for the application is identified e.g. drugs (Misuse of Drugs Act 1971), stolen goods (s.26 Theft Act 1968), material of 'substantial value to the investigation of a serious arrestable offence' (s.8 PACE 1984).
- Written information is required.
- Separate paperwork and separate consideration for each application.
- Officer must be sworn or affirm.
- Check that premises to be searched are clearly defined e.g. garage at rear of ...., flat number ...
- Identify the articles being sought.

Questions to ask

The occupiers

- Who is the likely occupier of the property?
- What is known about him?
- Has he got any previous convictions?
- Is he currently the subject of criminal proceedings?
- Are there any young children or other vulnerable occupants?
- If so, what arrangements are in place to care for them during the search and in the event of arrests? e.g. officer to accompany for specific purpose and local social services office informed.

The information source

- What is the nature of any police surveillance of the property?
- When was the information received?
- Is the informant registered?
- Has the informant previously been used and found to be reliable?
- If anonymous source, what steps have been taken to corroborate the information?

The area

- Is the area ethnically sensitive?
- If so, what steps have been taken to try and diffuse any problems? e.g. police to be accompanied by local group leaders and police community liaison officer.
- When is the warrant to be executed? If any delay is expected, why is this? If during the night, why is this necessary?

Before granting the warrant, the magistrate should have a picture of the property involved and the probable people inside. Is it reasonable to issue a search warrant in all the circumstances? It is appropriate to ask whether a previous application has been made and refused. If so, there must be additional grounds for a second application.

On granting the application, the date and time of grant must be noted on the information and both the information and the warrant must be signed. The information is retained by the court and the police must forward the search warrant after 1 month at the latest, executed or not, endorsed as to whether the articles were found and whether any other articles were seized.

The execution of a search warrant is a serious interference with the right to private and family life (Article 8) and the questions must be considered:

1. Is the action legal, clear and accessible? e.g. s.8 PACE 1984 provides legal criteria (above).
2. Does the intrusion pursue a legitimate aim? e.g. to prevent crime and protect the rights of others by retrieving stolen goods.
3. Is it proportionate to issue a warrant in this particular case? i.e. is it really necessary to possibly break down the door of this house to retrieve these goods in this way?

The police are a public authority and in terms of practical execution they also have responsibility for ensuring compliance with the Human Rights Act. Operational issues should be left to the police. If the court feels tempted to impose conditions e.g. not to execute during the night, then it is unlikely that the statutory criteria of urgency are met!

2.40 Utilities and others

Applications may be made for various purposes, for example for entry to read a meter or to cut off a power supply following non-payment of the bill. An electric/gas supply may be cut off where the customer has not paid within 20/28 working days of a demand in writing and after 2/7 days notice of his intention to cut off the supply. This power is not available if there is a dispute as to the amount owed.

After appropriate notice, an officer of the supplier may at all reasonable times enter the property for the purpose of cutting off the supply. The right of entry may only be exercised with the consent of the occupier or by warrant.

The court may grant a warrant on sworn information in writing and the magistrate must be satisfied that:

- Notice of the application has been given to the occupier (right to fair trial).

- Admission is reasonably required for the specified purpose.
- The applicant has a right of entry to the premises.
- The requirements of any enactment have been complied with – a code of practice exists to avoid cutting off vulnerable people during the winter months if at all possible.
- That relevant notices have been given.

Premises must be left secure following entry and any damage must be made good.

2.41 Statutory declarations

Statutory declarations are a regular feature of magistrates' court work and are frequently made particularly in order to declare that the maker was unaware of criminal proceedings in order that his case may be re-opened. They may also be used for a multitude of other reasons e.g. to declare that educational qualifications have been attained; that pawn tickets have been lost rather than sold on and also to change name.

The words for a statutory declaration are as follows:

"I, ... do solemnly and sincerely declare and affirm that the contents of this declaration are true to the best of my knowledge and belief, and I make this solemn declaration conscientiously believing the same to be true and by virtue of the provisions of the Statutory Declarations Act 1835."

The maker of the statement itself need not read the document, nor need the magistrate consider whether he believes what is said or not. The magistrate's role is simply to attest that he is present and hears the maker declare that the contents of the document are true. An untrue statement may render the maker liable for perjury.

2.42 Children Act Emergency Protection Orders

This order authorises the removal of a child to accommodation provided by the applicant e.g. to a foster parent or prevents removal e.g. from hospital. It may be granted by any single justice, although the preference will always be to use a family panel magistrate if available.
(See 9.18 for full discussion).

2.43 Passport endorsements

A magistrate may countersign an application for a passport and certify the photograph as a true likeness <u>if</u> he has known the applicant personally for at least 2 years. When this is not the case, the applicant should be referred on to any professionally qualified person who has known the applicant personally. A Justice of the Peace is simply one of a list of suitable signatories and the essence is personal knowledge of the individual applicant by a person of some 'standing'.

2.44 Limits of JP's powers

What is the limit of a magistrate's powers? Whenever you are uncertain, ask. The bench chairman or the Justices' Clerk may not know the answer either, but they are likely to 'know a man who does.'

CHAPTER 3
COMPETENCE 3
Thinking and acting judicially

Demonstrating knowledge of the full implications of the judicial oath
"Do right to all manner of people"

This chapter focuses on the practicalities of personal compliance with the Judicial Oath:

> JUDICIAL OATH
> **I ... do swear that I will well and truly serve our Sovereign Lady Queen Elizabeth the Second in the office of the justice of the peace, and I will do right to all manner of people after the laws and usages of this realm, without fear or favour, affection or ill will. So help me God.**

An affirmation may be made as an alternative to the oath.

3.1 Different cultures and ethnic minority communities

A multifaith, multicultural, multiracial society makes special demands on magistrates as it poses challenges in court which require an immediate and well-informed response as soon as they arise. In the words of the Lord Chief Justice (Lord Taylor) 'there is a great deal more to understanding the feelings and concerns of ethnic minorities than simply being polite and patient.'

Anyone who appears before the court basically wants to feel that they have been dealt with fairly and equally 'no matter where they come from and what they come with.' Whether they come from Africa or from the notorious estate in town; whether they come with intelligence and articulation or with learning difficulties, anger and ignorance. They may well be dealt with equally but the true test is how the individual perceives the fairness of the court process.

Everyone must be dealt with as an individual. Judges are urged to warn juries of the dangers of using their own assumptions to evaluate the behaviour of those whose cultural conventions are different from their own. The significance of many acts and behaviours cannot be judged effectively without making appropriate allowances and without consideration of any relevant cultural code.

> Example:
>
> In some South Asian, African and Caribbean cultures it is considered to be appropriate to look away from a person in authority to indicate deference and respect. It would be wrong therefore to interpret 'failing to look in the eye' as an indication of telling lies.

The concepts of institutional racism and unwitting discrimination further increase the importance of some knowledge of social diversity, all of which are discussed further.

3.2 National and local population statistics

The 1991 census is unfortunately the most recent census at the time of print and statistics are therefore a little stale. At that time, 5.5% of the population were of ethnic minority origin. Nearly half of Britain's population who were not white had been born in the United Kingdom, and about 3/4 of them were British citizens.

The ethnic composition of the population in Great Britain in 1991 was as follows:

Total population	54,888,844	100%
White	51,873,794	94.5%
Black Caribbean	499,964	0.9%
Black African	212,362	0.4%
Black Other	178,401	0.3%
Indian	840,255	1.5%
Pakistani	476,555	0.9%
Bangladeshi	162,835	0.3%
Chinese	156,938	0.3%
Other Asian	197,534	0.4%
Others	290,206	0.5%

(Source: Owen, D, 1992-1995 Commission for Racial Equality factsheet)

In West Yorkshire, all groups were represented in each area and the following groups represented more than 1% of the total population:

Bradford	457,344	Pakistani	9.90%
		Indian	2.56%
Calderdale	191,585	Pakistani	3.28%

Kirklees	373,127	Black Caribbean	1.19%
		Indian	3.19%
		Pakistani	4.68%
Leeds	680,722	Indian	1.45%
		Pakistani	1.37%
Wakefield	310,915	No groups over 1%	

(Source: 1991 Census County Reports, OPCS, HMSO 1992)

The Labour Force Survey 1998 breaks down the population of British nationals aged 15-64 as 94.9% white, 1.5% black, 2.8% South Asian and 0.8% belonged to different ethnic groups.
(Statistics on Race and the Criminal Justice System – Home Office 1999)

3.3 Disadvantaged and vulnerable groups

Many such groups exist. A few are selected for discussion as being the groups which we tend to see in the courtroom most frequently.

3.3.1 People with a disability

Various guidance has evolved which includes the following:

- Talk directly to the person with the disability. This includes those with a learning disability. It is tempting to speak instead to the person accompanying him as they will very often be making the responses on behalf of the person.

- When talking to a person with a hearing difficulty, make sure that your face is in the light, look at them directly and speak clearly and naturally in a strong volume which you can maintain. Keep your hands away from your mouth. Ask them if you are speaking loud enough rather than shouting at the outset.

- When talking to a blind person, introduce who you are and ask each speaker to introduce themselves before beginning their speech so that the person can orientate himself first.

- Ask if a person needs any help, but wait until it is accepted before doing anything.

- A wheelchair is part of the body space of the person using it and nobody in the court should simply move it without permission.

The Disability Discrimination Act 1995 places a duty on the court to make reasonable adjustments to prevent disadvantages arising from the design of the premises and outlaws the harassment of people with a disability.

3.3.2 Children

Children may be called as witnesses in adult court and obviously require every possible support in order to give their evidence as confidently as possible. A parent should accompany and remain next to the child throughout. First names should be used. A child under 14 will give evidence unsworn and should be presumed competent unless the contrary is shown.

Screens may be considered in order to avoid intimidation. Video recordings of interviews may be admissible in certain circumstances, notably involving sex and violence. At the hearing itself, video links may be used. The child remains in a private room with a parent (and possibly a witness support officer who is familiar with the equipment) and communicates with the chairman and advocates by television screen. See 5.29. Where a child is the alleged victim, it is possible for some types of cases to be 'transferred' to crown court without the necessity for committal proceedings.

A press restriction direction should always be considered whenever a child is a party or witness in proceedings in adult court. This will prevent publicity which reveals particulars which are calculated to lead to the identification of the child. In considering whether to make an order the court must weigh the public interest in full reporting of the crime, including the identification of the defendant, against the need to protect the victim from further harm. It is particularly important when an adult is charged with sexual offences and child victims are named in the charge and therefore in open court.

Press restrictions apply in youth court unless dispensed with. This may arise if the court considers that it would be in the public interest to do so and the child has been convicted or to prevent injustice to the child. The DPP may also apply to the court if the child is charged or convicted of a serious violent or sexual offence and it is necessary for the purpose of apprehending the child.

The court has power to clear the court if a child is giving evidence in a matter involving decency or morality.

3.3.3 Homosexuals

Various prejudices and stereotyping occur towards those who are gay or lesbian and as with all situations concerning court users and decision-making, it is important to 'acknowledge and abandon' them at the court door.

The level of approval and acceptance by society varies but homophobia (hostility and fear towards homosexuals) is widespread and this may well contribute to feelings of isolation by those who do not currently have a partner or a supportive network of family and friends.

A research project by the London Lesbian and Gay Teenage Group provides an insight into the lifestyle of some homosexuals which may be helpful for magistrates to be aware of. 416 individuals completed the questionnaire as to whether they felt that the various situations applied 'because they were lesbian or gay':

- 6 in 10 had been verbally abused
- 1 in 5 had been beaten up
- 1 in 10 had been thrown out of their home
- 1 in 5 had attempted suicide
- 1 in 5 had had contact with the police
- 1 in 2 had had problems at school

3.3.4 Transsexuals

Some awkwardness may occur particularly for transsexuals who are in the process of change. The treatment usually involves living in the new role for at least a year, usually on hormones and then undergoing a series of operations to bring the body into line with the chosen gender. Whether they are 'pre-op' or 'post-op' they should be referred to by their new gender. Transsexuals normally change their name by statutory declaration.

The process is complex and it is important to the person concerned that the new name is used with ease and acceptance rather than incredulity. 'Jane' Smith may well have some facial hair but that is 'her' name.

3.3.5 'The poor and ignorant'

The words above the Old Bailey summarise a crucial duty upon the court, to 'protect the poor and ignorant.' Words and behaviour can be misinterpreted if the expectations and evaluations of them are based on the code of the 'richer and wiser.'

Examples:

- A defendant attends court and wears dirty, torn clothing. Is he being deliberately disrespectful and provocative? Is he making some kind of political statement? Is he making the point that he cannot pay a high fine?
  or
  Is he wearing the only clothes he has?

- A defendant says that he has nothing to say about the offence. Is it because he has no mitigation at all? Is it because he might make matters even worse for himself? Is he purposely refusing to show appropriate remorse?

  or

  Does he feel too intimidated, too inadequate or too inarticulate to speak up?

Being open to various possibilities and interpretations is important to social justice.

3.3.6 Women

Women can feel particularly vulnerable in a court situation. It is less 'normal' for a woman to appear before the court than a man. The experience is far less likely to have been shared by female friends and family. The 'code of behaviour' may remain something of a mystery until the day of the court appearance.

Similarly the imposition of a custodial sentence on women is a relatively infrequent occurrence compared to men. In 1998 there were 57,751 men and 2,642 women in the prison population.

How may a woman be put at ease? It is helpful to determine the appropriate title of address. Given the comparatively low numbers of women attending court as defendants and witnesses, it is suggested that the usher may have the opportunity to check whether it is 'Miss' 'Mrs' 'Ms' or otherwise when registering the names outside the court. When called into court the defendant may be announced as 'Mrs. Jane Smith'. This saves the chairman having to guess (is she wearing a ring?); questioning title in a manner which may indicate to her that marital status is somehow important, or alternatively using all names throughout the case and avoiding any reference to title. In terms of maintaining some dignity and some warmth it seems far preferential to use a title.

"Without fear or favour, affection or ill will"

3.4 Discrimination and its impact

3.4.1 Definition and legislation

The Oxford dictionary definition of discrimination is to 'make a distinction, especially on the grounds of race or colour'.

The Race Relations Act 1976 makes it unlawful to discriminate against anyone on the grounds of race, colour, nationality or ethnic or national origins. It is concerned with people's actions and the effects of their actions and not their intentions. It is not good enough to say 'I meant no harm'. What would a reasonable bystander have thought about the action or the comment?

The criminal justice system has the capacity for both indirect and direct discrimination. Direct racial discrimination occurs when an individual is treated less favourably than others. Indirect discrimination occurs when treatment may be equal in a formal sense between different racial groups but it is discriminatory in its effect on one particular racial group.

There are certain situations where discrimination is more likely to occur. These include where decisions depend on subjective (i.e. personal) judgements rather than, or in addition to objective criteria and where there is considerable scope for the exercise of discretion. These are situations which magistrates deal with on a daily basis.

It is worth considering some of the features which appear in the sentencing guidelines.

Examples:

- Remorse? How is it recognised? How much depends upon demeanour in court? Can the sentencer be sure that they have interpreted the behaviour correctly?

- Co-operation with the police? Are all members of society as likely to co-operate with the police? Young people, for example, who challenge authority? Black people, who may feel victimised by being repeatedly stopped and searched? (5 times more likely to be stopped than white people in 2000). Should a failure to co-operate always be an aggravating factor?

- Timely guilty plea? African Caribbean people are more likely than white people to seek trial by jury. There may be many reasons. One explanation is the lack of confidence in the system and a hostile attitude based on perceptions of unfairness. Should this be considered? Interestingly, research suggests that the CPS discontinued a higher proportion of cases involving black defendants as compared to white defendants at the crown court in 1999.

(The Royal Commission on Criminal Justice Discrimination 'Ethnic Minorities and the Criminal Justice System', Home Office 1993. Statistics on Race and the Criminal Justice System, Home Office, 1999).

3.4.2 The Stephen Lawrence Inquiry Report

The content of the report is highly relevant to the magistrates' courts. The Inquiry, published in 1999 pursued explanation into the police enquiry following a fatal stabbing of a black student by a group of white youths at a bus stop in London in 1993.

The report is clear in its purpose to restore and improve confidence in the criminal justice system. The Home Secretary referred to it as a 'watershed in our attitudes to racism'. The following key extracts relate to racism:

'There is a striking and inescapable need to demonstrate fairness, not just by the police services, but across the criminal justice system as a whole in order to generate trust and confidence within minority ethnic communities, who undoubtedly perceive themselves to be discriminated against by 'the system.'

'Institutional racism consists of the collective failure of an organisation to provide an appropriate and professional service to people because of their colour, culture or ethnic origin.' ...

'It can be seen or detected in processes, attitudes and behaviour which amount to discrimination through unwitting prejudice, ignorance, thoughtlessness, and racist stereotyping which disadvantage minority ethnic people.' ...

'The majority of police officers who testified before us accepted that an element of the disparity was the result of discrimination' (regarding 'stop and search' statistics) ...

Concerns were expressed about the 'patronising and thoughtless approach' of some officers towards Stephen's parents and the side-lining of his friend, who survived the attack; the refusal of at least five officers to accept that this was a purely racist murder and the use of inappropriate and offensive language by some police officers.

(The Stephen Lawrence Inquiry – Report by Sir William MacPherson of Cluny, 1999).

3.4.3 Impact on the magistrates' court

If we accept that institutional racism does exist and some groups in particular have been exposed to discrimination in their encounters with state systems, it is hardly surprising that some will appear before the court with cynicism and suspicion. This may be demonstrated in various ways. It could well inspire an attitude of non-conformity with the court's expectations.

In the case of some African-Caribbeans there is a high value placed on personal dignity and many would rather 'take the pressure' than bow to what they perceive to be unjust systems and demands. Any distrust will only be confirmed and exacerbated if their behaviour is met with aggression and impatience from the bench. The cycle will simply go on and strategies of resistance will continue as a matter of course. Taking the defendant's perspective into account and showing that authority can be fair, sensitive and reasonable to each individual and the 'baggage' they bring with them may help 'authority' to turn the corner.

3.4.4 What can be done by magistrates to fight discrimination?

- Make it clear to colleagues and court users that racist language, racist assumptions and gross generalisations are not going to be tolerated by you as an individual and have the confidence that you are speaking for the bench as a whole.
- Be specific and objective rather than criticising the speaker personally, make it clear how you feel and suggest an alternative expression. This is a sensitive and complex area and most of us do not want to set ourselves up as experts or indeed, lose friends. A balance can be made though which does not patronise and does not take away any dignity from the individual concerned.

Example:

'I wasn't very comfortable about you describing the defendant as 'a queer' in the retiring room. May I suggest that you say 'gay' instead in future. I'm no expert in modern terminology but I've just recently done some reading about it and 'queer' can be considered to be an offensive description. I'm just trying to save you any embarrassment in future rather than being judgemental.

- Demonstrate an equality of social approach to colleagues who are from minority groups. Are they side-lined in any way? Are they left 'to keep themselves to themselves?' Are colleagues afraid of 'saying the wrong thing?' Are relationships secure enough for views to be openly shared with them? Are they used as a valuable resource to develop local understanding of racial issues?

- Recruitment action directed towards minority groups who are not reflected adequately on the bench as a reflection of the local community, particularly by practical liaison with community groups. In 1998, 6.8% of new appointments nationally were from racial minority groups. Of existing magistrates the figure was 4.4%. Positive (and legal!) action may be necessary in some areas. This means adopting imaginative schemes to encourage more applications and ensure that those who are interested are equipped to make an effective application.

- Ensure that the court is demonstrating its openness by open days and reminders in the press that the court is open to visitors.
- In 2001 the Magistrates Association are offering 4-day training courses to experienced trainers about incorporating fair treatment and diversity awareness into all magistrates' training.

3.5 Relevant equality legislation

s.95 Criminal Justice Act 1991 creates an obligation on the Home Secretary to publish information to try to avoid discrimination "on the ground of race or sex or any other improper ground" in the administration of justice. This information is published each year and includes statistics on 'stop and search', arrests and prosecutions by police force and sentencing in magistrates' courts relating to the ethnic appearance of the relevant persons.

The Crime and Disorder Act 1998 places an obligatory duty upon the court to treat any racial aggravation as an aggravating feature to increase seriousness. The Act also created specific racially aggravated offences which carry higher penalties than the 'basic' offence e.g. racially aggravated criminal damage, public order offences, harassment.

Article 14 Human Rights Act 1998

'The enjoyment of the rights and freedoms set forth in this Convention shall be secured without discrimination on any ground such as sex, race, colour, language, religion, political or other opinion, national or social origin, associated with a national minority, property, birth or other status.'

This article does <u>not</u> create a new right to avoid discrimination – it is only invoked in conjunction with another right e.g. right to a fair trial under Article 6. The meaning of discrimination under Article 14 is a difference in treatment which has 'no reasonable and objective' justification.

Oaths

The common law originally held that atheists and agnostics could not give evidence in court or serve as jurors, as they could not swear an oath. Religion therefore became a basis for inequality. The affirmation to tell the truth followed and the current law is contained in:

s.5 Oaths Act 1978 allows any person who objects to being sworn to make a solemn affirmation instead of taking an oath. Furthermore, when it is not reasonably practicable without inconvenience or delay to administer an oath in the manner appropriate to religious belief, an affirmation may similarly be made. The section states clearly that 'A solemn affirmation shall be of the same force and effect as an oath'.

Obviously it is important to try to make readily available the appropriate holy book namely the Old Testament for Jews; the Qur'an for Muslims; the Gita for most Hindus and the Sunder Gutka for Sikhs. The books should be covered and kept scrupulously clean and facilities should be made available for washing and cleansing prior to taking the oath. Unless the appropriate care is taken, objection may be taken to taking the relevant oath.

When an oath is taken on the holy book of a faith other than a faith of the person taking the oath it is nevertheless held to be binding if it appears to be binding on the conscience of the witness and if the witness himself considers it to be binding upon his conscience e.g. a Muslim giving evidence on the New Testament rather than upon the Qur'an.

3.6 The exercise of fairness, impartiality and equal treatment

Article 6 Human Rights Act 1998 – Right to a fair trial.

This Article is perhaps the most significant to court process and magistrates should be familiar with the rights as summarised below with important interpretations under Convention case law in parentheses:

Civil and criminal matters.

- A fair and public hearing (+ opportunity for effective participation).
- Within a reasonable time (i.e. not left in a state of uncertainty for too long).
- By an independent and impartial tribunal (see 3.12).
- Judgement must be pronounced publicly unless specific exceptions apply i.e. reasons for the decision must be given.

Criminal offences.

- Everyone charged with a criminal offence is presumed innocent until proved guilty according to law.

- To be informed promptly and in a language which he understands, the nature and cause of the accusation against him.
- To defend himself in person or through legal assistance of his own choosing, <u>or</u> have free legal assistance if of insufficient means and the interests of justice so require.
- Time (and confidential) facilities to prepare defence.
- To examine or have examined witnesses against him.
- To obtain attendance and examination of witnesses on his behalf under the same conditions as the witnesses against him (and obtain disclosure of material for and against him).
- To have the free assistance of an interpreter if he cannot understand or speak the language used in court (see 3.9).

There are clearly greater rights in respect of 'criminal' matters. Convention case law has applied a wider interpretation of 'criminal' than simply looking at the domestic classification. It also considers the nature of the offence or conduct in question and the severity of any possible penalty i.e. does it have a deterrent purpose or carry imprisonment? On this test, proceedings for non-payment of community charge were concluded to be 'criminal' and therefore carried the right to legal aid. The fine default situation is analogous and the duty solicitor should therefore be offered if there is a real likelihood of imposing imprisonment in default.

The principle of 'equality of arms' underpins Article 6 as one feature of the concept of a fair trial. Essentially this means ensuring that one party is not placed at a procedural disadvantage as against the other party.

HOW TO REACH IMPARTIAL DECISIONS

3.7 One's own conditioning and personal prejudices

Prejudice is defined in the Oxford Dictionary as 'preconceived opinion'. That is all that it is and as life goes on we are likely to formulate many prejudices/preconceived opinions based upon our own experiences and conditioning. Prejudice is not a problem in court as long as it is recognised as such and forms no part at all in making any decisions. Decisions must be based on specific individuals and specific facts and never ever on prejudices. Pre-conceived opinion is not a basis for judicial opinion.

Prejudices may be based on specific personal experiences or attitudes and they can be managed simply be recognising them for what they are and putting them to one side when making a decision or dealing with a situation.

ALLPORT LADDER OF PREJUDICE – diagram 3.7

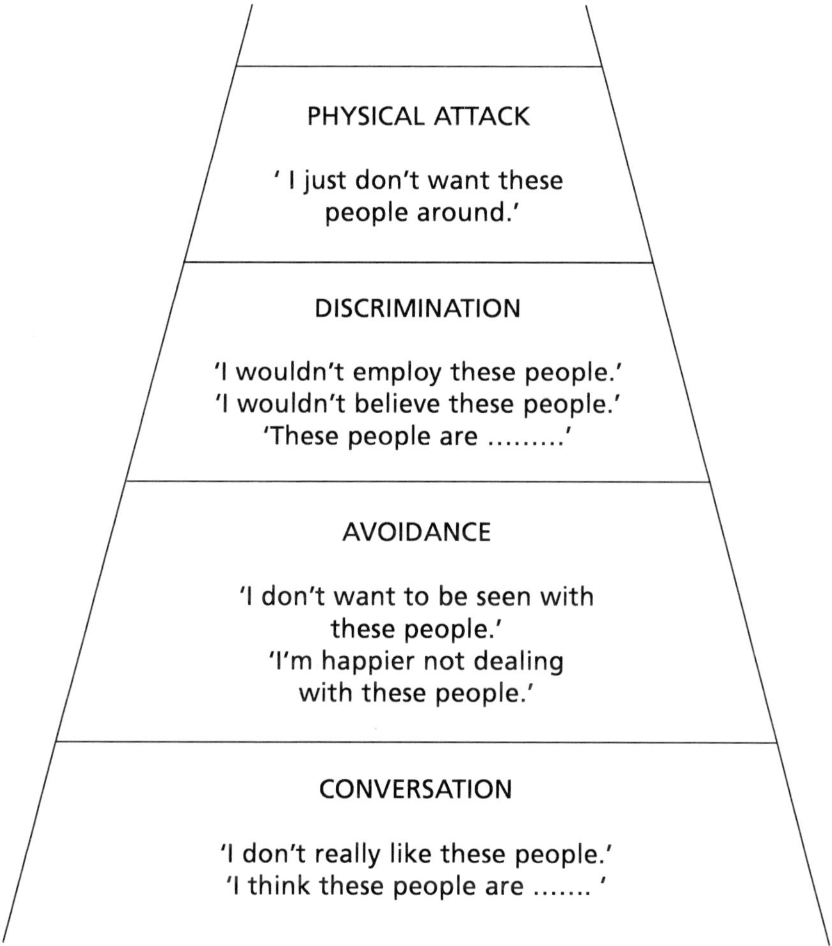

Not easy, as it needs some careful soul-searching to distinguish relevant hard facts from personal prejudices. Once prejudice in a particular area is identified and acknowledged, it is possible to check that it has not influenced any magisterial decision. A deliberate thought process can also be made at the outset of any relevant decision-making to 'acknowledge and abandon' any prejudices which could affect the decision

There is also the danger of over-compensation. Personal prejudice may be recognised, but it does not mean 'back off and be lenient; this is an uncomfortable decision for me'. It means, recognise and be fully independent and if necessary, make the uncomfortable decision. Just check that you would have made the same decision even without the uncomfortable element e.g. a prejudice against drunken women – would you have convicted on these facts, whatever the gender?

Allport Ladder of Prejudice

This diagram is based on the work of Professor Gordon Allport (Harvard University) with the addition of examples given which are relevant to the court. It is a simple summary of many theories in respect of prejudice and how it can move from personal thought, into conversation with others, and then into actions against others.

Defendants with prejudices

Prejudice must also be considered from the vantage point of the particular defendant. What are their 'preconceived opinions'? Is there some basis for them? Is it understandable that there is some lack of confidence and even distrust by some defendants towards the justice system?

Example:

- The 2000 Home Office Report, Statistics on Race and Criminal Justice System, states that black people were overall five times more likely to be stopped and searched by the police than white people and only 8% of all arrests resulted from stop and search. (800,000 recorded stops and searches – 8% black people, 4% Asian). Does this provide a basis for prejudice? Does it potentially explain a particular attitude towards the criminal justice system by a black or Asian defendant?

One court appearance may begin to dispel the prejudice.

3.8 Labelling and stereotyping

3.8.1 Stereotyping

Stereotyping can be summarised by the following statements:

- Generalised perceptions leading to predictions of behaviour.
- Stereotypes or mental short-cuts are categories, which generate in people's minds certain expectations about the characteristics of individuals and groups.
- Stereotypes can also be regarded as selective perceptions – we see what we want to see.

We need to avoid stereotypes because they can incorrectly influence judgements. The labelling which follows can be too broad and too rigid, e.g. all men with dreadlocks are cannabis users; all heroin users commit offences to finance their drug habit; all teenagers on a particular estate are criminals.

It is similarly dangerous to make assumptions and take a view based on one's own knowledge and experience without direct information about the person or situation concerned. Assumptions can be defined as 'taking things for granted' e.g. all magistrates are broad-minded.

3.8.2 Naming systems and forms of address in court

It is surely a basic issue that names and forms of address are used appropriately in court if we are to demonstrate some personal sensitivity and ensure that personal dignity is instigated and preserved on both sides of the bench. Most defendants would feel at least patronised, probably insulted and possibly even pre-judged if they were referred to purely by surname. Similarly, by using the first name only there could well be a feeling of over-familiarity by the chairman and the formality and authority of the court may well suffer.

Much detail has been written about various naming systems but the best advice is the simplest:

1. Ask how someone wishes to be referred to in court. The usher may well be happy to do this outside court when taking names and then refer to the preferred name when calling the case into court e.g. Mrs. Ann Smith, Jaswinder Kaur Gill, Mohammed Rahman Khan, Aziz Ullah Choudhury.
2. Check pronunciation and note it phonetically on the register as the defendant or witness says it. Even the simplest names can be misheard and we have probably all had the irritation of being referred to incorrectly!

3. Use all names if in doubt. In Sikh naming systems, Singh (male) and Kaur (female) are religious designations and it is normally inappropriate to treat these as surnames without permission e.g. Mr. Kamarjit Singh and Miss Jaswinder Kaur should therefore be referred to by both names.
4. Traditional Muslim male names most commonly consist of a personal name and a religious name - either may come first and the personal name is only used by family and friends. There may also be an hereditary name. All names should therefore be used e.g. Mr. Mohammed Rahman, Mr. Mohammed Rahman Khan. Referring to Mohammed Ali as Mr. Ali can be likened to saying 'Mr. God'.
5. Female Muslims should also be referred to by both names, usually a personal name and a title or second personal name e.g. Mrs Amina Begum, Miss Yasmin Nesa. Referring to Mrs. Begum can be likened to saying 'Mrs. Mrs.'

It is not an answer to say that no one has complained. Arguably this could suggest that the level of expectation of respect is fixed at a very low level!

3.8.3 Appropriate language

This summary gives some alternative descriptions which are less likely to cause offence and will retain the dignity of the court and show an appropriate lead from a judicial, public body, rather than laying it open to criticism.

✗ Coloured, Negroid – considered to be patronising or offensive
✓ Black people (Caribbean or African origin), Black British

✗ Asian <u>if</u> exact origin is known
✓ National origin e.g. British, Indian, Pakistani, Bangladeshi
✓ Region of origin e.g. Punjabi, Bengali, Gujarati
✓ Religion e.g. Muslim, Hindu, Sikh

✗ West Indian <u>if country</u> of origin is known
✓ Jamaican, Guyanese, etc

✗ Afro-Caribbean
✓ African Caribbean

✗ Half-caste
✓ Mixed-race

✗ Non-white as it indicates a deviation from the norm
✓ Black, Asian, Chinese, etc.

✗ Wheelchair-bound
✓ Wheelchair-user

✗ Handicapped, invalid, cripple, spastic, disabled
✓ Person with a disability

✗ Mental, mental handicap
✓ Person with a learning disability

✗ My dear, love, son
✓ Use their name!

✗ Queer, bent
✓ Homosexual, gay, lesbian

✗ Your husband? wife? – assumes traditional family
✓ Your partner?

✗ Ethnic minority = distinct from the majority in terms of ethnic or cultural identity
✓ Minority ethnic communities = this emphasises that even the majority is also an ethnic community.

3.9 Language and cultural differences

Best current estimates are that there are more than 3 million speakers of other languages in England and Wales. In 1991 the census revealed that Punjabi was the most commonly spoken South Asian language among British Asians, followed by Urdu, Hindi and Gujarati. It is estimated that probably only 1% of the population cannot speak English at all. However, it has to be recognised that it is one thing to 'get by' in another language on a 'needs must' basis and it is quite another to present mitigation confidently or withstand rigorous cross-examination.

Article 6 of the Human Rights Act gives a person charged with a criminal offence the right to the free assistance of an interpreter if he cannot understand or speak the language used in court. The free assistance is unconditional and does not depend on the financial circumstances of the defendant. The right includes verbal translation of all disclosed documents.

The court must check that the interpreter has the relevant linguistic skills with a fluent command of the dialect which the person actually speaks and also of the English language. If the interpreter has not met the defendant before the proceedings it may be useful to allow them a few minutes together so that understanding and procedure can be checked between them and a bond can be made.

It is good practice for the chairman to invite the interpreter to ask for any of the parties to speak up, slow down or even stop from time to time.

3.9.1 Religion

An awareness of a person's religion is an integral element of being aware of equal treatment issues and it is often a key element of a person's identity and family life. There follows a few key points in respect of some of the religious groups insofar as they may relate to court. In an effort to provide useful information, it is necessarily generalised. It is fully acknowledged that everyone must be treated as an individual who may hold individual beliefs and individual choices of manifestation. More detailed information and a wider range of religions are covered in the Equal Treatment Bench Book produced by the Judicial Studies Board.

3.9.2 Hinduism

This is an extremely diverse tradition with a wide range of beliefs and practices which continue to diversify. It does not require an express commitment to one particular core belief or doctrine and not to one deity. Hindus may worship many different gods and goddesses on different occasions.

Hindu culture has developed a complex system of social organisation which is encapsulated in the caste system which is based upon groupings as intellectuals, rulers, common people and servants.

Many Hindus do not smoke tobacco or drink alcohol, or sometimes tea and coffee, which are also considered to be intoxicants. Avoid suggesting 'go for a coffee' until the case is called.

Marriage is valued as the key institution and is arranged in accordance with rules of caste. Divorce is relatively uncommon and is stigmatised, especially for women, because it represents a violation of ideal norms.

3.9.3 Jews

The main elements of Jewish faith are as follows:

- The Torah as the revelation of God's will to Moses, which contains 613 commandments.
- That humanity is made in God's image.

- That God's compassion permits the atonement of sin.
- The sabbath which begins an hour before dusk on Friday and ends at nightfall on Saturday as a day for worship and family life.

Friday afternoons should be avoided for cases during the winter months and some care should be taken in ordering attendance at the Attendance Centre on a Saturday. Men may wish to keep their head covered at all times. In Orthodox Judaism neither men nor women are permitted by Jewish law to take an oath on the Hebrew Bible/Old Testament and they will affirm.

3.9.4 Muslims

The Islamic faith involves:

- Belief in the Oneness of God, Allah, to whom every individual is responsible on Judgement Day.
- The Qu'ran, the Holy Book of Islam, as the word of God.
- Belief in all the prophets and messengers of Allah including Jesus.
- Saying of prayers five times a day, with special importance for males on Friday at midday.
- Fasting from dawn to dusk in the month of Ramadan.
- Pilgrimage to Mecca once in a lifetime.

Men may wish to keep their head covered at all times. Muslim women may wish to remain completely veiled and this may cause some difficulty in communication, but it is not a refusal to co-operate but in response to Islamic teaching to wear modest dress which covers the whole body and to avoid unnecessary contact with strangers.

Most marriages are arranged in some form by the families involved. Monogomy is the norm but polygamy for men is allowed in certain circumstances. Divorce is met with disapproval.

3.9.5 Rastafarians

The two central beliefs are that:

- Ras Tafari, the former Emperor of Ethiopia is the true and living God and
- Salvation can come to black people only through repatriation to Africa.

Rastafari has links with Christianity and Judaism and was inspired by Marcus Garvey in Jamaica in the 1930s. A man and woman who cohabit are automatically treated as husband and wife by the community and fidelity is considered to be very important.

Men may wish to wear distinctive caps (tams) which may be made of knitted material, leather or cloth, often in the traditional colours of the Ethiopian flag, namely red, gold, green. They may wish to keep their heads covered in court. Women may choose to wear a head wrap.

3.9.6 Sikhs

The main features of the Sikh religion include the following:

- Founded by Guru Nanak, born of Hindu parents, who went on to create a new religion.
- The lowest is equal to the highest in race, creed, political rights and religious hopes.
- Belief in one God and the teachings of the 10 spiritual masters (Gurus).
- Rejection of the caste system.
- The five Ks (uncut hair; comb; bangle; underpants; sword) which should not be removed other than by the wearer.

A turban may be worn. Sikhs may wish to carry a ceremonial sword (kirpan) at all times which symbolises fearlessness and independence. The Lord Chancellor has provided guidance to court security staff that this should be limited to 6" and should be worn beneath clothing whilst in court.

As Hindus, some Sikhs may also abstain from drinking tea and coffee. Marriage is regarded as a person's entry into a new spiritual stage and from a religious point of view it is regarded as indissoluble.

3.10 Body language

The expectation of the court is quite understandably that a defendant or witness will stand up straight and look the chairman in the eye as a sign of respect and deference to the court. There may be good reasons though why some defendants and witnesses do not follow this expectation and it should not be held against them as 'best evidence' of attitude.

Within European culture a person's willingness to sustain a direct gaze is routinely taken to be an indicator of honesty and sincerity. In many African, African-Caribbean and Asian contexts, it is taken to indicate impudence, insult and disrespect for a young person to look an authority figure in the eye. In some South Asian societies it is considered by women that eye-contact with any man is brazen and immodest. In such situations any parties in court may feel that they are in fact acting appropriately to the situation by averting their eyes from the bench.

Some African-Caribbeans tend to be particularly expressive and 'speak with their hands' – it is not a mark of disrespect but a normal method of communication.

Many teenagers adopt a body language with hunched shoulders, a sullen expression and possibly chewing gum, which is considered by them simply to be 'cool' (particularly if accompanied by their peers!), rather than being deliberately provocative to the bench.

HOW TO MAINTAIN THE INTERESTS OF JUSTICE

3.11 That the interests of justice are seldom, if ever, those of any one party

The need to demonstrate 'equality of arms' as required by Convention case law is highly relevant to the notion of equality of treatment. This requires the court to ensure that domestic legal processes do not place one part at a procedural disadvantage as against the other party.

> Example:
>
> A professional prosecutor is unlikely to have any diffidence at all in letting the court know if he cannot hear what the defendant or a witness is saying. A defendant should equally be able to hear what the prosecutor is saying about the case so that he may participate effectively. However he is likely to be far more reticent or may well feel that 'this is how it is done' if the prosecutor directs a quiet, fast outline for the magistrates' ears alone.
>
> Equality of arms requires the bench to ensure that both parties can equally hear exactly what is said. Move the defendant; move the prosecutor; ask him to 'shout up and slow down'; look and see whether the defendant is responding; make it clear that it is 'o.k.' to say "I can't hear.'

Equality of arms requires each party to be afforded a reasonable opportunity to present his case under conditions that do not place him under any substantial disadvantage *vis-à-vis* the prosecutor, or opponent.

Although a victim is seldom a party to the criminal proceedings much work has been done over recent years to acknowledge the importance of looking after the victim's interests. This includes various scenarios. The victim who attends court as a witness in the trial should be advised about procedures beforehand, whether by written material sent out in advance or by having a look inside the courtroom before the case begins and having a word with the clerk.

The 'invisible' victims are the ones who do not attend court but the outcome of the case may affect their pocket, or more importantly, their peace of mind. They will have a strong view on whether or not they have received justice? Has compensation been awarded? If not, was there a good reason? What was it? Has the perpetrator been released from custody on bail or not? Reasons must be given – someone always has a right to know why.

3.12 The perception of the reasonable person in the public gallery

3.12.1 Impartiality

"It is not merely of some importance but is of fundamental importance that justice should not only be done but should manifestly and undoubtedly be seen to be done."

This quotation comes from a 1924 case and is usually quoted as the guiding principle in court, although cases and statutory guidance have followed. Under Article 6 of the Human Rights Act, everyone is entitled to an 'independent and impartial tribunal'. On the bystander test, the question is whether or not there are 'ascertainable facts which may raise doubts as to his impartiality.' If there is, then the magistrate should offer to withdraw.

In a recent case it was stated clearly that a judge could not be challenged purely on the basis of 'religion, ethnic or national origin, gender, age, class, means or sexual orientation' (Seer Technologies Ltd. V. Abbas 2000).

Specific disqualifications

In the following situations the domestic law is clear that magistrates should not adjudicate:

- Magistrates who are members of a local authority must not sit on any cases brought by or against the authority.

- Magistrates who have dealt with a bail application and considered previous convictions must not sit on a trial of the same defendant in the same proceedings. Similarly magistrates sitting on a trial who are aware of previous convictions through dealing with a legal aid application in the same proceedings should not sit. Any pre-trial involvement which does <u>not</u> involve prejudicial information is unlikely to breach Article 6.

- Previous convictions become known during the course of a trial – a trial before a fresh bench will be usually be required. Disclosure of other allegations or future trials is not of itself a basis for disqualification.

- Any direct pecuniary interest, however small, in the outcome of the proceedings – 'nobody may be a judge in their own case'

- The Lord Chancellor has issued guidance to local advisory committees as to various situations which may require care in the selection process e.g. applicants who are related to local serving police officers.

Whenever a magistrate knows that there could be an objection to his sitting on the case, he should let the chairman know so that the matter can be brought to the attention of the parties with the intention of withdrawing from the case. Arguably the withdrawal should take place by remaining in view of the parties by moving well away from the bench or sitting in the well of the court. The difficulty of simply going into the retiring room is that the bench may subsequently wish to retire and discuss the case. An alternative suggestion is to leave by the public entrance if the situation is likely to embarrass the defendant and affect his communication if the magistrate remains.

Magistrates must be seen to give their undivided attention to the case before them and this must be actual <u>and</u> apparent. Appeals have been successful when one of the magistrates has 'appeared to be asleep', has been looking at length through a bench guide, and has been signing warrants during the course of a case.

At the end of the day, it is really about 'Do as you would be done by.'

CHAPTER 4
COMPETENCE 4
Working as a member of a team

INTRODUCTION

This particular chapter forms the principal basis for a winger court appraisal. All competences are observable by the appraiser and most of them will additionally demonstrate some understanding of the relevant basic law and procedure.

PARTICIPATE EFFECTIVELY ON THE BENCH

By undertaking particular pre-arranged roles

4.1. As a note-taker

What is the legal responsibility of a magistrate to take a note? None. The clerk does have specific legal responsibility to take a note of any full argument for bail and also 'the substance' of oral evidence in family proceedings. The 2000 Practice Direction at paragraph 8 states that:

'At any time, justices are entitled to receive advice to assist them in discharging their responsibilities. If they are in any doubt as to the evidence which has been given, they should seek the aid of their legal adviser, referring to his/her notes as appropriate.'

This carries the inference and expectation that the legal adviser will take a note. What are the practical advantage of magistrates taking a note?

- Assists an individual to concentrate on the case.
- Visibly creates an impression of careful interest being taken.
- Useful to refer to and check back in the decision-making process.
- Assists in drawing up reasons for a decision.
- Assists if the magistrates are asked to state a case.

In the trial scenario there is a school of thought that notes should not be taken during the opening and closing speeches, but only of the actual evidence. This is to emphasise that the magistrates are not considering mere opening representations as evidence.

Fortunately it is becoming more common for advocates to disclose the basis of the 'not guilty' plea at the outset and this assists in identifying the relevant key issues e.g. descriptions, timing, words spoken and these matters can be noted more fully and underlined for easy reference.

When taking notes on a matter for sentence some magistrates find it helpful to head up and split the notes in readiness for the decision making process under the headings:

Example:

An offence of assault.

- Aggravating features
  Laid in wait outside victim's home at 2am
  'I've got something for you' – 2 blows to the face – clenched fist
  Deliberate and planned
  Black eye – some swelling to nose – no break
  Defendant on bail – trial next month for driving over prescribed limit
  One relevant previous conviction – assault last year – compensation £250 ordered (check is it paid?)
  Victim of a different race (check – is that aggravating on these facts?)
- Mitigating features
  Provocation – flirting with defendant's partner – some taunting
  Both parties in drink – both asked to leave club
- Offender mitigation
  Immediate admission to police – arrested at home at 4am
  Guilty plea today – 1st appearance 3 days after incident
  21 years old – partner and child of 2 – full-time work as trainee supermarket manager – good employment record – family responsibility
  Visited victim to apologise – hard evidence of remorse
  Self-motivated referral for help with drink problem
- Options
  Entry point – custody.
  Compensation – £180 per week income? Rent £40 per week. Council tax £6 per week. Partner doesn't work. No debts.
  CSO? – suitable? – can't do weekends or some evenings.
  Combination order? – punish + address drink problem? + compensation.

Failure to make notes is not a sign of incompetence. Some magistrates have excellent memories and the appraiser will see that they are contributing fully in the decision-making process and have clearly missed nothing. Most of us simply do not have that facility!

4.2 As a keeper of/referrer to handbooks/guidelines

The principal reference in court must be the sentencing guidelines. It is well worth spending a few minutes familiarising with the way they are set out so that there is not a protracted period of flicking from page to page in court. There is now a single contents page for the detailed guidelines which lists criminal offences and then the motoring matters which appear most regularly before the court. Other motoring matters are listed at the back.

As a test of familiarity, check that you can readily locate the following:

- Compensation guidelines - black eye now £125.
- Speeding – e.g. exceeding a 30 mph limit by 25 mph – band B + 6 points or disqualify up to 56 days.
- Drive with alcohol over the prescribed limit – breath reading of 80 – band C + disqualify 24 months.
- Driver failing to supply details (speed camera cases) – band B + 3 points.
- Insecure load (vehicle up to 3.5 tonnes) – band A.
- Insecure load (vehicle over 3.5 tonnes) – band B (distinguish the different weight factor).

It is important to turn quickly to the relevant pages and understand any tables involved so that the minimum time is spent looking at paperwork and the maximum time is spent looking at the defendant and listening to the case.

4.3 Observing particular people/conduct

The chairman cannot see everything in a busy court and it is helpful for the wingers to make any relevant observations. This might include various situations, for instance:

- People talking in the gallery.
- 'The head round the door' trying to attract the usher's attention.
- The witness who has reached the stage of looking exhausted.
- The court probation officer who is trying to attract attention to make a comment.
- The clerk from another court who has come along to take some work.

When there is a bench of three nobody in the court should be ignored.

4.4 Appropriately drawing the chairman's attention to particular points of evidence or procedure

What is appropriate? This will vary with the urgency of the situation and the preferences of the particular chairman. It may well be appropriate to pass a note to the chairman bearing the word 'COSTS' as an *aide-mémoire* to add them to the penalty just announced.

It is also relatively straightforward to underline key words in your notes if you feel that the chairman should consider asking further questions or seeking clarification of issues.

It is more difficult to stop a chairman in his tracks from saying or doing something which is seriously wrong e.g. agreeing to an adjournment without consulting wingers. There is a balance of upholding the dignity of the court and measuring whether you are concerned as a matter of principle or whether you seriously disagree with the decision. If it is the latter then it may be necessary to ask for some consultation on the matter. If it is simply a matter of principle it is nevertheless important to raise your concern with the chairman at the end of the court.

PARTICIPATE EFFECTIVELY IN DISCUSSION IN THE RETIRING ROOM

Active involvement

4.5. Contributing to a structured decision making process. See 2.11 (trial) 2.13 (sentencing) and 2.29 (bail) for details of the process.

The contribution can begin on the bench by turning to the relevant guidelines for sentencing cases or to a copy of the bail form for bail cases and by making relevant notes. In the retiring room it is important to encourage others to use a structured approach. This means avoiding the temptation to join in any immediate judgements e.g. 'I think community service would be a good idea', or 'Perhaps we could let him out on bail but with stringent conditions.'

The 4 'O' approach to sentencing (2.13) and the 'ABC' approach to bail (2.29) take just a few minutes and ensure that all relevant matters are considered and all members of the bench are aware of the agenda.

4.6 Helping identify the issues.

4.7 Helping keep the focus on the evidence as presented.

This involves breaking down the information into what is agreed and what is not.

Example.

Trial of a criminal damage allegation.

> The defendant accepts the written witness statement that he damaged the door and the cost, but he disputes that he caused the damage intentionally or recklessly. There is little point in hearing sworn evidence about the colour of the door and the type of wood – it is agreed – there is no issue about it. The emphasis of the evidence should simply be about who did what and who said what when the damage was actually caused. The question becomes, 'is this evidence helping us to decide about whether this was done intentionally or recklessly or not?' If not, suggest that the chairman asks where the questions are leading.

Even in a guilty plea case it is important to identify whether there is any significant variation in the version of events between prosecution and defence. Does the mitigation provide explanation for the facts or does it create a different version of the facts? If so, the court may have to order a Newton hearing and hear evidence if the different versions of events would lead to different penalties.

4.8. Challenging any views that seem to be partial or discriminatory.

See 3.4 , 3.7 and 3.8.

It would be a strange world if we did not build up preconceived ideas based upon previous experiences. In the main that is how we learn. Sometimes we would be the first to accept that we can make leaps of belief which have no hard factual basis. Sometimes that might be a good thing – 'once bitten twice shy' may sensibly create some caution for the future. When it comes to making judgements on others it has to be a bad thing. There is no real basis. No facts. No evidence. Only personal feelings based on odd anecdotes, some thoughts, an odd incident, propaganda, an unfortunate personal experience – maybe several.

Challenging partial and discriminatory views does not have to be from a standpoint of 'holier than thou'. It is more important to recognise that we all have our prejudices and be grateful for someone to pull us up <u>if</u> they are entering into decisions about others.

Example:

Retiring room.

> 'Well I think he's guilty of stealing the car. They're all the same on that estate – it's a disgrace, all the burnt-out cars up there. They

just take whatever they fancy and then burn the evidence. Why pay for a taxi or wait for a bus? They're into a car in just a few minutes. There was a programme about it last night.'

'I think he's on drugs as well – with those dark shadows under his eyes. Probably dealing – he's dressed in expensive designer gear and he can't afford that on benefits. My son paid over £200 for a jacket like that. It would be as well for him to get some rehabilitation in prison and break the drugs ring.'

THE CHALLENGE!

'Yes I've been in that area and there are a lot of burnt-out cars around (*some appreciation of the point of view)* BUT what's the actual crime rate up there? Not very much different to the rest of the city? *(question to check out any actual facts*). Not 100% anyway! That's the fact isn't it? We must be careful to treat this defendant fairly. Let's go through the actual evidence ...

4.9 Contributing to discussions with the court clerk as appropriate.

Most chairmen prefer to act as the spokesperson to the clerk and it is usually easier for the clerk to act as impartial adviser to the bench as a whole through one person. It also means that the chairman can take the matter through discussion of the facts with colleagues and then identify the areas on which 'the bench' require legal advice.

Obviously there are times when the chairman will be quite happy for wingers to ask additional questions or seek clarification.

Discussions with the court clerk should be solely about the law, practice, procedure, penalties and structure and in the main should begin with '<u>we</u> would like to know' from the chairman rather than '<u>I</u> would like to know' from a winger. Identifying the issues for the clerk is a team effort.

The clerk also has the responsibility to assist, where appropriate in the formulation of the reasons and the recording of the reasons. Provided that the chairman has led a structured decision-making process the reasons will flow from the chairman's lead. Contribution to the decision-making therefore runs in tandem with contributing to the formulation of the reasons.

4.10 Assisting in the formulation of announcements to be made in court.

(See also 6.5 'consulting colleagues and preparing what is to be said'.)

Most courts have a set of guideline pronouncements but it is unlikely that any one of them will totally fit a particular case as there are endless permutations of penalties, explanations, warnings and money payment rates. A vigilant winger can helpfully remind the chairman about the costs order, the warning for failing to surrender to bail, the requirement to pay the fee for the drink/drive rehabilitation course.

Added to this there is of course the requirement to give reasons and set out the aggravating and mitigating features which have affected penalty. Reasons are discussed in chapters 2 and 3, and a specimen checklist for sentencing is produced at 2.13 – this is not the property of the chairman, it is the property of the full bench and equal input must be given by all members.

Any defendant must be aware of the basis of the decision. Why did they sentence in my absence? Why did they fine me this particular figure? Did they take any notice of my mitigation? Clear, succinct answers in reasons will enable a defendant to decide whether they should ask for the case to be re-opened or appealed. Good reasons should avoid appeals rather than create them!

CHAPTER 5
COMPETENCE 5
Adult Court Chairmanship
Managing people and processes and leading the team

CONSULTING WINGERS ON THE BENCH

5.1 Encouraging full participation on all decisions (except possibly contempt)

Encouraging participation on the bench requires additional skills to those required for encouraging participation in the retiring room (see competence 5.14). In the retiring room there is the privacy for frank interchange and the 'round table' discussion ensures that all contributions can readily be seen and heard.

On the bench there is the disadvantage of whispered comments along a lateral seating arrangement.

Discussion on the bench in such circumstances should therefore be limited to interchanges which are straightforward and where agreement is likely to be reached quickly. The chairman may usefully open discussion with a clear and concise opening suggestion which requires a brief (but important) comment by each winger.

Examples:

Traffic offences attracting guideline fines.

C. 'Are you content to impose the guideline figure of £150 based on his net income and guilty plea or do you feel that it should be increased or decreased?'
W.1. 'I think it should be £200 – there's the previous conviction last year and he can afford £4 per week to clear it within the year'
W.2 'Yes, I agree with that'
C. 'So do I'.

Adjournments.

C. 'Are you happy with the suggested adjournment for 4 weeks for medical evidence?'
W.1. 'It seems unrealistic to me – surely 8 weeks would be more appropriate – he doesn't even have an appointment yet.'

W.2. ' I just wonder whether we could actually go ahead today. Could we ask whether the injuries are agreed and whether there are any photographs on file?'
W. 1. ' It's a good idea but I didn't know that we could do that.'
'I'll have a word with the clerk first.'

Bench participation must be based on 'no assumptions' and genuine contributions. It may well be helpful to discuss the sentencing approach to be taken at the beginning of special court lists e.g. a list of parking offences, TV licence cases and agree the fine to be imposed in the absence of mitigation or means information. The assurance can then be given that there will be discussion if a defendant does respond or attend.

Where substantial discussion develops it is preferable to retire so that communication is more effective. It is difficult for a winger to effectively argue in whispered tones for a conditional discharge if colleagues are minded to impose a community penalty. The gap is great and a winger should be given the opportunity to ask for a retirement in order to gain the benefit of full expression.

Contempt proceedings are discussed at 5.23 and it is clear that a chairman may well have to act very quickly to ask for the removal of an unruly person. The full bench would however be fully involved in deciding upon any subsequent action.

5.2 Ensuring a three way conversation is seen to take place

Looking ahead and saying 'OK?' is not a 'conversation'. It is beneficial for the chairman to draw back his chair and so allow the wingers to draw closer and turn towards each other for discussion. This avoids the situation of a chairman having to relay the wingers' views to each of them.

The danger of turning to each winger is that one will give a full view and the other will repeatedly simply be asked whether they agree with the first view or not. Natural instinct leads us to turn one way more easily, but it is important to take first views from different sides.

Never let a member of the public believe that the wingers are simply administrative aides!

5.3 Ensuring all pronouncements are agreed

Most benches have standard pronouncements which serve as a starting point reference. Whilst they are naturally adapted for the particular individual and circumstances, the essential ingredients must be covered i.e.

the detail, the explanation, the reasons and necessary warnings. The format of most pronouncements must therefore be agreed by the full bench.

Whenever a homily is to be delivered it is important for the bench to agree what is to be said. Wingers should not be put in a position of demonstrating by their body language that they do not wish to be associated with unexpected tirades or threats. The chairman's authority is clearly dissipated in the face of the court by such actions. Check that there is to be a united front first!

5.4 Ensuring wingers have opportunity to put questions through the chair

In a trial this is relatively easy because there is a specific point in the proceedings for questions from the bench and wingers will have made their notes during the proceedings as prompts.

It is more difficult where the proceedings require the chairman or clerk to effectively conduct a cross-examination e.g. fine defaulters and arguments to prove 'exceptional hardship', or encouraging an unrepresented defendant to mitigate. The chairman must make it clear to the wingers that he will consider their questions and when that will happen. The assurance must be genuine and not a dismissive 'any questions?' Ask it and mean it before asking any person to sit down again. Check that you've done it before moving into decision-making mode!

The wingers are in a better position than the chairman to listen and to observe the defendant. They will often pick up points missed by the chairman who is obviously more involved in talking than listening. If the wingers really are the eyes and ears of the bench then they must be encouraged to process and pursue the information trail.

Many wingers are anxious that their questions may be inappropriate or inadmissible and unfortunately it is very easy to destroy confidence in this important area. The clerk will be happy to explain any legal difficulties. Explanation should always be given if a question is not appropriate, together with reassurance to encourage questions in the future.

LEADING DISCUSSION IN THE RETIRING ROOM

5.5 Apply structure to the decision making process

The three most complex decision-making processes apply to bail, sentencing and trial and suggested structures are covered in detail in competence 2 as follows:

Bail – 2.29.7
Sentencing – 2.13
Trial – 2.11

By applying a structure to the discussion, the reasons will simply flow!

5.6 Getting the discussion started – identifying the issues

It is usually helpful for the chairman to establish first of all what is agreed before identifying the issue for discussion. Use lots of questions to check out understanding and ensure involvement.

Example:

Agreed relevant facts: "I suggest that the agreed facts are that the defendant struck a blow to the victim causing a black eye. Both the defendant and the victim are about the same age and physical build and one cannot be seen as physically superior to the other. Are we agreed?"

Issue for discussion: "The defence is that the blow was given in self-defence. The prosecution evidence is that the defendant struck the first and only blow, following a heated exchange. The defence evidence is that the victim pushed the defendant violently at the outset and raised his fist to strike him in the face.
Is that a fair summary?
Are we agreed that the only issue is whether there is any basis for self-defence?"

Moving into discussion:"Shall we discuss each of the witnesses' evidence in turn?"

5.7 Consulting with colleagues

Example:

"Mrs. Brown, would you like to start? What was your impression of the victim's evidence?"

A wide open invitation without any indication of personal opinion.

5.8 Listening actively to colleagues

Make it clear that time is available and you want to hear what is said. No decision is obvious and no contribution can be overlooked or side-lined. One view can change the whole approach. Active listening is about showing open body language – leaning forward, arms uncrossed, eye contact and prompting if necessary. Avoid the temptation to interrupt, finish statements, jump to conclusions or do too much talking yourself. Reflecting back any feelings or comments is evidence of good listening.

Example:

"So, Mrs. Brown, you've identified an important inconsistency in the victim's evidence. Your note is very clear that in evidence in chief he said that there was no conversation at all but under cross-examination he admits that there was an interchange in which he swore at the defendant. This seems to be affecting how you regard his truthfulness generally. Is that correct?"

5.9 Ensuring that discussion is purposeful and relevant

It may be necessary to repeat the issue for discussion in order to keep on track and prevent wingers from 'jumping the gun' and/or confusing issues for verdict with mitigation.

Example:

Winger : " I think there was a lot of provocation here and I do have some sympathy with the defendant. He was driven to it by the abuse."
Chairman : "If we were to find him guilty then we would have to consider provocation. For the moment we need to stick to the issue of self-defence and identify whether the defendant really believed that he was about to be physically struck or not?"

The most common difficulty when sentencing is to maintain discussion about the offence itself before moving on to discuss the offender. The defence solicitor will have had the last word and it will have been predominantly about the offender rather than the offence. The prosecution outline about the offence can easily recede into the background. It is understandable to enter the retiring room and immediately begin a discussion about the offender and suggested disposals. It is important therefore to set the agenda at the outset and deal with items in turn. The seriousness of the offence must be determined first, in order to establish a level of seriousness – it may even be beyond the magistrates' courts powers.

5.10 Ensuring chairman speaks for the bench

The easiest discipline is to ensure that each decision and reason begins with 'we' and check whether it is true.

5.11 Inviting the clerk, where appropriate, to give advice

See 5.16 - 5.20 for full Practice Direction 2000.

This is a very important area, particularly for chairmen and the main points are summarised as follows:

- Responsibility to advise in the following listed areas, whether or not the justices so request:
  Questions of law, and mixed law and fact
  Matters of practice and procedure
  Range of penalties available
  Relevant decisions of superior courts or other guidelines
  Other issues relevant to the matter
  Appropriate decision-making structure.
- Responsibility to assist the court, where appropriate, as to the formulation of reasons and the recording of those reasons.
- Must play no part in making findings of fact but may assist the bench by reminding them of evidence, using notes.
- Request to join in retiring room should be made in open court, in the presence of the parties.
- Retiring room legal advice is 'provisional' and should be repeated for representations in open court.

How should the invitation be made for the clerk to join the magistrates in the retiring room at a later stage?

A suggested form of words is:

'We shall ask the clerk (legal adviser) to join us when we have made a decision in order to formally record our reasons'.

This specific assistance is likely to be required in most cases involving retirement. It makes the situation clear that the bench are responsible for the decision, but the clerk (legal adviser) has a formal role to play in respect of reasons. Formulation of the reasons may properly include some or even all of the other listed areas of assistance and the final decision may well be modified as a result. A request to join the bench in order to give 'advice on the law' is arguably too restrictive and it should ideally be sought and given in open court before the bench retire.

USING WINGERS EFFECTIVELY

5.12 Delegating key tasks e.g. note-taking, consulting bench guidelines

Delegation is a management skill and is more than simply 'asking someone else' to do a job. The chairman retains accountability. Any decision to delegate will therefore depend upon the ability and experience of the winger. The winger will naturally wish to do the job well and will appreciate the opportunity to either say 'no' or question exactly what is required. What exactly do you want them to do? As in any other setting, what does a 'good job' look like to you? Tell the winger.

Examples:

> Consulting the bench guidelines – depending upon your personal preference, suggest that they should be turned up whilst the defendant is being identified rather than during the prosecution or defence submissions. Stress that it should not be done during any interchange between the bench and the defendant or defence solicitor. If there is any problem or delay then make it clear that it is important to wait until the case is concluded rather than flicking through the guide while the case is going on.
>
> Completing a fine default checklist – make sure that the winger is familiar with the form and the requirements before delegating the task.

5.13 Encouraging wingers to prompt

- Be clear as to your preferred method e.g. nudge, note, cough. Be clear that you do not want to be loudly interrupted in mid-flow in court. It may be necessary to refer to a major prompt openly in court by saying, for example "I'm grateful to my colleague for reminding me that we also agreed that you will pay costs of £40." This explanation will make it clear that it is an oversight rather than an addition which has come solely from the winger concerned.

- A prompt is a reminder to include information which is either agreed by the bench or is standard information. It should not be seen as an opportunity for a winger to be making additional contributions during a pronouncement.

5.14 Ensuring full participation

- Beware of being the chairman with whom all wingers agree. Agreement may be more apparent than real. Many people acquiesce and this can easily be mistaken for real agreement. Acquiescence can exist for various reasons – a wish to 'fall into line', a lack of confidence, or a feeling that any views will not be heeded in any event. It is important to check out whether the agreement is genuine through conversation and observation of body language.

- Open questions are least threatening and most likely to generate a helpful contribution "What do you think is the most suitable option?" is a more useful line than saying "Shall we go with the report for probation or not?" Consider whether each winger has said anything positive about the proposed decision – is there a real commitment by both?

- Is each winger fully engaged e.g. maintaining eye contact with you and leaning forward into the discussion. If not, ask yourself whether you reached agreement by participation or by acquiescence?

UNDERSTANDING THE CLERK'S ROLES AND RESPONSIBILITIES

5.15 Agreeing speaking roles

- This may vary between various partnerships and may require some clarification before the court begins. It arises most significantly in fine default means enquiries where there is a danger of clerk and chairman jockeying for questions between them. This can be disconcerting for the defaulter and also confusing for the wingers who are trying to follow through a line of enquiry. Who is going to do it? Is there permission and understanding for supplementary questions at the end?

- After making complicated pronouncements, it may be helpful to say "Is there anything you wish to add learned clerk?" This provides a dignified opportunity for the clerk to cover any explanations or warning which may have been omitted. The chairman may then make the formal dismissal of the defendant.

5.16 - 5.20 Relationship with the court clerk

The Practice Direction (Justices:Clerk to Court) 2000 is set out in full:

(1) A justices' clerk is responsible for:
a. the legal advice tendered to the justices within the area;
b. the performance of any of the functions set out below by any member of his/her staff acting as a legal adviser;
c. ensuring that competent advice is available to justices when the justices' clerk is not personally present in court.

d. the effective delivery of case management and the reduction of unnecessary delay.

(2) Where a person other than the justices' clerk (a 'legal adviser'), who is authorised to do so, performs any of the functions referred to in this direction he/she will have the same responsibilities as the justices' clerk. The legal adviser may consult the justices' clerk or other person authorised by the justices' clerk for that purpose before tendering advice to the Bench. If the justices' clerk or that person gives any advice directly to the Bench, he/she should give the parties or their advocates an opportunity of repeating any relevant submissions prior to the advice being given.

(3) It shall be the responsibility of the legal adviser to provide the justices with any advice they require to properly perform their functions whether or not the justices have requested that advice, on:
(i) questions of law (including ECHR jurisprudence and those matters set out in s.2(1) of the Human Rights Act 1998)
(ii) questions of mixed law and fact;
(iii) matters of practice and procedure;
(iv) the range of penalties available;
(v) any relevant decisions of the superior courts or other guidelines;
(vi) other issues relevant to the matter before the court;
(vii) the appropriate decision making structure to be applied in any given case;

In addition to advising the justices it shall be the legal adviser's responsibility to assist the court, where appropriate, as to the formulation of reasons the recording of those reasons.

(4) A justices' clerks or legal adviser must not play any part in making findings of fact but may assist the Bench by reminding them of the evidence, using any notes of the proceedings for this purpose.

(5) A justices' clerk or legal adviser may ask questions of witnesses and the parties in order to clarify the evidence and any issues in the case.

(6) A legal adviser has a duty to ensure that every case is conducted fairly.

(7) When advising the justices' clerk or legal adviser, whether or not previously in court, should:
(i) ensure that s/he is aware of the relevant facts;
(ii) provide the parties with the information necessary to enable the parties to make any representations they wish as to the advice before it is given.

(8) At any time, justices are entitled to receive advice to assist them in discharging their responsibilities. If they are in any doubt as to the evidence which has been given, they should seek the aid of their legal adviser, referring to his/her notes as appropriate. Where the justices request their adviser to join them in the retiring room, this request should be made in the presence of the parties in court. Any legal advice given to the justices other than in open court should be clearly stated to be provisional and the adviser should subsequently repeat the substance of the advice in open court and give the parties an opportunity to make any representations they wish on that provisional advice. The legal adviser should then state in open court whether the provisional advice is confirmed or if it is varied the nature of the variation.

(9) The performance of a legal adviser may be appraised by a person authorised by the magistrates' courts committee to do so. For that purpose the appraiser may be present in the justices' retiring room. The content of the appraisal is confidential, but the fact that an appraisal has taken place, and the presence of the appraiser in the retiring room, should be briefly explained in open court.

(10) The legal adviser is under a duty to assist unrepresented parties to present their case, but must do so without appearing to become an advocate for the party concerned.

(11) The role of legal advisers in fine default proceedings or any other proceedings for the enforcement of financial orders, obligations or penalties is to assist the court. They must not act in an adversarial or partisan manner. With the agreement of the justices a legal adviser may ask questions of the defaulter to elicit information which the justices will require to make an adjudication, for example to facilitate his or her explanation for the default. A legal adviser may also advise the justices in the normal way as to the options open to them in dealing with the case. It would be inappropriate for the legal adviser to set out to establish wilful refusal or neglect or any other type of culpable behaviour, to offer an opinion on the facts, or to urge a particular course of action upon the justices. The duty of impartiality is the paramount consideration for the legal adviser at all times, and this takes precedence over any role he or she may have as a collecting officer.

It is proper for the court to delegate the task of assisting an unrepresented defendant to the clerk e.g. to assist in framing questions, clearing up ambiguities and ordering the defendant's evidence into a clear sequence. This particular task should be delegated early in the proceedings.

Not surprisingly most unrepresented defendants have enormous difficulty in phrasing questions for cross-examination and will quickly lapse into making statements. The clerk can simply hear the various statements and then phrase them into questions, perhaps by going through the various relevant parts of the evidence and asking whether the defendant agrees or not. Whilst this is time-consuming it is far more just than taking away a defendant's confidence by expecting him to conduct a professional cross-examination and then frequently reminding him that he must not make statements and disallowing his 'questions'.

In open court, it is no longer appropriate for the clerk to be giving advice in a whispered tone to the chairman. Article 6 requires a fair trial and a fundamental feature is that all aspects of the adjudication are heard clearly by the parties. Open discussion and advice removes any appearance of inappropriate intrusion by the clerk into the decision-making arena and also ensures that legal issues can be properly commented on by the advocates.

Once in the retiring room, it is helpful to the clerk if the advice is sought by the chairman and then for the chairman to ask the wingers if there is anything else which they wish to clarify. This avoids the situation of three magistrates firing questions and also the difficult situation of inexperienced wingers asking questions which are teasing the clerk into giving a personal opinion towards the decision – the 'fourth magistrate' scenario.

CREATING A WORKING RELATIONSHIP

5.21 Agreeing speaking roles

This agreement is largely based on local bench practices e.g. in some divisions all chairmen will put breaches of conditional discharges, whilst in others it will always be the clerk. Sometimes it will be based on particular chairmen who may not feel confident about certain parts of the proceedings e.g. giving the witness requirement warning on committal to crown court. As a chairman it is helpful to the clerk to identify any particular requirements before court e.g. for the clerk to conduct a full means enquiry if the bench are minded to impose a financial penalty, for the clerk to make a calculation to assess net income.

A small but important aspect is the 'permission to sit/requirement to stand.' This is one of the earliest instructions and some chairmen understandably wish to use the opportunity to show who is in charge. Others take the view that this is the dividing line between identification/charge or case history by the clerk and once he has asked the chairman whether the defendant may be seated, he has 'clearly finished for the time being' and 'handed over the proceedings'.

When nothing is said by either chairman or clerk for a few seconds, the clerk (or even the prosecutor or defence solicitor) will often jump in and simply tell or motion to sit down/stand up. Given that the exercise may well be repeated several times during a case it is helpful for a dignified team effort to determine who is going to deal with this courtesy, which can also double as a helpful cue in and/or an indication of who is in charge.

5.22 Holding a pre-court briefing

This is something beyond the enquiry "Is it a heavy list? What time can we expect to finish?" It is the opportunity to be prepared for the types of case you will have and the kind of information you will need to hand.

Examples:

(i) Any bail applications? A bail form with the list of exceptions and reasons might usefully be requested as an *aide-mémoire*. Check out whether there are any new local practices regarding regular bail conditions e.g. police reporting conditions, bail support schemes.

(ii) Any committals for trial? A copy of the committal pronouncement and witness warning. Ask the clerk to advise on the committal of any other matters along with the principal offence.

(iii) Any non-police prosecutions? Check out the current 'going rate' for fines e.g.parking offences.

5.23 Keeping the clerk properly informed

Whenever a decision is well outside the guidelines or against the representations of both of the advocates it is always advisable to inform the clerk of what you are minded to do. You may feel fully confident and the decision is likely to be entirely appropriate but a quick word of information may generate a new line of considerations or the assurance that 'it is entirely a matter for you.'

It is also helpful to provide some sort of time indication if retiring to reach a decision. This is more commonplace in the family court, but with the additional requirement of drawing up reasons in all courts, it is courteous to all concerned to release the parties from the courtroom for a period and give the clerk some indication of when he may be required.

5.24 Ensuring the clerk has sufficient time to do his/her job properly

This relates predominantly to the completion of paperwork or entering information into the computer. A compensation order is announced. At this point the clerk has to complete the details, obtain the name and address of the victim, record any reasons for ordering a lesser amount, record how it will be paid and possibly complete the notice to the defendant. Whilst there is always the opportunity for some catching up during the next case, it is far preferable to deal with one case at once. It does take a few minutes and for accuracy it is helpful to feel that there is no pressure to hurry.

During a trial it is helpful if the chairman can ask the witness and questioner to be guided by the clerk's pen in terms of breaking up the information and pausing until each part of the evidence is noted. Some clerks can keep up a fast pace alongside the evidence, but would appreciate a break in the proceedings after a couple of hours of note-taking.

When evidence is being taped, it is helpful if the chairman can pause the proceedings whilst the tapes are being changed or if there appears to be a technical problem.

Finally it is sometimes necessary for a clerk to seek authorities or a second opinion. Again, it assists the quality of the task if time can be given and the court possibly cleared for a coffee break 'whilst the legal points are researched.'

5.25 – 5.26 Establishing trust and co-operation, not competition and ensuring mutual feedback after court

Helpful feedback will only happen if there is some trust and co-operation between clerk and chairman. It is easy to avoid due to tiredness after a busy court, other duties and late finishes. Unfortunately it is human nature to avoid any form of feedback. Being on the receiving end may mean criticism. Being on the giving side may result in upsetting someone and after all, the court is over and next time will be different anyway.

'No feedback' is almost tantamount to saying 'no learning'. Every court is a unique learning experience and we all have the potential to develop. Someone else's perceptions can help us to do that.

What did the clerk do well – or different in a positive way to the norm? Tell them. If you were together again how might you suggest that things could be done more effectively? Share the idea. No criticism of the person, but possibly of what they did or how they did it today e.g. "I find your advice very helpful and clear but I had some difficulty in catching what you said when you remained seated to give the advice. When you stood and faced me I found it much easier. I realise it's a bit of an imposition but would you mind doing that each time? "

Then ask for feedback on your performance.

A few minutes and the clerk will reinforce the good behaviour and probably change approach in others. Remember to thank them next time round if the changes happen e.g. louder voice, slower pace, more timely interruptions, standing to give advice. An open discussion may similarly generate some changes in your approach e.g. announcing that "credit" is given for a guilty plea rather than your previous reference to "discount" for a guilty plea.

HANDLING ROUTINE PROCEDURES COMPETENTLY

5.27 Dealing competently with

5.27.1 Adjournments

The important point is that adjournments (delays!) are granted by the court and should be seen as an area for careful decision.

A basic adjournment checklist would be:

- What is the reason for the adjournment?
- How many previous listings?
- What was the anticipated action today?
- What steps have been taken to prepare for or resolve the difficulty?
- Can it be resolved today/differently?
- If not – what is the realistic, minimal period for progress?

Reasons for adjournment tend to fall around various regular scenarios and relevant specific enquiries may be follow:

(i) For production of insurance policy

The Crown Prosecution Service will normally only withdraw a case if an original certificate is produced. This does not preclude the court from hearing evidence and making a decision on the balance of probabilities that the defendant did have insurance. An adjournment 'to produce the certificate' may be futile if several weeks have already elapsed since the incident and there is still no progress. When a defendant states that it was his employer's vehicle, explore through your legal adviser whether or not the statutory defence may apply if the vehicle was being used in the course of employment and it may be possible to proceed immediately.

Consider how long ago was the offence – the original request to produce? What steps have been taken to produce the policy? Why are there grounds for optimism that it will actually materialise for the next hearing? Are the prosecution statements accepted? (usually a statement from the roadside officer and a statement from the nominated police station). What evidence other than the policy itself would the defendant wish to offer? e.g. bank statement showing a monthly direct debit to the insurance company, friend coming to court to say that permission was given for cover on his policy.

If no such evidence is to be called by the defendant and he accepts the statements then proceed as a trial today. If there is genuine 'other evidence' then adjourn for a 10 minute trial as soon as practical.

(ii) Absent witnesses

What directions were made regarding witnesses at the pre-trial review? When were they told about the hearing date? Are they contactable by phone or visit? Have they actually been interviewed? Have they supplied a witness statement? What is the nature and significance of the evidence? Should the case proceed in any event? Should the case go as far as possible as a part heard case? Is a witness summons necessary?

(iii) Tying up or linking with other matters

Are the offences of a similar nature and gravity? What stage has been reached in the other matters? It is more appropriate to tie to a case if it is a convicted matter and a report is already commissioned, than to a 'not guilty' case set down for pre-trial review and the prospect of a trial is many weeks away with possible acquittal! Can the other matter be brought forward and resolved today? A penalty of fine or community order can always be remitted or discharged if the defendant is sentenced to custody on a later date. Consider doing what you can when you can! Consider the benefit of the defendant being physically present today!

(iv) Breach of community order adjournments

Is it admitted or denied? Is it possible to obtain breach information today? How soon is the next breach court? Is it likely that the defendant will attend court after an adjournment? Disciplinary breaches should be dealt with promptly so that orders can be re-commenced. Very often the breach is due to failure to attend – surely this is a powerful indicator of dealing with the defendant whilst he is in court today! Compliance, or otherwise, may well have an affect on other matters in the system for sentence. Breaches which involve re-sentencing may have to be adjourned following plea for the CPS file to detail the original offence/previous convictions. Entering the plea will at least ensure that some progress is made.

5.27.2 Bail applications

A full discussion of bail law may be found at 2.29.

5.27.3 Not guilty pleas
5.27.4 Cases involving an unrepresented defendant

Specimen script and procedure checklist for chairmen:

1. EXPLAIN PROCEDURE TO DEFENDANT e.g. "The prosecutor (name?) will tell us about the case and will then call witnesses to give evidence. After each witness has given evidence, you will have the right to ask questions of the witness. After that, you have the right to give evidence and to call your witnesses. Finally, you can address the court before we retire to consider our decision.
   Have you brought any witnesses. Names? The witnesses will have to wait outside the court until called, which is likely to be about .... (prosecutor's estimate). In the meantime the usher will show them where to wait.
   Do you require a pen and paper to make notes?" (Seating with a table).

2. PROSECUTION OPENING SPEECH
3. CLERK WILL EXPLAIN THE IMPLICATIONS OF ANY STATEMENTS BEING READ OUT TO THE COURT

4. EXPLAIN PROCEDURE TO PROSECUTION WITNESSES
   e.g."The prosecutor (name) will ask questions first and then the defendant (name) may ask you questions. Please keep your voice up and please speak slowly because notes are being taken – keep any eye on the legal adviser's pen as you speak. Would you prefer to sit down as you give your evidence? "

5. EXAMINATION BY PROSECUTOR

6. EXPLAIN RIGHT TO CROSS-EXAMINATION TO DEFENDANT
   e.g. "You will have the chance to state your own side of the case later. At this stage, you may ask the witness questions about anything he has said, especially if you disagree, or about anything he may have left out. We would like the legal adviser to help you to frame the questions if necessary."

7. RE-EXAMINATION BY PROSECUTOR

8. QUESTIONS BY THE BENCH – check with both wingers and ask through the chair. Usually begin by, 'May we clarify...'

9. THANK WITNESSES FOR ATTENDING

10. CONSIDER WHETHER THERE IS A CASE TO ANSWER
    Is there any missing evidence required to prove an essential element? e.g. intention to permanently deprive the owner of the property on a theft allegation.
    Is the evidence so discredited as a result of the cross-examination or so manifestly unreliable that no reasonable tribunal could safely convict? e.g. witnesses describe widely different circumstances and give different versions during their own evidence.

11. EXPLAIN RIGHTS TO DEFENDANT
    e.g. " You can now make your defence to the charge. You do not have to say anything unless you wish to do so. However I must warn you that the court may draw its own conclusions and feel that you may have something to hide if you choose not to give evidence.

    If you want to say anything in your defence, you must give evidence on oath, and afterwards answer questions put to you by the prosecutor. Again, if you do not answer any questions without good reason, then the court may draw its own conclusions.

    Do you wish to give evidence or not?"

12. DEFENDANT'S EVIDENCE
    - Legal adviser requested by the bench to assist in presenting relevant evidence in a logical sequence.
    - Cross-examination by the prosecutor.
    - Questions by the bench.

13. DEFENCE WITNESSES
    - Explanation as for prosecution witnesses.
    - Cross-examination by the prosecutor.
    - Re-examination by the defendant.
    - Questions by the bench.
    - Thank the witnesses for attending.

14. DEFENDANT'S ADDRESS
    "Now is your chance to summarise your case and draw to our attention any particular points which have been made in the evidence given."

- Prosecutor may reply on legal points and with leave may call rebuttal evidence if unforeseen evidence is put to the court.

15. RETIRE
   - " We will retire now to consider the evidence. Would the clerk wish to advise us on any points of law before we retire?"
   - " We expect to take at least half an hour and you may wish to go for a coffee, and let the usher know where you are so that we can call you back into court".
   - " When we have reached a decision we will call for the legal adviser to formally record our reasons".

16. VERDICT – STRUCTURED APPROACH IN RETIRING ROOM
See example at 2.11.

17. VERDICT GIVEN and if guilty, APPLICATIONS BY PROSECUTION AND DEFENDANT'S ADDRESS ON DISPOSAL

Seek advice on the costs situation – witnesses are entitled to their expenses whether or not the decision is guilty or not guilty.

18. STRUCTURED APPROACH TO SENTENCE
See example pro forma at 2.13.

5.27.5 Binding over

Chairmen should be particularly aware of the procedure as set out below because the order may be made on the court's initiative as well as by complaint to the court. It is not intended to be a punishment but to prevent apprehended future danger.

In making a binding over order the court should follow steps below:

1. Hear the prosecution outline of the incident and consider whether evidence exists to suggest that there is a real risk of a future breach of the peace, not merely a possibility of a breach of the peace. Alternatively, the misbehaviour may well have arisen in the face of the court.
2. Indicate to the person concerned that the court intends to bind over and give the reasons for it e.g. the circumstances of the disturbance and the fear that it could arise again.
3. Indicate the intended type of binding over order: binding over to keep the peace; binding over to be of good behaviour with specific detail e.g. not to assault/molest/interfere with ...., or repeat the following

behaviour .... (JCS 2000); binding over to keep the peace and be of good behaviour, namely .... No other conditions may be inserted.

4. Seek representations. If consent is given, the court is relieved of the duty to allow an opportunity of showing cause why a binding over should not be made.
5. Obtain details of means in order to fix the amount of the recognisance.
6. Seek acknowledgement of the binding over and the indebtedness to the Crown as the court cannot make a unilateral order. A refusal may result in committal to prison for up to 6 months or earlier consent in respect of a party over 21. There is therefore no sanction for the under 21s. However in terms of proportionality under the Human Rights Act it is difficult to envisage a situation where the behaviour complained of, would be serious enough to justify custody beyond a very short detention in the courtroom or the cells.

5.27.6 Acceptable guilty pleas

A guilty plea may only be accepted by the court if it is unequivocal and unambiguous. The 'guilty but ...' and 'guilty because I want to get it over with' pleas cannot be accepted.

A stand down to consult the duty solicitor or short adjournment should be offered so that advice may be taken as to the correct plea. The papers should be clearly marked that a guilty plea was tendered so that appropriate credit can be considered if the matter does go to trial following advice and then a conviction follows. This ensures that the defendant is not prejudiced by the court's failure to accept a guilty plea as offered by the defendant the first occasion.

5.28 Identifying the elements of the offence charged

Example:

Theft requires the following elements to be proved:

- 'Dishonesty' e.g. defendant takes neighbour's lawn-mower – does he reasonably believe that he had the owner's consent? If so, there can be no conviction without proof of a dishonest intention.
- 'Appropriation' - assumes owner's rights and uses the property as if it belonged to him.
- 'Property' - a lawn-mower is 'property' – land is not, for the purpose of the Theft Act.
- 'Belonging to another' - the neighbour had possession and control.
- 'With the intention of permanently depriving the owner' did he intend simply to borrow it for an hour and then return it? (This is

one of the main reasons for the offence of taking a motor vehicle without the owner's consent – theft is rarely intended!.)

In dealing with a trial it is important to identify which element of the offence is denied so that the bench can concentrate on the relevant parts of the evidence. It is also important to spell out in the reasons, what has to be proved in order to convict of the particular offence. The clerk will assist.

5.29 Ensuring observation of the rules of evidence

Whole textbooks are devoted to the discussion of evidence and this summary seeks only to give general guidance.

1. Evidence must be relevant. It is relevant if it is logically probative or disprobative of some matter which requires proof. Evidence, for instance which goes beyond proving the essential elements of a strict liability offence is inadmissible as it may unfairly influence the decision.

2. Evidence is generally admissible if it relates to the facts in issue e.g. the quantity of alcohol drunk by a defendant pleading not guilty to being drunk and disorderly.

3. Hearsay evidence of a statement made by someone else is not admissible to prove the truth of the statement in criminal proceedings. The maker is not present to be cross-examined and the information may have been incorrectly heard, interpreted or recalled. Exceptions do exist.

4. Leading questions cannot be asked by advocates when questioning their own witness. A leading question is one which tends to suggest the answer and can often be answered therefore by a 'yes' or 'no' e.g. " is it correct that the thief had ginger hair and wore red jeans? This would not be admissible as it suggests the answer and cannot be a test of the credibility and weight of the evidence given.

5. Evidence of disposition, character or previous convictions is inadmissible in civil and criminal cases. It is dangerous to assume that facts will necessarily repeat themselves and a bad reputation in particular may be unfairly prejudicial. Exceptions do exist.

6. A person who is charged and called as a witness cannot be asked any questions which tend to show that he has been charged or convicted of any other offence. Exceptions do exist.

7. Inferences may be drawn from silence in court and failing to answer questions. Similarly, the court may take into consideration, silence at the time of arrest and failing to give an account for an object e.g. a jemmy; substance e.g. controlled drug; mark e.g. grazed arms; or failure to account for his presence at a particular place (e.g. burgled premises). Inferences from silence can never be used alone in order to convict.

8. The Court of Appeal guidelines, also referred to as the 'Turnbull guidelines' are relevant when the issue is disputed identity based on brief sightings. The court should have regard to the following points:

   - The possibility that a mistaken witness may be convincing (consider mistakes regarding friends and relatives) and a number of witnesses could all be mistaken.

   - 'Consider the circumstances of the identification; how long seen, how far away, in what light, was observation impeded, had the witness seen the accused before and if so how often, if only seen occasionally had he any special reason for remembering the accused, how long was there between the original observation and the subsequent identification to the police, was there any material discrepancy between the witness's description of the accused given to the police and the accused's actual appearance?'

9. Special measures directions may be made in respect of vulnerable and intimidated witnesses, which includes all children under 17. Special measures include video recorded evidence, use of screens, exclusions from the courtroom. Exceptions apply.

10. An accused person may not directly cross-examine a person who is a complainant where the proceedings are in respect of a sexual offence nor a 'protected witness' i.e. children who are witnesses to specified crimes.

APPLYING POWERS
USING KNOWLEDGE OF SENTENCING POWERS AND PROCESS

5.30 – 5.33 Using structured approach to sentencing and knowledge of range of penalties and any restrictions.

See 2.13 for detailed discussion.

5.34 Consulting the clerk to see if the sentence may be imposed

Some sentences are straightforward e.g. a tariff fine offence where there are no significant mitigating or aggravating features and the defendant can afford to pay within 12 months. Other sentences are more unusual and lie at the other end of the spectrum e.g. a combination order including an accredited programme, together with a reduced compensation order and a 'no costs' order. In such circumstances, consultation with the clerk is a competence rather than a sign of uncertainty.

5.35 Ensuring that the defendant understands

A good pronouncement will always include a clear explanation of the requirements of any sentence. The defendant may well convey through words or body language that certain aspects are not understood e.g. the right to seek review of a community service order. It may be necessary then to enlarge on this e.g. 'this means that if your circumstances change, for instance if you become ill, then you can apply for the order to be changed – possibly to another type of community order.'

Uncertainty should be resolved either by the chairman, the legal adviser or the probation officer. To rely on the defence solicitor is often unrealistic if he has other clients waiting in other courts.

Asking the question 'Do you understand?' is insufficient on its own. The answer is likely to be 'yes', whilst the reality from the quizzical look (if observed) is 'no'. Occasionally it may be helpful to ask a defendant to repeat the decision for his own benefit e.g. bail conditions, the total fine and when the first payment is due.

Relying upon a written notice of decision is insufficient on its own. Many defendants cannot read – even more, do not.

5.36 Following the correct order of proceedings

See competence 5.27.3 for a detailed description. It is helpful to an unrepresented defendant if the order is summarised at the outset along with an indication of who is who. He is then well aware that 'his turn will come.' It is then helpful to explain each stage as it comes along in a little more detail e.g. "Mr X, the prosecutor will now outline the case. Listen carefully, because in a few moments we will ask you to tell us your side of the story." Most defendants desperately want 'to <u>do</u> the right thing at the right time' in court. The chairman can ensure that at least that concern is allayed and leave the defendant free to consider the crucial aspect of what he needs to <u>say</u> to the court.

CHAPTER 6
COMPETENCE 6
Adult Court Chairmanship - Communication in court

SPEAKING EFFECTIVELY IN COURT

MAKING CLEAR PRONOUNCEMENTS

6.1 Using simple language without jargon

We would all no doubt say that we do not use jargon. The reality is that court jargon gradually becomes part of our day-to-day language and it is actually quite difficult for us to spot the jargon and translate it as necessary. There are a number of regularly used expressions which may need interpretation.

Examples:

'Adjourn' = 'put off ' to another day.
'We feel that you may fail to surrender because ... = 'We feel that you may not attend court for the next hearing because ....
'Advance disclosure' = information about the case against you.

6.2 Maintaining eye contact (where appropriate)

Eye contact is extremely helpful to assess whether a defendant or witness is engaged with the chairmen or not and whether there are indications of understanding or otherwise. It is accepted in case law that it is unnecessary to hold eye contact for prolonged periods and it may indeed be 'disquieting' to do so.

Assumptions may be made that direct eye contact by the defendant or witness may indicate honesty and veracity, but care should be taken in interpreting the response to eye contact in this way. Chairmen in particular should be aware that in African-Caribbean culture it may be considered impudent to look at a person in authority directly in the eyes and in some South Asian cultures it is considered appropriate to look away from a person in authority to indicate deference and respect.

6.3 Ensuring defendant and all in court understand

The most obvious way of checking is to ask, 'Do you understand?' In reality it is unlikely that a defendant will reply honestly in the negative, given the environment and the occasion. A more realistic way of checking is to look at the body language and determine whether the defendant is looking receptive, 'switched off' or quizzical and expand or change tone as appropriate. Occasionally it may be helpful to ask a defendant to repeat back his understanding of the decision e.g. date to return to court.

Sometimes there are implications for others. Does the probation officer understand which options should be covered in the pre-sentence report? Does the victim understand that the compensation will be paid in instalments rather than by a lump sum? Does the dock officer understand that the one day detention is deemed to have been served? Does the press officer understand that reporting restrictions apply?

6.4 Speaking clearly and concisely

The most common criticism of pronouncements is that they are rushed. This may be due to reading rather than communicating; nerves; or a lack of confidence in the content. The words of a pronouncement are important and the defendant deserves a professional and dignified approach. This message is going to affect his future in some way. It matters, and time and space are needed for it to be digested.

It is rarely resolved simply by 'slowing down'. It is more likely to be resolved by consciously breaking up a pronouncement into 'digestible chunks'. Keep a steady pace and give yourself and the defendant some space in the pauses to give and receive the information. A few seconds for the defendant to digest that the penalty is community service and not custody, before moving into the explanation of what will be required. Unfortunately in a busy court it is easy to overlook the value of silence – the pauses between each piece of information. Use them and make them work.

It is also common for volume to be low. By reading a pronouncement, it is easy to project downwards instead of upwards. Nerves can make a lengthy pronouncement into a breathless race. A lack of confidence can give the impression of 'simply wanting to get it over with.' The old-fashioned advice of taking a deep breath and giving yourself plenty of fuel is good advice. The volume should be loud enough so that everyone in court can hear easily without having to strain. Low volume is irritating to try to hear, immediately detracts from authority and reduces the likelihood of interaction.

Finally, a change of tone can help to get the message across. The tone of explanation may well be warm and friendly to engage attention, but can create a misleading impression if it continues into the warning element. The defendant deserves to be made aware that there are serious implications and the tone should convey this.

Sound as if you believe each part of this information is important. It really is. The most flattering response is for a defendant to ask a question at the end. He was listening and he trusts you to have the answer! (You may well deflect it to the legal adviser though.)

6.5 Consulting colleagues and clerk in preparing what is to be said.

Virtually every pronouncement has the same constituent parts which may serve as a checklist of information to check out with colleagues and the clerk particularly if the circumstances are unusual.

Pronouncement elements.

• The reasons	What is the basis for the decision? What has been taken into account?
• The detail	What? When? How? How long?
• The explanation	"You must .... Because ....."
• The warning	"Or else ...."
• Check understanding	"Do you understand?" Ask and observe!

Reasons must be given in accordance with Article 6 and the requirements of a fair trial. (See 6.7). Some chairmen prefer to detail the penalty first, but the pro forma produced in the sentencing guidelines gives the reasons before the penalty.

The detail is in the decision and it is worth considering whether all aspects of the decision are covered at the point of decision, rather than tackling elements piecemeal during the pronouncement. The question of costs is often tagged on at the end of a pronouncement and yet it may constitute the most onerous aspect of the decision. How much is claimed? Can the defendant afford to pay in full, or indeed, at all? What instalment rate would be considered appropriate?

The explanation may need to be checked particularly when imposing relatively new orders and ancillary orders. It may be appropriate to arrange for the clerk to explain complex orders e.g. football banning orders. The explanation that credit has been given for a guilty plea should be worded carefully so that early co-operation with the courts is seen to be rewarded. Unfortunately this message does not yet seem to be widely understood by the criminal fraternity.

The warning element is essential. The defendant must understand the full implications of the order. It is not common knowledge that a missed fine instalment renders the whole amount due. It is not common knowledge that non-payment can result in imprisonment. It is not common knowledge that failing to attend on court bail can result in arrest and imprisonment until the time of trial. These examples are particularly relevant to the first time minor offender. Prison does not equate in a layman's mind to failing to pay a television licence or speeding. Warnings are not the function of the defence solicitor, but the court.

Remember to use the word 'we' and operate as a 'we,' rather than 'I' in making any pronouncement.

6.6 Avoiding patronising tone

It is a thin line between exercising appropriate authority and behaving condescendingly. The balance probably lies in demonstrating common courtesy and respect for the defendant, whatever the decision of the court. Expressions such as 'my dear' and 'son', and body language such as peering down over the top of bi-focals can be perceived as patronising rather than authoritative.

An objective judgement delivered with some respect is more likely to be received and acted upon with respect, on an adult to adult basis. An adult reaction could be one of 'I'm not happy, but it's fair enough and I'll do it and get it over with'. A pronouncement delivered as a strict parent to a naughty child may generate quite a different reaction which may well reduce the motivation to comply. Treat as a child and you'll face a child.

6.7 Giving reasons clearly and concisely when required

Article 6 of the Human Rights Act states that 'judgement shall be pronounced publicly (subject to exceptions, principally where the interests of juveniles or the protection of private life so requires). Convention case law is clear that the giving of reasons is a part of the right to a fair trial, with two main purposes:

- To ensure that justice is done and is seen to be done by the person to whom the decision is addressed and by the community at large. (1998 British Crime Survey – 4 out of 5 respondents thought that the courts were too lenient in dealing with offenders. Will the giving of reasons dispel this perception?)

- To enable an aggrieved party to consider whether to exercise his right of appeal against the decision.

This is not a requirement to give 'a detailed answer to every argument', but to 'indicate with sufficient clarity the grounds on which they base their decision'. There has been a build up of specific requirements over recent years in domestic law e.g. when refusing bail, when imposing a custodial sentence, when finding special reasons for not endorsing a licence, when refusing to make a compensation order.

An example of reasons on verdict is given at 2.11, and a suggested checklist in delivering a sentencing pronouncement at 2.13.

The tests for adequacy of reasons are:

- Would a reasonable person with notice of all the facts and representations made to the court be able to understand the decision itself and the basis of that decision including the conclusions reached by the justices on disputed facts or contentious submissions and why such conclusions had been reached?
- Would a reasonable person with notice of all the facts and representations made to the court be able to properly consider whether to exercise his right of appeal in respect of either a finding against him or the decision made by the court?

Quite apart from the requirement under the Human Rights Act, there are also specific statutory requirements to give reasons in particular scenarios e.g. custody, refusal of bail, separate penalty points:

Examples:

(a) Custody because ... this was an unprovoked attack on an elderly, vulnerable victim whilst you were on bail for a similar offence of assault ...
(b) Custody for fine default because ... we have considered all alternatives and have discarded each option in turn for the following reasons, ...
(c) Bail is refused as we feel that you would not attend court because ... you have previously failed to attend court on three previous occasions in the past 2 years.
(d) Separate penalty points because ... the offence of speeding is an entirely different type of offence to the matter of using the car without any insurance and we feel that separate penalty points are therefore appropriate to distinguish the driving and document offences.

6.8 Using precedents appropriately

Suggested pronouncements are available from various sources and are helpful to ensure that all aspects have been covered. There has always been debate about whether it is appropriate for pronouncements to be 'read'. Provided that there is eye contact at relevant points, a chairman may feel more confident and delivery may therefore be of a higher calibre if a pronouncement is read. There are two issues worth considering before reading from a standard pronouncement:

Personalise as much as possible. As any sales representative is well aware – get hold of the name – keep saying it and you have more chance of your audience being hooked!
On the same basis, use the word 'you' and 'your' at every opportunity e.g. 'your' case/adjournment/fine etc.

Understand the content so that you are either able to clarify personally or alternatively calmly deflect to the clerk.

LISTENING ACTIVELY

6.9 Being attentive and being seen to be attentive in court

Justices should be seen to be paying attention and it is irrelevant that every word has been heard and understood, if the justice is giving the impression of being uninterested. Injustice has been held to have occurred where a witness had not received the undivided attention of one member of the bench, because the magistrate had been reading a bench guide during some of the evidence.

How can attentiveness be demonstrated positively? Expressions such as 'I see', 'And then what happened?'. Behaviour such as a gentle nodding from time to time (not nodding off!), making a note of what is being said, repeating back to check information 'So, you say that ...'

This is distinct from making constant interjections which can be un-nerving and distracting for a witness or advocate.

As a chairman it is important to take responsibility for wingers and check that they are engaged in the case. This may involve a suggestion that a break should be taken for the benefit of everyone involved in a lengthy case.

6.10 Making accurate notes

The key to note-taking is often found in the prosecution outline when the crucial issues are highlighted e.g. disputed identity defence would urge a fuller note and direct quotation at the point of description and apprehension in the actual evidence. Time can be saved by asking whether a copy of the interview can be handed to the bench for reference through the evidence.

Again it is important for the chairman to be 'winger-aware' and 'clerk-aware' and remind the witness from time to time that notes are being taken and give wingers and clerk the permission to interject if the evidence is coming too quickly or is not clearly heard.

Checking for accuracy of important parts of the evidence is an important part of the retiring room discussion.

6.11 Maintaining eye contact with the speaker

See 6.2 above.

QUESTIONING APPROPRIATELY

6.12 Asking relevant and appropriate questions

The single question for the bench is always the same. Do we have the fullest picture possible or not? If the answer is 'no', then consider whether questions may resolve and ask. Questions can set the ball rolling, open up communication and if nothing else, questions show an interest and attentiveness.

The use of open questions is important, particularly when dealing with unrepresented defendants e.g. Why did you do it? What happened next? Why do you need to keep your driving licence?' Tell us what you spend each week? Such questions cannot be answered simply by a 'yes' or 'no' and build on the reasonable assumption that generally people do want to tell their story. The question 'Do you have anything to say?' carries a possible message that the answer is quite likely to be 'no'. 'No' is so much easier and will get the case finished with much more quickly. Make it clear that the expectation is that you want to know and the time and space are there to be used. A quality decision needs quality information.

Obviously the chairman can then go on to ask closed and detailed questions and funnel the information into a tight picture e.g. Does your contract actually require you to drive or not? How much is outstanding on the hire purchase?

Whatever the scenario, whether it be extracting mitigation, clarifying the prosecution application, dealing with a means enquiry or avoiding unnecessary adjournments, the line of questioning must be kept firmly on the relevant track of achieving an effective decision.

Example:

An application for an adjournment.

- What is the reason for the adjournment?
- How many previous listings have there been?
- What was the reason for the last adjournment?
- What action/response has taken place during the adjournment?
- What exactly is going to happen if we adjourn again?
- How quickly can this realistically be achieved?

6.13 Ensuring that questions are understandable

Keep the questions short. Explain, if necessary why you need to know. The defendant may well misinterpret what you are asking and may be unnecessarily wary of giving the answer. Be ready to re-phrase if there is no helpful response.

Example:

Who lives with you? No response. Defendant may not wish to give names or relationships in open court.

Re-phrase:
We need to have picture of your financial situation so that we can fix a fair fine. Do you have any dependants to support out of your income?

6.14 Accurately relaying questions from the wingers

The winger has an ownership of the information as well as the chair and may well pick up points which a busy chairman has overlooked. Make sure that colleagues feel that they can properly contribute to the information trail and that you will relay their line of enquiry accurately.

How do you wish the winger to indicate to you that they have a question? What should the winger do to gain your attention? What is your preferred method? A jab in the arm? A note pushed across in front of you? Simply waiting for you to give the opportunity from time to time by turning to each winger? The assurance that you will ask before any decision is made?

6.15 Demonstrating a positive manner

Words and body language from the chair have to convey an active and interested attitude in the proceedings. This image is most likely to be tested towards lunchtime and during lengthy trials. At such times – put yourself into the shoes of the person speaking. Does the chairman look as if he wants to be here or not? If the answer is 'no' – ask a question, make a comment or take a break.

6.16 Demonstrating an unbiased approach

Examples:

- Thank the defence witnesses as well as the prosecution witnesses for attending court.
- Beware of nodding as some witnesses speak and raising eyebrows at others.
- Apologise to the defendant as well as the solicitor if the case has been held back in the list.

DEALING FAIRLY AND IMPARTIALLY WITH ALL COURT USERS

6.17 Ensuring equality of treatment to all court users

See 3.5 and 3.6.

6.18 Demonstrating a non-prejudicial attitude

See 3.7.

6.19 Addressing the defendant in an appropriate manner

The mode of address will often set the tone for the proceedings and may well establish a rapport between chairman and defendant.

A male defendant is more likely to respond positively if referred to as Mr. Smith rather than 'Smith.' So far as women are concerned it is not quite so straightforward and proceedings can become embarrassing in court if the chairman is asking 'Is it Miss or Mrs?' 'No, it's Ms'. It may be helpful for the usher to check out the title when taking the name outside court and then announce, 'Miss Ann Smith'.

When dealing with Sikh and Muslim naming systems it is of course preferable to find out how the defendant wishes to be addressed. In the absence of any specific request, if there are two or three names, it is most appropriate to address the defendant by using both or all names e.g. Mr. Amarjit Singh, Mr. Malik Ali. The second name is not a 'Christian name.' The religious name, whether first, second or third, should not be used in isolation. See 3.8.

6.20 Ensuring that all before the court understand what is going on

This will usually be satisfied if there is a commentary from the chair about who is doing what as the case proceeds and how it impacts on the defendant.

> 'The prosecutor (nod towards prosecutor) is going to tell us what the case is about so far as the police are aware and then you will have your opportunity to tell us your side of the story. '

Many defendants fully expect the arresting officer to be present in court and the notion of a crown prosecution service is not understood. They may wonder whether evidence is going to be called. Most importantly they need to be reassured that their turn will come.

> 'The clerk is telephoning the office to arrange a date for your trial. When we have a date we'll check whether it is convenient to you'.

The pregnant pauses in proceedings can be the most disturbing to a defendant. What is going on? Why is a telephone call being made? Is the case still going on? Are the police being called to court – possibly even for escort to prison?

> 'The probation officer (point out who he is) will need to speak to you before you leave the building to make arrangements for the preparation of the report'.

The after-court 'swoop' of officers/ushers should be announced. Who is going to speak to the defendant and why? Most importantly it is made clear that it is actually part of the official process and co-operation is required.

6.21 Showing appropriate concern for distressed parties and witnesses

Distress in court is common and understandable. It can take away self-control, dignity and confidence. The serious consequence is that a party is then unable to proceed in a helpful manner. Distress may manifest itself in angry, irrational outbursts or at the other end of the spectrum in a taciturn silence. Composure can be regained if there is a dignified acknowledgement of the feelings shown and then perhaps a pause in the proceedings. 'We can see that you're upset by what is being said and you may find it helpful if we take a short break. The usher will provide the parties (equality of treatment!) with a glass of water and we'll come back to court in a few minutes'.

The worst scenario is to ignore distress and let defendants soldier on and 'get it over with' – court proceedings are too important for a short-term fix.

MAINTAINING THE DIGNITY OF THE COURT

6.22 Ensuring that all appearing before the court treat it with respect (using common-sense)

With the exception of a small minority, most defendants would wish to treat the court with appropriate respect. The difficulty is that they frequently do not know what is expected of them. Once in court, they are immediately in the spotlight and there is no time to 'get the feel of the situation' and take the 'cue from others'. 'Do I stand?' 'Do I sit?' 'How do I address the magistrates/judges?'

The issue for the chairman is not so much one of being a disciplinarian as being able to talk a defendant through the case so that he knows that he is presenting himself in the best possible manner.

Various strategies can be adopted. The court usher will often take the opportunity to give some advice as the defendant comes into court e.g. 'stand up as the magistrates come into court and call the chairman 'sir.' It is easy enough and so very helpful for the chairman to tell the defendant that he 'may remain seated except when he is speaking to the magistrates '.

Different chairmen expect different standards of behaviour and this may depend upon the particular defendant. Some will take the view that a defendant who is chewing gum and standing with his hands in his pockets is necessarily being disrespectful and should be reprimanded immediately. Maybe he is nervous, maybe he is demonstrating an expected bravado in front of his friends, or maybe, he is in fact being deliberately difficult. Maybe? The danger of making a false assumption is that the situation can escalate. A defendant could immediately feel at a disadvantage and will go on to act as he is being treated - a 'naughty school-boy' role. He would then find it impossible to rise to the occasion on an adult to adult basis with the chairman. Protracted episodes of finding paper for the disposal of chewing gum and hands moving from pockets into an arm-folded stance are unlikely to generate an atmosphere for meaningful communication. At the end of the day, he has at least attended court!

The common-sense element of the competence is to recognise that sometimes it is just not worth jeopardising perceptions of justice purely to create a particular standard of presentation.

Prevention is better than cure. The vigilant court usher should be thanked and encouraged for taking the many unobtrusive actions and 'quiet words' which so often avoid such incidents and preserve the respectful atmosphere which is so important.

Solicitors are in a different category and must be expected to set an appropriate tone for others. Solicitors who begin a whispered conversation whilst waiting for their case to be called can be very distracting for those involved in the present case, and of course the bench. A short reprimand on the lines of 'we are finding it difficult to concentrate on the case before us because of the noise – could we ask for silence please.'

6.23 Dealing effectively with unruly defendants, witnesses and spectators

A suggested procedure would be:

(i) A firm, but polite request to refrain from the inappropriate behaviour 'so that the bench can concentrate properly on the case before the court.'

(ii) A general warning of the court's powers which could be invoked if the misbehaviour continues i.e. removal from the court, and being charged with contempt which carries imprisonment.

(iii) The court to retire to enable the person concerned to have a few minutes for reflection. This court action is recommended by the Court of Appeal 'so that those who wished to behave badly could so in its absence'.

(iv) Any person may be ordered to leave the court if the court is sure that removal is necessary to enable it to administer justice properly. If he refuses then an officer of the court or a police officer should be ordered to remove him or take him into custody. He should be told that he will be re-admitted or released as soon as he is prepared to behave. The case can proceed in the absence of the defendant in these circumstances but it may be more appropriate simply to put the case to the end of the list.

(v) The court may bind over any person who uses 'disrespectful or unmannerly expressions' in the face of the court, or if he disparages a magistrate or insults an officer of the court outside the courtroom. The court can proceed immediately to pursue the binding over order based upon a recognisance in the normal way. The person must of course be given the opportunity to comment on the proposal.

(vi) Contempt proceedings are the last resort. A person may be found guilty of contempt if he:

- Wilfully insults a magistrate, officer of the court or a solicitor or barrister during his attendance at court or
- Wilfully interrupts the proceedings or
- Wilfully misbehaves in court (s.12 Contempt of Court Act 1981).

The penalty is a fine to a maximum of level 4 and/or imprisonment for one month. Shouting from the gallery, 'terrible' and 'disgusting' in relation to the pronounced sentence was met with 7 days imprisonment which was appealed and reduced to a fine (R v Lewis and others 2000). Custodial sentences should only be imposed where there is no practical alternative. Legal advice must be offered and the defendant must have the opportunity to apologise and purge his contempt at any stage.

MANAGE BEHAVIOUR

EXERCISING AUTHORITY

6.24 Requiring explanations from those who have caused delay

There are two aspects to delay. Delay on the day and delay during the course of adjournments. On the day it is irritating to be in a situation where defendants are present and the court is ready to proceed but solicitors have not arrived. This also causes additional stress to the waiting defendants. Some chairmen take the view that the bench should always appear at the beginning of the court session if only to show that the court is ready and waiting and to emphasise that they did come into court at the appointed time.

Explanations should be sought as to why the client and the court have been kept waiting. This is not about reprimanding irritating behaviour or poor planning, but making it clear to the defendant that the court itself was ready to go ahead at the time stated on the bail form or summons.

Similarly the unrepresented defendant should properly be expected to explain any reason for late arrival and the court may well consider a charge of failure to surrender to the court at the appropriate time.

Delay which causes adjournments must always be questioned. A full discussion of appropriate questions for various situations can be found under competence 5.27(a).

6.25 Ensuring that witnesses are not bullied

There is a fine line between robust cross-examination and bullying of a witness, but it must not be crossed. The chairman may consider various interventions:

- Summarise what the witness has answered e.g. that he cannot remember, and suggest that the advocate now moves on.
- Suggest that the witness may need a short break and the bench will retire e.g. after a particularly lengthy or emotional line of questioning.
- Allegations of lying/covering up/making up should be cut off with the statement from the chair that they are matters for the court to determine after hearing all of the evidence.
- Summarise the point which the advocate has made and ask whether it need be pursued any further e.g. that the witness admits that he was under the influence of drink at the time.
- Ask where the line of questioning is leading if it is becoming protracted and unclear.

6.26 Dealing with discourteous or unhelpful advocates

Comment has to be made in such circumstances with the intention of avoiding repetition. It is important to recognise that the client wishes to feel that he is being well represented and that his choice of advocate is respected by the court. The typical discourtesies of late arrival at court or inadequate instructions can be dealt with more sensitively after the client has left the court. Check that your perception is shared by the wingers and check that they wish you to take some action.

As with any criticism, assume first that there is a perfectly good explanation and allow the opportunity for it to be given. Express your concern or difficulty clearly and check your facts e.g. 'we were ready to proceed at 10 a.m. as were the 4 witnesses. We were concerned that you did not arrive until 11 a.m. and then had to be given further time to take additional instructions. The witnesses were kept waiting for nearly 2 hours to give their evidence. The case has been fixed for trial for 6 weeks. Why were you not here at 10 a.m. with full instructions and ready to go ahead?'.

Ignoring such situations is to the detriment of witnesses and defendants on the day and encourages similar repetitions.

6.27 Coping with the unexpected

People do lose their temper and people do become suddenly ill with the stress of court proceedings. It is not expected on a particular day but is likely to happen at some time within a magistrates' period on the bench. Preparation is advisable. What are you going to do? A dignified withdrawal is usually the key. Who do you need to assist? e.g. 'We will retire and ask the clerk to contact a first aider/security officer/police officer.'

Be equally ready for the defendants who leave court and thank the court for their decision!

CHAPTER 7
COMPETENCE 7
Youth

INTRODUCTION

s.37 Crime and Disorder Act 1998

'It shall be the principal aim of the youth justice system to prevent offending by children and young persons'.

'In addition to any other duty to which they are subject, it shall be the duty of all persons and bodies carrying out functions in relation to the youth justice system to have regard to that aim'.

This statutory requirement, along with regarding the welfare of the child discussed at 7.6, is the guiding principle of the youth court and its decision-making process. How does the bench prevent this particular youth from further offending?

The strategic lead in youth justice is now taken by the Youth Justice Board which was established by the government in 1998 to monitor performance of the youth justice system, identify and disseminate good practice, advise the Home Secretary and hold a budget. The Board comprises 12 experts and a staff. It has 6 objectives which are also central to the work of the courts and the youth agencies.

These are to prevent offending by children and young people by:

1. The swift administration of justice so that every young person accused of breaking the law has the matter resolved without delay.
2. Confronting young offenders with the consequences of their offending.
3. Intervention which tackles the particular factors which put a young person at risk of offending.
4. Punishment which is proportionate to the seriousness of the offence.
5. Encouraging reparation to victims by young offenders.
6. Reinforcing the responsibilities of parents.

The Board's aim is 'to prevent offending by children and young people so that young people can have more fulfilling lives, families are strengthened and communities feel safer and more harmonious'.

SPECIAL/RELEVANT LEGISLATION

7.1 Constitution and jurisdiction of the youth court

7.1.1 Constitution

Outside of the metropolitan area the youth court is made up of either a district judge or up to 3 members of the youth panel. A youth panel must be elected for each petty sessions area and the only criteria in the rules is that the appointed justices must be 'specially qualified for dealing with juvenile cases'. The Lord Chancellor expects panel members to sit for a minimum of 13 youth court sittings per annum. The panel is appointed every third year at the October Annual General Meeting, with the next full panel appointment in October 2003. Provisions exist for the combination of youth panels; the appointment of panel members from within the commission area and temporary transfers between petty sessions areas if necessary. Youth panel members receive specialist training and are appraised on the youth court competences.

The lay bench must include a man and a woman unless a man or woman is not available due to unforeseen circumstances e.g. illness, disqualified from dealing with the particular case. The bench must consider in open court whether it is 'inexpedient in the interests of justice' for there to be an adjournment. Representations should be sought from prosecution and defence and relevant factors may include the gender of the bench and the defendant and any victim; the nature of the charge and the implications of further delay.

The chairman or a deputy chairman must normally chair each bench. There are two exceptions:

- A chairman is not available due to unforeseen circumstances, when members of the court may choose one of their number to take the chair e.g. a competent adult court chairman or the most experienced youth panel member.

- A panel member is nominated to take the chair under the supervision of a chairman e.g. for training and appraisal purposes.

7.1.2 Jurisdiction

Basically all criminal matters concerning youths (age 10-17) must be dealt with in the youth court. There are 4 exceptions:

1. Youth is jointly charged with an adult. The case must be listed in adult court initially. The court must then consider the following:

- Is it in the interests of justice to keep the youth with the adult in the adult court, or indeed commit to the crown court for trial together with the adult? or

- Remit the youth to the youth court to be dealt with, whether for trial, or for the benefit of the full range of youth court sentences? or

- Deal with the youth on conviction in the adult court by way of a fine/ discharge/ binding over of parent or guardian - the only sentences available to the adult court in respect of youths?

2. Offence arises out of the same circumstances as an adult, or aiding and abetting etc. an adult or vice versa. These matters may be dealt with in the adult court at the court's discretion e.g. youth charged with theft and adult charged with handling the stolen goods; youth charged with driving without insurance and adult is charged with permitting the use.

3. Remand applications. A single adult justice may deal with remand applications for youths.

4. A charged youth becomes 18 after his first appearance in youth court. The youth court may at any stage remit the case to the adult court.

7.2. The Children Act

The Children Act 1989 placed the statutory general duty upon every local authority to:

'Safeguard and promote the welfare of children within their area who are in need; and
so far as is consistent with that duty, to promote the upbringing of such children by their families ... by providing a range and level of services appropriate to those children's needs.'
(s.17 Children Act 1989)

The Act also provides that local authorities must provide accommodation for any child who requires accommodation because they are lost, abandoned, without any person with parental responsibility or where their carer is prevented from providing suitable accommodation or care. Various duties also arise specifically in respect of children who are accommodated by the local authority e.g. to maintain, advise and befriend.

Schedule 2 of the Act sets out the provisions for support and services for children and families, including the duty to take reasonable steps to encourage children within their area not to commit criminal offences and to avoid the need for placements in secure accommodation.

It must therefore be emphasised that local authority involvement in court proceedings is by no means restricted to assisting in the sentencing decision of convicted youths. Whether convicted or not, whether adjourned or finalised, the local authority's responsibilities may well be triggered by information given in court.

The court also has a welfare duty (see 7.6) and no child should walk out of the youth court without a request for local authority intervention if the court has any serious concerns about the child's welfare, particularly regarding accommodation.

7.3 Education Acts

The relevant statutory provisions are contained within the Education Act 1996. It is the duty of every local education authority to 'secure that efficient education is available' for the population in their area. It is the duty of parents to cause their child to receive efficient full-time education either by regular attendance at school or otherwise, and proceedings may be taken against the parent in the adult court if appropriate.

The local authority may serve a notice on parents at any time if they have concerns about a child's education. The notice requires the parent to satisfy the authority that their child is receiving suitable education and if the local authority remain dissatisfied they may make a school attendance order requiring the child to attend a named school. Failure to comply with the order is an offence. The only defence is that the child is receiving suitable education otherwise than at school.

Parents may also be found guilty of an offence of failing to secure regular attendance at school. The penalty is currently a level 3 fine. This will increase to level 4 and carry imprisonment of up to 3 months, which will enable the court to enforce parental attendance at court for such offences (s. 72 CJCSA 2000 when in force).

Before taking proceedings against a parent the local education authority must consider whether it would be appropriate to apply for an Education Supervision Order (ESO). The ESO is made by the family court and the supervisor is required to advise, assist, befriend and give directions to the supervised person and parent to secure his education. The order is effective for a year initially and a parent may be liable to pay a fine if he persistently fails to comply with directions. Interestingly the fine is the same maximum as for the offence itself – level 3.

When the local authority decide not to pursue an ESO following breach of an attendance order or on a charge for failing to secure regular attendance,

the court may direct that such an application is made. Reasons must be given within 8 weeks if the local authority fails to apply.
In fact very few ESOs have been made.

The court may also make a parenting order following a conviction for failing to comply with an attendance order or failing to secure regular school attendance (see 7.14.3).

The process of ensuring regular school attendance varies from one authority to the next and it is helpful for magistrates to be made aware of the steps taken locally and the timetable before proceedings are taken. This will enable the chairman to question the parent about whether difficulties have been aired and whether steps have been taken to address them. It may also avoid an unnecessary referral for an ESO or consideration of a parenting order if it becomes clear that all efforts for co-operation and resolution have been rejected.

The youth court is required to take school record into consideration as necessary to enable it to deal with a case in the youth's best interests and the pre-sentence report will cover this aspect. However, if there are particular concerns, the local authority/local education authority are under a statutory duty to provide information as to school record if requested by the court and this may occasionally form the basis of a special report.

See also 7.26 Truancy.

7.4 Age limits

'Child'	= age 10 to 13
'Young person'	= age 14 to 17
'Youth'	= age 10 to 17

Age 10 – conclusively presumed by statute that no child under 10 can be guilty of an offence. However the local authority may bring proceedings in the family court under the Children Act 1989 and child safety orders and child curfew orders may be made under the Crime and Disorder Act 1998.

- Age 10 to 13 – fine limit of £250.
- Age 14 to 17 – fine limit of £1000.
- Age 10 to 15 – parent must pay <u>unless</u> .., parent must be bound over <u>unless</u> ..., parenting order shall be made unless ...
- Age 10 to 15 – curfew orders for up to 3 months.
- Age 12 to 16 - may be remanded to secure accommodation if criteria apply.

- Age 15/16 (males) – may be remanded to remand centre/prison if criteria apply.
- Age 16/17 – parent *may* be ordered to pay, parent *may* be bound over, parenting order *may* be made.
- Age 16/17 – probation order, community service order, combination order, drug treatment and testing order may be made, curfew orders for up to 6 months.
- Age 17 – treated in the same way as adults for the purpose of police interview, detention and court remands.
- Age 18 – attaining 18 during the course of the proceedings enables the youth court to retain jurisdiction or alternatively remit the defendant to the adult court.

7.5. Youth jointly charged with adults

See Jurisdiction at 7.1.

PROCEDURE

7.6 Welfare orientation of the youth court

Arguably the most important statutory requirement on the youth court was formulated as long ago as 1933:

'Every court in dealing with a child or young person who is brought before it, either as an offender or otherwise, shall have regard to the welfare of the child or young person, and shall in a proper case take steps for removing him from undesirable surroundings, and for securing that proper provision is made for his education and training.'
s. 44 of the Children and Young Persons Act 1933

No child should ever be dealt with in the youth court without the court having a picture of where they live, who they live with and the assurance that there is some support available to them. The local authority's duties are wide and referral may well be made through the court officer quite independently of the outcome of the case.

Understandably concerns are occasionally dealt with by a request for pre-sentence reports in order that 'matters can be properly looked into' and a supervision order can be explored. The danger is that a youth with welfare needs can find himself being sentenced in the community band when the offence seriousness does not reach the 'serious enough' level.

The serious implication is that re-sentencing on breach may lead to a custodial sentence. It is stressed that welfare needs can be referred by the court to the local authority without the unnecessary (and unfair) implications of a statutory supervision order.

7.7 Protocol of the youth court

7.8 Pre-court intervention by the other agencies

Most youth courts have a protocol which basically sets out 'who will do what and when they will do it' in order to deal expeditiously and fairly with young offenders. Following the introduction of the 'Narey' provisions, most youths are now before the court within a week of charge and pre-court intervention is largely unrealistic because of the short time-scale. However this is outweighed by the benefit of an early clarification of plea and court managed action from the point of first appearance.

7.9 Cautioning and procedures under PACE

7.9.1 PACE requirements

There are additional requirements under PACE in respect of arrested youths, namely:

- An 'appropriate adult' is required to be present during interviews between the police and the youth.
- It must be 'exceptional' to interview a youth at his place of education and must be with the consent of the principal.
- When a youth is arrested, the arresting officer is bound to try to notify a parent or guardian.
- If detained in custody at the police station the custody officer must inform him of his rights to have someone informed of his whereabouts and to have access to legal advice.
- A youth must not be detained in a police cell without good reason and should be visited frequently.
- When charged a youth should be transferred to local authority accommodation unless the custody officer certifies that it is impractical or that the secure accommodation criteria are satisfied and there is no such accommodation available.
- Except in cases of urgency, youths should not be interviewed or asked to sign a written statement in the absence of the appropriate adult. If cautioned in the absence of the adult, the caution must be repeated in the adult's presence.

- A youth held in police detention should not be detained or conveyed with an adult offender unless charged with a joint offence.

7.9.2 Warnings and Reprimands

The familiar caution process enabled many youths not to enter the criminal system and estimates of around 80% of cautioned youths did not subsequently come to the attention of the police. The criticism was that the decision to caution rather than charge and the actual process of the administration of the caution was inconsistent across the country. Some youths gathered a number of cautions based on police discretion whilst others came into the court process at a much earlier stage.

Cautions are now replaced by warnings and reprimands. A reprimand is similar to the caution, whilst a warning brings with it some form of intervention. The police retain discretion as to whether to take no formal action, issue a warning, a reprimand or prosecute.

Reprimands and warnings may only be given if:

- A constable has evidence that a youth has committed an offence and he considers that there would be a realistic prospect of conviction if prosecuted but is satisfied that it would not be in the public interest to prosecute.
- The offender admits the offence and has not been convicted of an offence previously.

A reprimand may only be given for a first offence.

A warning may be given instead of a reprimand even for a first offence if the constable considers that the offence is so serious as to require a warning. A warning may be given in 2 situations:

- No previous warning, <u>or</u>
- Previous warning and the offence was committed more than 2 years after the date of that previous warning and the constable considers the offence to be not so serious as to require a prosecution to be brought. Effectively this provides a potential rehabilitation period of 2 years.

An appropriate adult must be present during the administration of a reprimand or warning to a youth under 16.

When a warning is administered the YOT are notified and contact is made with the youth to arrange an initial assessment meeting to create a programme aimed at rehabilitation and prevention of offending, and an

ASSET assessment must be carried out within 10 working days. Reasons must be given to the youth, his parents and the police if a programme is not deemed to be appropriate. From July to September 2000, prevention programmes supported 46% of final warnings.

Any victims are notified that a warning has been issued and the programme may include reparation either to the victim or to the community at large (see 7.14). The programme may also include counselling, health, education and building parenting skills. Breach of the programme may be notified to the court if there is any further offending as an indicator of non-compliance with community orders.

Reprimands and warning are notified to the court together with any information about failures to comply with a post-warning programme. When an offence is committed within 2 years of a warning, the sentencing court may not make an order for conditional discharge unless there are exceptional circumstances and reasons must be given.

7.10 Effects/handling of delay

There are two aspects to handling delay in the youth court. First, the specific targets which apply to all courts in respect of 'persistent young offenders' and secondly the need to avoid unnecessary delays for all youths.

7.10.1 Persistent Young Offenders (PYOs)

Based on the statistic that 3% of young offenders commit approximately 25% of offences the PYO initiative was created in order to prioritise those particular offenders and deal with them quickly. The government target is to achieve an average of 71 days from arrest to sentence for 50% of PYOs, increasing to 70% by 2002. The 'magic' of 71 days is that it is exactly half of the average period of 142 days when the pledge was made in 1997.

A PYO is defined as a youth aged 10-17 who has been sentenced on 3 or more separate occasions for one or more recordable offences and the last one is less than 3 years ago.

Example:

Age 16
Theft in June 1998 – Compensation £40
Theft in June 1999 – Supervision Order for 12 months
Burglary in June 2000 - Attendance Centre Order for 12 hours

Charged with assault in May 2001
Sentenced 3 times – last time was within 3 years = PYO.

Local fast track procedures are implemented from the point of charge through to sentence. The police are responsible for identifying the PYO and this is marked on the charge sheet so that all court officers are aware of the need to expedite. This may involve early preparation of papers for pre-trial review; setting up a special court for trial within 28 days of plea; expedited pre-sentence reports and prioritising warrants for arrest which may be required along the way. At the present time, PA Consulting have been given the responsibility of monitoring results on a countrywide basis in each court, sharing good practice and giving advice to improve performance.

In 1996 the national average was 142 days from arrest to sentence and in November 2000 the figure had dropped to 96 days.

7.10.2 Reducing delays generally

The government requires detailed monitoring of local statistics. There can be no argument that youths should be dealt with at the earliest possible opportunity to either resolve the matter without conviction or to be sentenced as soon as possible after the relevant offence. Various strategies are used, which include the following.

1. A philosophy of 'do what you can, when you can.'

Unfortunately youths tend to commit offences in groups and a large proportion go on to commit further offences whilst on remand. The practice of adjourning to tie up the case with other offences in the pipeline or with other defendants can string matters along for months. The question must always be – can the other matters be brought forward for progress today? If not, better to sentence for the offence today and thereby take some action here and now to prevent offending e.g. by an action plan order/compensation and then discharge or review <u>if</u> he is eventually found guilty and sentenced for another offence by a custodial sentence.

Statute specifically provides that the youth court shall not be required to adjourn any proceedings for an offence by reason only of the fact that it commits the accused to crown court for another offence or simply because the accused is charged with another offence (s.47 CDA 1998).

The exceptions to this robust approach are:

(a) When a youth is on remand in custody or in local authority accommodation. All options obviously cannot be considered in practical terms and he is already subjected to a remand regime which is aimed at preventing future offending.

(b) When pre-sentence reports are in the process of preparation for other offences. There is no uncertainty about plea or conviction and the sentence date is fixed and close. The court is dealing with a certainty and it is sensible to adjourn and request that the new matter is included into the report and its proposal.

So far as co-accused are concerned it is clearly helpful to deal with them all together and attempts are usually made to do this. A line has to be drawn though, either when a co-accused does not attend court or certainly if a warrant is not executed for the next hearing date. A note of the sentence can be made on the prosecutor's file for the information of the court dealing with the co-accused. However, the reality is that there are so many aspects and options to youth sentencing that a simple yardstick no longer measures parity in any event. It is helpful to seek representations from the prosecution and defence as to any compelling reasons for keeping co-accused together. If none – split and sentence!

2. A presumption of progress.

Pro-active questioning is the key if an application is made for an adjournment.

What is the case set down for today?
This is only effective if the previous bench have made that clear and allowed sufficient time for it to happen. Arbitrary periods as a form of punishment and dates given solely as 'next available date' in the court diary are not careful, effective adjournments.

Is there any reason why pleas cannot be taken today?
The presumption of progress, along with the open question is more likely to provide productive information than the closed question of 'can pleas be taken?'

The 'other matters' – what stage are they at and is there any reason why they cannot be brought forward?
Adjournments 'to tie up with other matters' must be carefully explored. Where there is no plea to the new matter, it could well run and run – along with the existing matter! A 'Not Guilty' matter which is destined for pre-trial review and trial, arguably should carry a presumption of innocence and be ignored.

What is the attendance record of this defendant?
A good attender may well be given credit and the balance of any decision to adjourn may go in his favour. A defendant who appears on warrant should generate every effort to deal with him whilst he is present. This

applies particularly to youths who appear for breach of community orders. The information about any breach can often be obtained by a telephone call or from a statement on the original summons and they can be quickly re-introduced to the community option regime if appropriate.

Can venue be determined today on the grave crimes?
Whilst full instructions are required in order to enter a plea, the venue decision is based essentially on the worst scenario of the prosecution outline. A decision that a case is destined for the crown court enables the prosecution to prepare the committal file for the next hearing.

3. More 'stand-down' reports for specific sentences.

A large feature of delay is the period required for the preparation of unnecessary pre-sentence reports coupled with the high number of defendants who fail to co-operate with the report or fail to attend at the next hearing. In 2000, almost 1/3 of defendants on remand for reports in Leeds City, either failed to attend for report preparation or failed to attend court.

Adjournments for 'unnecessary' pre-sentence reports feature as one of the main reasons for delay. An 'unnecessary' report can be defined as any report which results in an outcome which could have been imposed on the day of plea or proof e.g. community orders.

A full pre-sentence report (as opposed to a specific sentence report) is not legally required for action plan orders, attendance centre orders, community service orders, curfew orders, reparation orders, or supervision orders without requirements.

Even when a detention and training order is being considered, the court may legally refer to a recent old report.

Of course local agreements may for good reason require pre-sentence reports but magistrates must be aware of why they are required. For example, a supervision order may simply carry the basic requirements but the YOT officer may feel that a full report and home visit is essential to gauge suitability. Curfew orders may require discussion with family members who are not present at court.

In the absence of local agreements the court should always proceed as far as identifying the level of seriousness and potential order e.g. action plan order. The case may then be stood down for discussion with the court officer and a written action plan report. Of course this would not prevent the court officer returning to court and requesting a full report if this became necessary.

4. *Effective pre-trial reviews leading to effective trials*

An effective pre-trial review which allows plenty of time for informal discussion between the advocates can frequently result in matters being finalised. This may be achieved through a discussion of evidence and explanations which may result either in the case being withdrawn; guilty pleas to amended charges or a change of plea to guilty after agreement on the outline of the case to be put to the court. Interestingly half of the youth cases sent to court are dropped or end with the youth being discharged (Misspent Youth 1998).

Trials will always collapse on the day when the defendant finally accepts that he is guilty. This may be prompted by many reasons e.g. the fact that the witnesses have materialised and there can be no more prevarication, or possibly the first detailed discussion with his solicitor about the actual evidence. The latter reason is the one that can realistically be explored at a serious pre-trial review. What exactly is the evidence? Who is coming on both sides and what are they going to say? Is there any room for amending or reducing the charge?

Once the task of exploring the issues and the certainty of the 'not guilty' plea is complete, the enquiries move on to establishing how long each witness is going to take and how long the case should be listed for.

The final enquiries aim to ensure that the case will go on. Have the witnesses been interviewed yet? Is a witness summons required? A direction that application should be made within x weeks if contact has still not been made to secure voluntary attendance. A direction that telephone numbers should be available for all witnesses so that reminder calls can be made on the day if necessary. Possibly a condition of bail on the defendant to keep an appointment with his solicitor at least x days before the trial so that any changes of plan may be notified to the court, the prosecution and most importantly, prosecution witnesses.

POWERS OF THE YOUTH COURT

7.11 Adjournment, bail and remands to local authority accommodation and prison

7.11.1 Bail provisions in youth court

Basically the same considerations apply as for adults (see 2.28 and 2.29), even to the extent that a single magistrate in the adult court may deal with a youth remand, but there are a few differences and special features.

So far as conditional bail is concerned the court may order a parent or guardian to stand surety to a maximum of £50 to ensure that the youth complies with any requirement to which the parent or guardian has consented e.g. to abide by a curfew from 8pm to 8am.

The condition of curfew might usefully contain a proviso that the curfew should apply 'unless the youth is accompanied by a parent' or named adult. It is unlikely that the court would intend the younger defendants to be left at home unsupervised and rather than creating a resentful parent, the proviso may actually encourage some positive social interaction!

Curfews may also be considered for periods immediately after school or on Saturday afternoons if that is the time of offending. Consult the parent – what curfews are they imposing?

The Youth Justice Board has been keen to encourage a bail support facility for youths and such schemes are now widespread. National Standards require that each YOT must ensure that there is a local bail support and supervision programme.

Whilst there are regional differences, the provision is essentially an individual supervised programme and discipline during the bail period. A 'remand support' scheme is available in some areas for youths who are remanded into local authority accommodation. Bail support and remand support have the same purpose – support and prevention of further offending immediately following the alleged offence rather than weeks or months later following sentence. Significantly, the remand population dropped by 20% between March 2000 and January 2001, which may reflect confidence in the community alternatives. They will be further enhanced by the introduction of intensive supervision and surveillance programmes from 2001.

7.11.2 Refusal of bail

The Bail Act 1976 applies except that a youth may additionally be refused bail 'for his own welfare' e.g. in respect of a youth without any accommodation. A remand into police custody/cells for the purpose of inquiring into other offences is limited to 24 hours rather than the 3 day maximum for those aged 17 or more.

When bail is refused the outcome varies according to age and circumstances. A youth aged 17 is remanded into prison custody in the same way as an adult. The options for youths aged 10 – 16 are described below.

7.11.3 Remand to local authority accommodation.

The accommodation is provided by or on behalf of the local authority and may be a children's home, a foster home or even with the youth's own family or friends if considered suitable by the local authority.

If concerns arise about the youth absconding, coupled with a likelihood of significant harm or injury to the defendant or to others then the local authority may apply to the court for the remand to be in secure accommodation (s.25 CA 1989). Secure accommodation means accommodation provided for the purpose of restricting liberty. This application may be made at any stage during the remand provided that appropriate notice is given (see 9.20).

The length of remands and custody time limits apply to remands to local authority accommodation as for custody.

7.11.4 Remand to local authority accommodation with conditions

After consultation with the local authority the court may add conditions in the same way as for conditional bail e.g. a curfew. The court cannot impose a condition as to residence as this would inhibit the authority's discretion as to placement, but it may specify that the youth must not be placed with named individuals e.g. co-accused adult, a parent who has not demonstrated suitable care and control. Requirements may also be placed upon the authority to secure compliance with the conditions. Breach of the conditions carries a power of arrest – note that, as in adult court, there is no penalty for breach of a bail condition! In practical terms in youth court, bail has already been refused in this scenario and the reality is that he will be reprimanded by the court and returned from whence he came, probably with the same conditions!

Example:

- Curfew from 8pm (check usual curfew at the children's home) to 8am except when accompanied by a responsible adult nominated by the local authority (so that youth may accompany evening trips out or go out of the home with a parent or relative).

- Not to reside with co-accused adult, John Smith.

A remand into local authority accommodation engages the right to respect for private and family life. Such a remand must therefore be proportionate to the crime committed and particularly if a parent's right is also engaged through a condition that the child may not reside with him.

7.11.5 Remand to remand centre/prison of males aged 15-16.

The remand is to a remand centre or prison if the following criteria are met:

(a) Youth is charged or convicted of a violent or sexual offence, or an offence punishable in the case of an adult with imprisonment for 14 years or more; or
(b) Youth has a recent history of absconding (single previous occasion is sufficient) while remanded in local authority accommodation, and is charged with or has been convicted of an imprisonable offence alleged or found to have been committed while so remanded,

AND the court is of the opinion that only remanding the youth to a remand centre or prison would be adequate to protect the public from serious harm from him, following consultation with the local authority. (If the youth is deemed vulnerable, he may instead be remanded to secure accommodation if a bed is available – same criteria apply.)

In procedural terms there is an element of law and an element of practical consultation before such a decision can properly be reached.

Example:

- Offence? - Youth is charged with robbery on a neighbour, by threatening with a knife. He has a recent record which includes offences of violence – assault, wounding. The criteria at (a) is satisfied as robbery carries 14 years or more imprisonment.

- Serious harm? - The court could reasonably be of the opinion that there is a risk of serious harm to the public. 'Serious harm' relates to 'death or serious personal injury, whether physical or psychological' (s.23 (13) CYPA 1969). The use of a knife and the threat may satisfy the risk element.

- The 'only way to protect the public'? - The court cannot draw this inference without further enquiry. What are the representations of the defence? What are the issues and concerns? Perhaps drug-driven crime to feed a heroin habit. What options are available to deal with the situation? Consultation with the local authority/probation/YOT is essential at this stage.

- Possible outcome? - Remand to local authority accommodation with a specialist remand foster carer away from the offence locality + remand support programme with high intervention and a drug rehabilitation programme + condition not to approach the victim or his address.

There is one exception to the remand centre venue. When a 15-16 year old is deemed to be 'vulnerable' the court may remand him instead to secure accommodation <u>if</u> a bed is available. Vulnerability ('physical or emotional immaturity or a propensity to harm himself') may take several forms but may well be transmitted from information on the ASSET form, and possibly from the history of previous custodial remands.

7.11.6 Remand to secure accommodation – Females aged 12 – 16 and boys aged 12 - 14.

Since June 1998 the secure accommodation facility has been available for all youths aged 12 -16. The criteria and process is the same as for the remand centre provisions above.

An opportunity must be given for the youth to apply for legal aid and reasons must be given for the decision.

7.11.7 Remand of 17 year olds.

The remand is in custody as for an adult.

7.12 Financial penalties

7.12.1 Fine

The maximum fine, which may be imposed on a child of 10 –13, is £250 and for a young person of 14-17 the maximum is £1000. These maxima must therefore be reflected in any tariff of fines in the youth court. Without a proportionate reduction in the guideline penalties, there is no recognition that the maxima are substantially different from the adult court. When fixing the fine, based upon the relevant band, there is argument to suggest that the 'top limit' should be reduced to a 3 month repayment figure rather than the 12 month maximum repayment as in adult court.

Most other penalties for youths now average out at a 3 month duration. It is the fixed period for an action plan order; the maximum completion period for a reparation order; the usual period for a 24 hour attendance centre order and possible period for a 60 hour community service order. Surely this adds strength to a realistic limitation and completion of a fine repayment within 3 months.

A local consistent approach to youth fines should be a priority matter for youth panels to determine, in respect of maximum duration and any presumption of the parent being made responsible for payment (see 7.13). During the first quarter of the introduction of the new penalties from July to September 2000, the fine remained the most popular sentence at 18.5% of penalties imposed in youth courts.

7.12.2 Compensation

The maximum compensation order is £5000 as for adult court and the same criteria apply. It is worth emphasising that compensation can be awarded for 'terror and distress.' In a far more victim-orientated sentencing field this should at least be considered more often than not as an obvious measure of restorative justice e.g. the householder who sees a brick coming through his window – compensation for the window and for the householder himself!

Swift justice can mean that compensation schedules are not always available at first hearings for specific losses. It is important to consider the likelihood of an award and if means are available and there is culpability then it is essential that victims are given the opportunity to substantiate their claims as compensation must either be agreed or proved.

7.12.3 Costs

The maximum costs order in youth court is limited to the amount of any fine if the youth is ordered to pay e.g. fine of £10 – costs must be reduced to maximum of £10. Costs must always be proportionate.

7.12.4 Who pays?

The parent or guardian of a child aged 10 -15 must pay any financial order, and in respect of a young person aged 16 -17 may be ordered to pay unless :

(a) The parent or guardian cannot be found, or
(b) It would be unreasonable to make an order for payment, having regard to the circumstances of the case e.g. the youth is in local authority care and has no contact with either parent.

The order may be made against the parent or guardian in their absence if they have been required to attend and have had the opportunity to be heard on the matter. This situation can be covered by issuing a summons for the parent/guardian to attend together with clear information about the court's powers. It may also usefully state that the court must assume that the family income is the national/regional average weekly income and an order will be made on that basis unless the court is told otherwise. This will make it clear that non-attendance does not mean 'no order' and may create an incentive to attend and put actual means before the court so that the penalty is fair.

When a local authority has parental responsibility through a care order it may be ordered to pay unless the court considers that this would be unreasonable because the authority has done everything that it reasonably and properly could to protect the public.

Who should pay when there is a discretion? Parent or youth? Various aspects should be considered. First, the emphasis is now firmly on the parent taking responsibility. Secondly, there must be some regard to the certainty of a youth's income (particularly pocket money and casual employment) and his actual capacity and ability to organise payment. Thirdly, there are enforcement implications if a youth is ordered to pay, which will certainly engage the Human Rights Act and issues of proportionality. The arrest of a youth for non-payment; sending the bailiffs to visit him; sending him to an attendance centre because he has failed to pay a small fine. Finally, there is perhaps an element of unfairness that a youth who has the wherewithal to hold down a paper round could find himself responsible for a fine, whereas his co-accused has 'no income' and 'mum pays'.

This scenario can also generate a disparity if the youth's fine is fixed on his £10 per week, whereas a fine made payable by a parent is fixed on perhaps £150 per week benefits. There is at least some measure of consistency of approach if the starting point is that it will normally be reasonable for the parent to pay, unless there is good reason to the contrary e.g. 17 year old is living apart and is financially independent, or child is in receipt of deductible pocket money in a local authority home.

Although reparation orders have largely take over from fines as an entry point penalty, the money order option should not be overlooked, particularly if there is a possibility of compensation as this is arguably the most obvious and tangible expression of remorse to a victim.

7.12.5 Enforcement if youth is ordered to pay

The adult options are available, namely, remission, rectification, search, setting a review date, money payment supervision order, attachment of benefits, attachment of earnings, distress and attendance centre order (see competence 12 for full discussion of options), but a youth cannot be detained for non-payment of the order.

The court has the additional powers to:

- Order a parent/guardian to enter into a recognisance to ensure that the defaulter pays – parental consent is required.

- Order a parent/guardian to pay following an opportunity to attend and make representations.

An order for parent/guardian to pay is enforced in the adult court with full enforcement powers including custody.

7.13 Parental responsibility, attendance, fines and binding over

The most effective supervisor/adviser/friend for any youth is almost always a parent. No one else is likely to come anywhere near in terms of the knowledge and energy that a parent can give. Others have to assess the baggage that comes along. A parent will usually have helped to pack it! It is essential that the court takes them on board as someone to help the court rather than someone who is 'in the dock' themselves. Inspiring, motivating, cajoling and occasionally imposing some sort of disciplinary incentive. The law provides some clear responsibilities and sanctions.

7.13.1 Attendance at court

- A parent/guardian of a youth aged 10 – 15 must be ordered to attend court unless the court considers that it would be unreasonable, having regard to the circumstances of the case.
- A parent of a youth aged 16 - 17 may be ordered to attend.
  (s. 32A CYPA 1933)

The provision relates to youths who are charged or brought before the court for any other reason. When the local authority have parental responsibility, a local authority representative should attend e.g. foster parent, social worker.

When a youth attends court without a parent/guardian the court must consider whether to proceed or whether to issue a summons, or even a warrant to secure attendance. In the case of a youth of 17 who is living independently, the court may feel content to proceed in the absence of a parent.

There are also limited circumstances when it may be appropriate to proceed if a responsible adult has attended instead of the parent. This may arise for instance if the parent is clearly well aware of the proceedings and the implications; a report covers parental involvement adequately; a community order is agreed and there is no question of the family bearing any costs. A set of circumstances which do not arise very often!

The absence of a parent causes the following difficulties:

- No order for fine, compensation or costs against the parent unless he has been given the opportunity to be heard i.e. adjournment required first. Orders made on the next hearing in absence and without means information usually create difficulties for all concerned.
- No possibility of making a binding over order on the parent.
- No background information about 'what the youth is like at home'.
- No possibility of referring the parent for assistance and advice, independently of any sentence.
- No possibility of seeking parent's views on the proposed sentence.
- No possibility of 'getting the parent on board' to work with the court in preventing offending and working with the YOT team in its plans.
- Possibility that the parent is unaware of the proceedings and any sentence of the court!

Whilst delays are regrettable, there is much to be gained from an adjournment to bring the parent before the court.

7.13.2 Fines (see 7.12)

7.13.3 Binding over

A parent/guardian of a youth aged 10 –15 must be bound over to take proper care and exercise proper control over a convicted youth if it would be desirable in the interests of preventing the commission of further offences. The maximum order is in the sum of £1,000 for a maximum of 3 years or until aged 18. Consent is required. Refusal to consent may result in a fine of up to £1,000 if the court considers that the refusal is unreasonable.

When a community sentence has been imposed, the recognisance may include a provision that the parent/guardian ensures that the youth complies additionally with the requirements of the sentence e.g. attends the attendance centre.

When the order is not made the court must give reasons in open court e.g. 'parent has taken all reasonable steps to control the youth'; 'the court does not foresee any further offending'.

A binding over order may be made on a parent/guardian of a youth aged 16 –17 and forfeiture proceedings may be taken.

7.13.4 Parent's views on proposed sentence

The parent/guardian is entitled to make representations to the court at any stage after the conclusion of the evidence. More specifically, the court must inform the youth and his parent/guardian (or any other person assisting him in his case) of the manner in which it proposes to deal with the case before announcing sentence and the parents/guardians must be allowed to make representations. (Rule 11 Magistrates' Courts (CYP) Rules 1992.)

This can bring up new information and representations.

> Example:
>
> 'We are considering making an Attendance Centre Order. This means that .... '
>
> 'Yes but, I work on a Saturday and he looks after the younger ones. I can't stay off work for 6 weeks. I suppose I'd just have to leave them on their own.
>
> ***Well if that is what he has to do, he'll have to do it, but he's got a football trial next Saturday and we really hoped it might get him away from these lads and give him something to do on a weekend.***
>
> Court reconsiders.....

Of course, the hope is that sufficient information is given to a court in advance, possibly through a stand down with a youth officer. However, answering questions and discussing possibilities in an informal 'stand-down' interview is not quite the same as facing a specific sentence in court and the reality is that crucial information is often generated at this critical point.

7.13.5 Parental involvement in community orders

In respect of action plan orders, the supervising officer must consider the attitude of the parents in the report to the court and then agree with the offender, the parents or primary carer how the action plan will be implemented (National Standards 2000).

In respect of supervision orders the supervising officer must show that every effort has been made to secure parental support for reparation and action to prevent re-offending by asking the parent/primary carer to sign the supervision plan.

7.14 Community penalties

7.14.1 Action Plan Order (APO)

Level and purpose

- Community penalty – offence must be 'serious enough'.

- Order is 'desirable in the interests of securing the offender's rehabilitation or preventing further offending'.
- Age group : 10 – 17.

Basics of the order

- Placed under supervision of a 'responsible officer' (probation officer, social worker or YOT member).
- Required to comply with officer's directions.
- Targeted programme of interventions.
- ⏲ Duration: 3 months (no more – no less!)

Restrictions

Already subject to an APO.
No combination with custody, a probation order, CSO, combination order, supervision order, reparation order or attendance centre order.

Procedural requirements

Written report is necessary (NOT a pre-sentence report) setting out:

- Proposed requirements.
- Possibility of reparation.
- Benefits to the offender.
- Attitude of parents/guardians.
- If under 16, information about the offender's family circumstances and likely effect of the order on those circumstances.

The court must explain the effect of the order, the consequences of non-compliance and the power to review the order by variation or early discharge.

A further hearing may be fixed not more than 21 days after making the order. The responsible officer will prepare a report and at this stage application may be made to cancel or insert any provisions depending upon how the order is progressing.

Practicalities

The APO may include the following:

- Reparation to specified person or to community at large
- Participation in activities specified in the order at a fixed time and place e.g. motor projects, drug rehabilitation, anger management

- Present himself to people specified in the order at specified times and places e.g. meet with social worker at 4pm after school each Monday
- Attend attendance centre for specified number of hours (if offence imprisonable)
- Stay away from specified place or places e.g. amusement arcades
- Comply with specified educational arrangements e.g. to attend at pupil referral unit on 3 days per week
- Attend a court review hearing.

Typically the core programme may consist of about 6 sessions of 2/3 hours each and cover the consequences of offending, victim issues, peer pressure and family and relationships. Additional requirements include reparation, mentoring, mediation.

Breach/variation/discharge

Application is made by the responsible officer concerning the failure to comply with any requirement. No more than 2 warnings may be given before court action is taken. The options are as follows:

- No action
- Fine
- Attendance centre order
- Curfew order
- Youth court orders - discharge the APO and deal with him in any way it could have done had the order not been made
- Crown court orders – commit to the crown court with view to discharge and re-sentence.

The court must take into consideration the extent to which the order has been complied with. Application may also be made for discharge and for variation.

7.14.2 Attendance Centre Order

Level and purpose

- Community penalty – must be 'serious enough.'
- The offence must be imprisonable.
- The purposes are basically discipline, social awareness and punishment for the offence.
- Age group: 10 –17.
- The Youth Justice Board are now responsible for the junior attendance centres.
- A 'taste of detention order discipline and regime?'

Basics of the order

- Attendance at a centre for 2-3 hours, usually on a Saturday, with a programme of activities which may include sport, team games, woodwork, needlework, cookery, discussion about offending, motor projects, First Aid and a range of guest speakers.
- Age 10 –13: The order may be reduced below 12 hours if this is considered to be excessive due to age and other circumstances.
- Age 10 – 15: Duration of 12 to 24 hours.
- Age 16 – 17 : Duration of 12 to 36 hours.

Restrictions

A report is not required when making an attendance centre order but the court must be satisfied as to suitability. This may be undertaken on a stand down enquiry or through questions from the court.

The reality is that a substantial number of orders are breached and some are replaced on re-sentence by supervision orders. It can be deduced that perhaps a supervision order might have been preferable at the outset.

There is an understandable temptation to select a straightforward punishment which requires no bureaucracy, but the offence is 'serious enough'; the order is onerous for some individuals and the question has to be seriously explored – would punishment in this way prevent this youth from offending? Some enquiry through the court is therefore essential.

Procedural requirements

Whilst a pre-sentence report is not required and consent is unnecessary, there are important factors to consider in assessing suitability and duration. This information may well be gathered during a short stand down.

The following questions are suggested:

- How accessible is the local centre?
- Does this youth have the independence to cope with making the journey?
- Can the family afford the bus fares? If not, what arrangements are made for reimbursement (if any)?
- Is an adult likely to accompany him on the first visit?
- Does the family ensure that he attends school?
- What is the school situation – excluded, truant, special needs? (This may affect suitability and activities at the centre)
- Is he going to be capable of fitting in with group work activities?

- Does he have any other commitments on a Saturday which may be helping to prevent offending and should be maintained e.g. a job, member of local football team?
- Is he likely to be susceptible to peer influences?
- Is he likely to see attendance as kudos rather than punishment?
- What has been his response to previous orders?
- Are there any welfare needs which ought to be explored first?
- Is it helpful to split co-defendants to different centres? e.g. if junior/senior centres take a common age group at 16-17 year old.

Practicalities

Magistrates are traditionally welcomed to make an appointment and observe at the centres and this is a well worthwhile experience.

Breach/discharge

The following options are available:

- No order.
- Fine.
- Revocation and re-sentence for the original offence – custody available if 'wilful and persistent.'

Application may also be made for discharge.

Combination order/Community punishment and rehabilitation order (see 2.13.8)
Community Service Order/ Community punishment order (see 2.13.6)
Curfew Order (see 2.13.9) – N.B. Maximum period of 3 months rather than 6 months for 10 to 15 year olds and additional requirement to consider likely effect on family circumstances.
Drug Treatment and Testing Order (see 2.13.10)

7.14.3 Parenting Order

Level and purpose

- In the youth court a parenting order may be made whenever a youth is convicted of an offence.
- A disposal designed to help and support parents/guardians in addressing their child's offending behaviour.
- The order must be 'desirable in the interests of preventing the conduct which gave rise to the order.'

- A subjective test is applied, similar to the test for the binding over of parents.

Basics of the order

- Attendance at counselling or guidance sessions (excusable by court if already attended) – parentcraft basis – as specified in directions given by the 'responsible officer' for up to once per week for up to 3 months and
- Further requirements as considered desirable in the interests of preventing repetition of the misconduct which led to the offences e.g. to ensure that a responsible adult is at home to supervise the child from 6 pm to 8 am, up to a maximum period of 12 months.
- A responsible officer is appointed.
- ⏱ Maximum order = 12 months. Maximum period for counselling/guidance = 3 months.

Restrictions

- Local arrangements must be in place for the provision of parenting orders and a place must be available.
- 'Parent' includes someone with parental responsibility for the child or has care of the child e.g. grandparent or family friend.

Procedural requirements

The court must obtain information about the family circumstances and the likely effect of an order if the child is under 16.

In the case of a youth of 10 –15 the court must make the order if the conditions are fulfilled and reasons must be given if the conditions are not satisfied e.g. parents are making reasonable efforts to control the child; parents are seeking voluntary support; parent has lost control and there is no real prospect of regaining it. The order is discretionary in the case of parents of youths of 16-17.

The court must explain the effect of the order and of the requirements to be imposed and that failure to comply with the order without reasonable excuse is a summary offence.

Article 8 will engage on the making of a parenting order as it restricts the parents' right to respect for private and family life. This is a qualified right and the 3 questions must be asked about the restriction of a parenting order.

- Is the restriction legal, clear and accessible? Yes, the Crime and Disorder Act criteria are clear.

- Does it pursue a legitimate aim? Yes, to prevent offending.
- Is it proportionate? Arguably it may be disproportionate if the parent(s) have already demonstrated a commitment to a voluntary programme and court sanctions may be unnecessary and disproportionate. Proportionality will also be measured by the extent of the intrusion into the family unit as a whole, the seriousness of the presenting offences and any other penalty imposed.

Practicalities

An order may be made, for example, on a father to attend parent–craft sessions on Monday evenings for 8 weeks. Additionally, he may be required to ensure that the child is accompanied to and from school by a responsible adult *(relevant if offences committed during truanting from school)*.

Breach/discharge/variation

If a parent without reasonable excuse fails to comply with a requirement in the order, or specified in directions given by the responsible officer, he will be liable on conviction to pay a fine not exceeding level 3 on the standard scale.

In the event of more than one unacceptable failure in a period of 3 months, the responsible officer must meet with the parents and any other agency involved to review the order and consider amendment/revocation or reporting for breach.

Probation Order/Community rehabilitation order (see 2.13)

7.14.4 Reparation Order

Level and purpose

- The reparation order is <u>not</u> a community penalty. It is available for any offence in the youth court as an 'entry level' disposal. The offence does not have to be 'serious enough'. Between September and December 2000, nearly 5% of convictions resulted in reparation orders.
- The reparation order is the most obvious example of a move towards restorative justice and victim awareness. The sentence is intended to demonstrate to the offender the distress caused to his victim; emphasise the link between offending and its consequences and provide an opportunity to take some responsibility for the offence.
- Age group : 10 – 17

Basics of the order

- Reparation must be made within 3 months of making the order.
- Reparation must be supervised by a 'responsible officer'.
- ⏱ No minimum period. Maximum of 24 hours – to be commensurate with seriousness.

Restrictions

- No combination with custody, CSO, combination order, action plan order or supervision order with any requirements. Compensation may be ordered.
- No reparation towards an individual without their consent – assessment and consultation necessarily takes some time.

Procedural requirements

Written report (NOT a pre-sentence report) setting out :

- The type of work suitable for the offender and
- The victim's attitude to the proposed requirements – contact by letter, telephone or home visit by a YOT member (possibly the police representative).

The court must explain the effect of the order, the consequences of non-compliance and the power to review the order.

The court must give reasons if it does not make an order where it has power to do so.

Practicalities

- Direct reparation to the victim - the victim's consent must be given in writing. If the consent is not given or the victim cannot be contacted then the YOT must make arrangements instead for reparation to the community at large. The work is supervised by a YOT member, partner agency of a YOT accredited volunteer. It may, for instance, involve tidying a garden, clearing grafitti or writing (or dictating) a letter of apology which may or may not be sent depending upon the victim's wishes.
- Indirect reparation to the community at large – examples may be working on a community farm, day centre assistance, victim awareness sessions. The reality is that indirect reparation is the 'norm' and efforts are made to try to place offenders in situations, which have some relationship to the offence committed.

Breach/discharge/variation

There must be no more than 2 warnings of non-compliance before commencing breach proceedings and breach may be taken without prior warning if so warranted. The options on breach are as follows:

- No action.
- Fine.
- Attendance centre order.
- Curfew order.
- Youth court orders – discharge the order and re-sentence in any way it could have done had the order not been made
- Crown court orders – commit to crown court with a view to discharge and re-sentence.

The court must take into consideration the extent to which the order has been complied with. Application may also be made for the order to be discharged or varied.

7.14.5 Supervision Orders

Level and purpose

- Community penalty – offence must be 'serious enough.'
- Age group : 10 – 17.
- Focus is on rehabilitation and prevention of further offending.

Basics of the order

- Placed under the supervision of a probation officer, social worker or YOT member acting as a responsible officer.
- The supervisor must advise, assist and befriend the youth.
- The order must name the local authority and petty sessions area where the youth lives.
- Duration : No minimum. Maximum of 3 years.

Restrictions

Before inserting specific requirements the court must consult the supervisor about the offender's circumstances and the feasibility of securing compliance.

Procedural requirements

A supervision order does not in itself carry any specific requirements or obligations on the part of the youth. However, most youth panels always incorporate the basic requirements to keep appointments as arranged with the supervising officer, receive home visits and notify any change of address.

Various additional requirements may be imposed if considered necessary to secure the youth's good conduct or to prevent further offending:

- To live at a particular place e.g. in a named hostel; with mother.
- To take part in various forms of activity or requirements.
- To remain at home for specified periods of not more than 10 hours between 6pm and 6am for not more than 30 (not necessarily consecutive) days in 3 months. The requirement does not apply if the youth is accompanied by a parent/guardian/supervisor/named person.

(This is arguably supplanted by the curfew order which has the benefit of a tagging device and effective enforcement).

- To refrain from taking part in specified activities, either on a stipulated day or days, or during the whole or a stipulated part of the supervision order – no 90 day limit.
- To receive psychiatric treatment, if satisfied on medical evidence that the youth's mental condition requires and is susceptible to treatment. Consent is required if the youth is 14 or over.
- To attend school or comply with other arrangements for education.
- Reparation requirement to the victim or to the community at large up to a maximum of 90 days.
- Residence in accommodation provided by or on behalf of the local authority for a specified period not exceeding 6 months. Specific conditions must be satisfied before this highly restrictive requirement is placed in a community level order.

Requirements should be carefully worded to ensure that the youth is absolutely clear about what he must do and so that breach action, which could include custody on re-sentence, is taken seriously. There is little point in detailing specific timetables to a youth who is living a chaotic lifestyle. He will sometimes be late. He will sometimes fail to attend. Does the court seriously intend that he should be arrested and punished every time? It is more important to detail the essential parameters which really call for breach action. For this purpose it is helpful to seek the supervisor's views on how much individual discretion they would prefer to work with.

Practicalities

During the first 3 months of the order the minimum contact must be twice-weekly; during the next 3 months once-weekly; after 6 months must be at least fortnightly.

There must be a supervision plan and this must address parental/primary carer involvement; work on offending behaviour; any substance misuse and healthcare needs; education, training or employment; work to address any previous experience of discrimination and plans for reducing any risks of significant harm. Efforts must be made to ensure that the parent/primary carer also signs up to the plan.

Breach

It is important to recognise that the commission of a further offence does not constitute a breach of the order. Unfortunately prosecutors in remand applications sometimes refer to youths being in 'breach of an existing supervision order by the commission of the offence'. This is incorrect.

It is also important to check that there is actually a requirement stipulated in the order and the wording. As stated earlier a 'straight' supervision order does not carry any requirements and is essentially unbreachable.

Unexplained missed appointments must be followed up by a YOT member with a visit or a telephone call within one working day. Breach action must be initiated within 10 working days of the most recent failure if there are more than 2 formal warnings in a 3 month period (National Standards 2000). The options on breach are as follows:

- No action.
- Vary the order – often a fair option when a breach is caused by inability/incapacity or lack of parental support and compliance is basically unrealistic.
- Fine.
- Curfew order.
- Attendance centre order
- Youth order – discharge and re-sentence for the original offence (age is relevant as at date of breach being admitted or proved i.e. now aged 16 – CSO would be available).
- Crown court order – may commit to deal with, with a view to re-sentence.

7.15 Custodial Penalties

7.15.1 Detention and Training Order (DTO)

This order provides for a single custodial order which replaces the secure training order and detention in a young offender institution.

The clear focus is on the prevention of further offending.

Criteria

15 to 17 year olds – any imprisonable offence which is either so serious or is a violent/sexual offence and only custody is adequate to protect the public from serious harm or failure to comply with a community order.

12 to 14 year olds – offence justifies custody and the court is of the opinion that the youth is a persistent offender. The term 'persistent offender' in this context is not the same as the definition used for 'persistent young offenders' in the delay strategy and pledge. It may simply be someone, without previous convictions at all, who stands convicted of more than one offence (R v. Smith 1999).

Duration

- Periods of 4,6,8,10,12,18 and 24 months (no variations!) or adult maximum if less.
- The 24 month maximum applies to youth court and the provision for committal for sentence to crown court is therefore repealed as it is no longer necessary.
- Maximum period is subject to any statutory maximum for the particular offence e.g. 6 months for drive whilst disqualified, conduct causing harassment.
- The total overall period for consecutive sentences is 24 months.
- Time spent on remand must be taken into account, unlike the adult custody provisions where the remand time is deducted after sentence. This information will usually be provided to the court by the YOT and it is conceded that this cannot be a strict mathematical calculation, especially if the period on remand is very short.

Features of the order

This is a two part order – the 'custodial' half and the 'community half. The custodial half will be served either in local authority secure accommodation, a secure training centre, a young offender institution, Glenthorne Youth Treatment Centre or accommodation as directed by the Secretary of State. The community half is supervised by the YOT in the community.

A supervising officer is appointed at the start of the sentence and he is responsible for the planning and supervision of the custodial element along with the secure facility staff and parent/carer if possible. The YOTs are expected to carry out the supervision, except where they nominate probation or social services colleagues as more appropriate.

An initial training plan must be drawn up within 5 days of admission. This must address the trainee's offending behaviour and educational and other developmental needs.

Example:

Objectives and targets in Training Plan:

- To complete a certain number of hours of literacy and numeracy tuition, with a view to demonstrating a specified improvement in reading age or numeracy skills.
- To complete satisfactorily an anger management groupwork programme, which would mean attending all the sessions, not being ejected from the group for disruptive behaviour and completing the pre- and post-group assessments.
- To write or telephone two colleges near home to request details of training courses.
- To apply for a training course and attend the interview if offered.
- To attend follow-up literacy and numeracy classes at a local college.

Joint Home Office/LCD/Youth Justice Board Circular 9.2.2000

Supervision – the 'community half'

A supervision notice is issued and read to the youth which contains details of all requirements. Post-transfer supervision begins on the day of release when the supervising officer sees the youth and makes a home visit within 5 days. Contact thereafter must be at least twice weekly during the first 3 months after transfer and then at least once every 10 days. For school age youths, the officer will monitor whether the home education authority is providing education of at least 25 hours per week and whether the health authority is providing planned services e.g. drug treatment.

Early and late release

The Home Secretary can release offenders one month early for orders of 8 – 18 months and one or two months early for orders of 18 months or longer. He may also apply to the youth court for late release for periods of the same length.

Breach of supervision

Where it appears that the trainee has breached one or more requirements in the supervision notice an information should be laid and the youth will appear before the court. Failure to comply may result in a fine (level 3 maximum) or an order of detention for a period of up to the rest of the DTO term or 3 months if this is less.

Other offences during the order

If a youth is found guilty of a further imprisonable offence during the order, the court can order an additional period of detention. The maximum period is the length of time between the date of the offence and the original DTO expiry date. The period may be served either concurrently or consecutively to any new sentence.

7.15.2 Committal to Crown Court – Grave crimes (previously known as 's.53' offences)

Long-term detention up to the maximum term punishable on an adult is available in respect of 'grave crimes' in the crown court. In respect of murder, the detention is 'during Her Majesty's pleasure.' Grave crimes are defined as:

- Offences punishable in the case of an adult with imprisonment of 14 years or more e.g. robbery, rape, house burglary, wounding with intent, handling stolen goods.
- Indecent assault.
- Causing death by dangerous driving if a young person.
- Causing death by careless driving while under the influence of drink or drugs if a young person.

A 'mode of trial' decision must be made at the earliest opportunity. This enables committal papers to be prepared. The youth court must ask itself whether the outline of the facts suggests that their powers are insufficient, notably:

- No power to detain a 12 – 14 year old at all <u>unless</u> he is a persistent offender.
- 2 years maximum detention and training order.

Representations must be allowed from prosecution and defence about venue before it is determined. The National Mode of Trial Guidelines provide some assistance in terms of identifying whether there are aggravating features. However it is essential to remember that the youth court now has the power to detain a youth for 2 years, whilst the adult court is restricted to 6 months for a single offence.

Intensive supervision and surveillance programme (ISSP)

The new programmes are to be available in some areas from 2001, for offenders who are appearing before the court either charged with or convicted of an offence if they have:

- Been warned or charged for an imprisonable offence on 4 or more separate occasions within the last 12 months
- Previously received at least one community or custodial sentence.

The programme will cover bail supervision, community sentence or the community element of a Detention and Training Order. The intensive supervision aspect will focus on education and training, literacy and numeracy, a restorative element, victim awareness, interpersonal skills, and family support.

The surveillance aspect is to ensure that behaviour is monitored and that the community has the reassurance of knowing that the youth is being carefully watched. It will provide monitoring by intelligence led policing, tracking, tagging, telephone contact by the youth using computerised voice verification, with checking by the YOT as to whereabouts at least twice daily. For those serving a community sentence the programme should last at least 6 months. For those who are bailed or in the second half of a detention and training order the period will be determined by the length of the order.

THE AGENCIES AND INSTITUTIONS

7.16 Role of the local authority and the YOT

7.16.1 Local authority

Whilst the Youth Justice Board are now responsible for monitoring the national picture, all local authorities with social services and education responsibilities retain the prime duty for the availability of youth justice services in the area.

The statutory duties on a local authority in relation to youths include the following:

1. Establish one or more YOTs for the area.
2. Formulate and implement an annual youth justice plan.
3. Investigate and provide information relating to home surroundings, school record, health and character on the request of the youth court.

4. Provide appropriate adults to safeguard the interest of youths detained or questioned by the police.
5. Provide placements in local authority accommodation for those remanded or committed.
6. Provide court reports in criminal proceedings.
7. Provide people to act as responsible officers in relation to reparation orders and action plan orders.
8. Supervise youths sentenced to supervision and detention and training orders.
9. Obligations under the Children Act (see 7.2).

7.16.2 Youth Offending Teams

Chief Officers of police, probation committees and health authorities are required to co-operate with the local authority in establishing such teams. There are 154 YOTs established.

YOTs must include at least one of each of the following:

- A probation officer.
- A social worker of a local authority social services department.
- A police officer.
- Someone nominated by a health authority in the area.
- Someone nominated by the chief education officers for the area.

A YOT may also include other people as appropriate e.g. representatives from voluntary organisations. The duties of the teams are to co-ordinate the provision of youth justice services for those in the area who need them and to carry out the functions assigned to the team in the Youth Justice Plan.

Before any intervention is made with a youth e.g. following a final warning, an assessment must be undertaken by a YOT member using the Youth Justice Board's 'ASSET core assessment profile'.

7.16.3 ASSET form

This is essentially an ongoing questionnaire and summary which brings consistency of approach across the country and continuity of information as a youth proceeds through the criminal justice system.

A – Assessment and diagnosis.
S – Structure, standardisation and scoring – use of relative weighting of offending factors.
S – Screening and suitability – matching of offender with proposed interventions.
E – Evaluation, effectiveness and evidence.
T – Target.

It includes care history, criminal history, analysis of offending behaviour, relationships, education, health, any indicators of serious harm to others, motivation to change and indicators of vulnerability. The document is basically a working document for YOTs to help provide information to the court from remand through to sentencing and to assist the YOT to develop supervision plans. An offender self-assessment form is also used. The court may order disclosure of the ASSET form to the defence if scrutiny is deemed reasonable e.g. to scrutinise a resulting pre-sentence report. The starting point must be that it belongs to the YOT and the youth rather than the court and any disclosure should be regarded as a rarity.

7.17 Young Offender Institutions

Youths sentenced after the 1st April 2000 to Detention and Training Orders may be ordered to serve the order in a young offender institution. The Prison Service recognise the changes which the new order brings with it as compared to the previous detention regime. Essentially this is to focus on the prevention of further offending and to reflect the principles and good practice of care required by the Children Act 1989.

In the year 2000, there was an 11% increase in youth custody. The Criminal Justice and Court Services Act 2000 abolishes the separate sentence of detention in a young offenders institution for the 18-20 year olds. This will enable the prison service to develop regimes for a wider age group, including those in their early 20s (not in effect at the time of print).

7.18 Attendance Centres (see 7.14.2)

7.19 Voluntary organisations' establishments for young offenders

There is a wide range of such organisations. Some make themselves known to the youth court and send literature and make efforts to involve magistrates and officers in their work. Others do not, largely because their work is involved in crime prevention and their focus is on youths who do not reach the court process.

The philosophy of the youth offending team is for multi-agency co-operation and co-ordination and undoubtedly some of the voluntary organisations will be involved in dealing with the new orders. The expectation is that the courts will become better informed about local organisations in this way.

7.20 Schools and education welfare (see 7.3)

SOCIO – PHYSCHOLOGICAL ISSUES

This section is largely made up of statistics but they do provide a helpful picture of youth crime and they are of interest ....

7.21 Predominant forms and patterns of youth crime

- About 3% of offenders are responsible for about a 1/4 of all offences.
- The peak age of self-reported offending is 21 for males and 16 for females.
- The seriousness and frequency of offending by males and females declines with age.
- Most offending by young people is theft-related. Only a small proportion is violent (about 10%).
- Overall crime rates are rising and have been doing so steadily in the last half of the 20th century with only a few national exceptions (Japan).
- In the 1950s there were 11 male offenders to each female offender; in 1995 the ratio had fallen to fewer than 4 males to one female.
- In 1999 a MORI poll of 11-16 years on attitudes towards crime came up with the following outcome. The fear of detection and/or parental reaction constituted the most effective deterrents, with the fear of punishment some way behind and the reaction of friends and the plight of victims considered to be relatively unimportant.

See also 7.31.

7.22 Child development

Usual development in children aged 10 –14:

1. Onset of puberty and physical changes.
2. A need to begin to assert independence from primary carers, to make important relationships outside the primary carers.
3. Coming to terms with strong emotional feelings, including sexual feelings.
4. Questioning of adult values and changing views of the world.
5. Changing views about self and experimenting with different forms of identity.

Usual development in children aged 15 – 18:

1. Less reliance on primary carers.
2. Greater financial independence.
3. Consolidation of identity.
4. More focus on friends.

7.23 Child abuse

There are 4 main types of child abuse though a child may experience more than one kind of abuse at any one time. The following definitions and statistics are taken from the NSPCC publication 'A guide to understanding child abuse.'

1. Physical abuse is when a child is hit, shaken, burned, punched or slapped, given harmful drugs or alcohol or injured in any way by an adult.
2. Emotional abuse is when a child is starved of love or affection or is constantly threatened or taunted.
3. Sexual abuse is when a child is being used sexually by an adult. This may involve anal, oral or vaginal intercourse, fondling and exposing children to pornographic material.
4. Neglect is when a child's basic needs for food, warmth, clothing and medical care are not met.

At least one child dies each week in this country as a result of cruelty. More than 35,000 children are at risk of abuse and have to be protected by the authorities. There are at least 11,000 adults in this country who have been convicted of sex offences against children.

7.24 Child prostitution

Whilst there are various routes into child prostitution it is likely that the majority are targeted by paedophiles who identify children who are vulnerable. These include children who are lonely, lacking in confidence, bullied, in care or away from home. Such children may be carefully groomed into sexual relationships through forming a friendly relationship, taking an interest in the child, offering gifts which may include alcohol, cigarettes and drugs and showing the value of money.

Unfortunately there is a market for child prostitution and unfortunately many of the victims are likely to be youths who come through the youth court. The possible short-term and long-term effects are horrendous. Whenever there are indications that a youth does not have 'secure' accommodation, money to live on and someone to show some affection the court must be alert to the potential danger of sexual abuse and prostitution. Possibly a minor offence – possibly a small fine, but the child must be referred to the local authority for help after court. The court has a welfare duty, whether sentencing or not.

7.25 Causes of anti-social behaviour

- Inadequate parenting; being brought up by a criminal parent; living in a family with multiple problems.

- Having siblings who offend.
- Poor discipline in the family and at school.
- Aggressive, hyperactive behaviour.
- Truancy and exclusions.
- Peer group pressure.
- Unstable living conditions.
- Lack of training and employment.
- Drugs and alcohol abuse.

7.26 Truancy

1. The most common age for truanting and running away from home is 14.
2. Two-thirds of those of school age who are sentenced in court have either been excluded or are known to be missing a significant amount of schooling through truancy.
3. In 1995 nearly 60% of convicted youths aged 16-17 were unemployed and not in training or education at the time of sentence.

The new orders, in particular focus on getting youths back into school, and even community service orders carry the option of some time being spent on numeracy and literacy.

See also 7.3 Education Acts.

7.27 Alcohol, drug and substance misuse

Regular consumption of alcohol often starts early on, with 89% of children admitting to having had their first alcoholic drink by 13 years of age. Alcohol abuse can be linked to poor school achievement, unsociable behaviour, truancy, unemployment, problems with relationships and delinquency.

Every other male and every third female have used drugs at some time. This is mostly confined to cannabis, which is consumed regularly (at least once a week) by one in 3 male and one in 5 female users.

There are 4 ways in which drugs correlate with crime:

- Offences are committed under the influence of drugs.
- Crime is committed in order to fund the purchase of drugs.
- Violence occurs between rival groups of drug dealers.
- Dealing or possessing controlled substances is a criminal offence.

Long-term users are unlikely to be rehabilitated at the first attempt and this should be seen as a reality rather than a once and for all failure. Drug rehabilitation options are likely to be required again ... and again until they are successful.

In the Audit Commission survey, half of the subjects on supervision orders said that they got drunk at least once a week and 70% admitted to taking drugs.

7.27 – 7.30 Local youth culture, alcohol and problem premises

Where do the local youth tend to congregate? What do they do? If you are 'in' with the 'in crowd' where would you be? Who would you be with? Are there areas and places where that is inevitably on the fringe of offending?

What is important to the youth of today? The same as ever – appearance, possessions, relationships with their families, performance in school, making friends, keeping friends and fitting in with peers. What are their concerns? Being liked, being healthy, feeling good, having a boyfriend/girlfriend and so on. Some may also have concerns about separation/divorce, abuse, domestic violence, bullying, racism, homophobia. There is a predominant theme of simply 'wanting to be accepted'. It sometimes carries a price and so often that is through offending.

It is easily said that the basis for an effective sentence is simply to identify the problem and provide appropriate support. Perhaps it is more about striving for that ultimate need for acceptance – but within a law-abiding and motivating lifestyle!

YOUNG OFFENDER PROFILE

7.31 Age, sex, ethnicity, educational, geographic and social background of young offenders before the court and the offences with which they are commonly charged.

See 7.21 and local documents, namely Chief Constable's Report, Community Safety Strategy, Youth Justice Plan and national Statistics on Race and the Criminal Justice System.

Youth Crime: findings from the 1998/1999 Youth Lifestyle Survey (published in 2000):

- 10% of juvenile offenders were responsible for nearly half the crimes admitted by the sample.
- Girls under 16 were most likely to be involved in criminal damage, shoplifting, buying stolen goods and fighting. Over the age of 16, they

were committing less criminal damage and shoplifting but were increasingly involved in fraud and buying stolen property.
- The average age at which offending began was 13 and a half for boys and at 14 for girls.
- Almost half of the 12-30 year olds involved in the survey admitted committing at least one offence at some point in their lives.
- The levels of offending were highest among 18-21 year old men.

Nationally 26% of known offenders are under 18.

The crime statistics published in January 2001 reveal the following profile of crime for the 12 months ending September 2000:

- Robberies rose by 20.8% (much of which is blamed on robberies of mobile phones from and by teenagers).
- Violent crime rose by 6.8%.
- Drug offences, particularly possession of cannabis down by 11%.
- Burglary down by 8%.
- Theft of and from motor vehicles down by 6%.

THE ABILITY TO UNDERSTAND AND COMMUNICATE WITH YOUNG PEOPLE BY

7.32 – 7.35 Listening closely, paying regard to the role of parents, helping maintain an appropriate level of informality, helping in the formulation of announcements so that they can be understood by young people.

The Magistrates Association's Youth Courts Committee makes the following recommendations to promote better communication in the youth court:

Court lay-out

Consider the lay-out of the court room so as to encourage easy dialogue between the bench, the youth and parents;

Consider if the language used is appropriate to the age, understanding and culture of the youth and parents;

Consider the communication and equal treatment skills of all panel members, bearing in mind the disparities between those on the bench and those appearing as defendants.

In the courtroom

- Give clear, simple explanations at the beginning and throughout the proceedings of who is who in the courtroom and what will happen;
- Establish an atmosphere of courtesy, attention and respect for all;
- If there is a lawyer, explain that you will wish to talk to the young person and parents when necessary;
- Encourage the young person and the parents to ask, and answer, questions so that they feel that their views are necessary and valued;
- Announce what the court proposes to do and invite representations;
- Ask the young person to explain the decision in his or her own words;
- Announce the decision in a clear, firm yet friendly manner and try to end on a positive note.

(The Magistrates Association. Youth Court Committee. Communication in the Youth Court.)

Demonstration projects

Between 1998 and 2000 demonstration projects were undertaken in Rotherham and Leicester which aimed to engage young offenders and parents in focusing on offending behaviour and encourage magistrates to talk directly with young offenders and their parents.

The Rotherham chairman's protocol is summarised below:

- Chairman to speak briefly with parent and child once brought in by the usher.
- Briefly introduce people in court and their roles.
- Explain how the hearing will be conducted.
- Stress importance and seriousness of occasion and that the young person and parent are the focus.
- Inform young person and parent when to sit/stand and when they will be invited to speak or ask questions.
- Stress that the young person is here because of what he has done, not because of who he is.
- Clerk to explain the charge in simple terms. Plea taken.
- Chairman to stress importance of defence solicitor.
- Following conviction, chairman to engage with young person and parent focusing on offending behaviour and how to change it.
- Defence solicitor invited to have the last word.

The project also involved moving the magistrates from a raised platform into the well of the court, enabling parents to sit next to their children and asking defendants and others to remain seated throughout the proceedings. Fears that the length of the hearing would extend and dignity would be lost were not justified in practice. In the Rotherham project, it was noted that the number of discharges and probation orders increased and the number of fines and custodial sentences decreased.

The projects also attempted to encourage victims to attend court but attendance was infrequent and unpredictable. The benefits of the dialogue and the environment are encouraged and full details of the project and guidance may be obtained from the Home Office (02072732564). (Evaluation of the Youth Court Demonstration Project. Home Office. HORS 214)

Announcements in the youth court are potentially more complex than adult court in that there may be numerous features to a single sentence, particularly an action plan order. In the informal setting there is a school of thought that the outcome should take the form of a two-way discussion rather than a bland one-sided pronouncement. Youths only have limited patience to listen for long periods. Furthermore, by checking each aspect, there is a greater sense of involvement and opportunity for clarification. The role of the wingers is important to prompt and suggest any supplementary aspects. Direct and very basic warnings should be considered.

> Example:
>
> 'If you fail to comply with the requirements, then enforcement action will be taken ...'
>
> What does this really mean?
>
> 'If you don't go to the attendance centre every fortnight, on time, and do as you are asked, then we can ...'

A youth is unlikely to 'speak up'; is unlikely to speak robustly and clearly; is likely to speak at a low volume and quickly and is likely to dry up completely if put off his stride. Encouragement and enormous patience is essential if he is going to tell his story and have his day in court to the same extent as an adult.

The youth is the only one with the answers to the many questions you need to paint a picture of who you are dealing with and how a life might just be changed for the better. If he hasn't spoken during the whole of the proceedings, it is unlikely that the court have got the full picture. Talk to them!

The parent is the best witness the court could possibly have. If they haven't spoken during the whole of the proceedings, a valuable source of information is left untapped and an essential support is left without encouragement. Talk to them! As any parent, they simply want 'what's best' for their child. Help them to get it.

CHAPTER 8
COMPETENCE 8
Youth Chairmanship

INTRODUCTION

The youth knowledge text is covered in chapter 7 and chairmanship skills in general are covered in chapters 5 and 6. This chapter simply highlights and expands on key areas.

8.1 Using a structured approach to bail and sentencing

8.1.1. BAIL – the 'ABC' approach

A = Adjournment (or not?)
B = Bail options
C = Custody provisions

A. ADJOURNMENT (OR NOT)?

Should the case be adjourned? The advocates will be aware of the basis for the adjournment and if they have no objection, will understandably focus their attention on the bail representations. However, the court must first consider carefully whether the case should be adjourned at all. Could it proceed today?

This is particularly relevant when the youth appears in custody on warrant having failed to attend an early first hearing or breach proceedings. A file should be readily available to CPS or the YOT representative as the case may be. A short stand down may be required to obtain the file, provide disclosure and take instructions. The expectation should always be for such cases to go ahead, at least to plea.

Doing 'what you can, when you can' is never more important than when there are grounds for a youth appearing in custody. Even more so if the court considers that he should remain so – even more so, if he is also a persistent offender.

B. BAIL

Offence

What is alleged by the prosecutor? What is conceded (if anything) by the defence? Provided that the evidence is strong, is the offence so serious that the youth may fail to surrender in view of the probable sentence? Is there a reliance on the prosecution witnesses and are they vulnerable?

Offender

Does the youth have a stable address? Does he have family or employment commitments? Are there any previous convictions? Is the bail record good or bad? What are the explanations/circumstances of any recent failures to attend? Was the youth on bail at the time of the alleged offence?

Options (non-custodial)

If there are no concerns (exceptions) found, then unconditional bail must be granted. Where there are exceptions with reasons, can they be allayed by relevant conditions? Define any conditions carefully so that both the youth and the police have the same understanding of what they mean.

Wording of compliance with bail support schemes should usefully be agreed with the local YOT so that arrest scenarios can be carefully discussed between the youth and the bail support officer.

Recent police curfew conditions which add a curfew check provision to answer the door to the police during curfew hours have been criticised by the Justices Clerks Society. Arguably the rider is intrusive and exceeds the provisions of the Bail Act and breaches the right to private and family life.

Check reasons with the clerk if granting bail in respect of murder, manslaughter or rape.

C. CUSTODY

When exceptions and reasons are found but conditions cannot safely be attached to allay concerns, then bail must be refused. Additionally, there is the added exception to bail for youths that 'custody is required for his own protection.'

Check that the bench have sufficient information on which to make a bail decision. If not, consider an overnight remand using the exception 'insufficient information' and identify exactly what information is required e.g. address to be checked out. Never adjourn for 8/28 days as a matter of course. How long is needed for the case to progress?

'Bail refused' in youth court = (i) local authority accommodation for the 10 –16 year olds (ii) remand centre/prison for the 17 year olds (iii) secure accommodation for 10 –16 year olds or (iv) remand centre/prison for 15-16 year old boys.

Secure accommodation and remand centre/ prison for boys of 15-16 (see 7.11)

When such remands are being considered the bench should approach the decision in 2 stages.

- Stage 1

Is the basic criteria satisfied for this youth?

> ➢ Youth is convicted of a violent or sexual offence, or an offence punishable in the case of an adult with imprisonment for 14 years or more: or
> ➢ Youth has a history of absconding (single occasion is sufficient) while remanded in local authority accommodation, and is charged with or has been convicted of an imprisonable offence alleged or found to have been committed while so remanded.

- Stage 2

Alternative bail packages and views on vulnerability of 15-16 year old boys provided by the YOT.

The court must then form the opinion that only remanding the youth to secure accommodation or a remand centre/prison would be adequate to protect the public from serious harm from him.

8.1.2 SENTENCING – the '4 'O's agenda

Offence
Offender
Objectives
Options

1. Offence

- What is the sentencing guideline entry point? e.g. community level.
- What is the nature and extent of criminal intent? A pre-meditated offence is more serious than a spontaneous offence.
- What is the nature and extent of any injury or damage to the victim? Personal injury is more serious than financial damage.
- Matters specific to the offence as listed in the guidelines.
- What are the aggravating features?
    - ➢ What are the relevant previous convictions (if any)?

- ➢ Was the offence committed on bail? (must increase).
- ➢ Is the offence racially aggravated? (must increase).
- ➢ Are there any failures to respond to previous sentences? (may increase).

- What are the mitigating features?
- What is the level of seriousness at this stage?

2. Offender

- Positive good character e.g. no relevant previous convictions, good school record, solid employment record, contributes to family
- Co-operation with the police and an early guilty plea will usually result in a discount of around 1/3 of the final sentencing option. Without other compelling features it would not be sufficient to alter the band of seriousness e.g. from custody to community band.
- Hard evidence of genuine remorse e.g. apology to victim.

If the offence is fuelled by drink or drugs – a genuine self-motivated determination to address the addiction.

Youth and immaturity would often justify a less rigorous penalty than for an adult (R v Howells 1998).

What is the level of seriousness at this stage?

3. Objectives

The principal aim in the youth court is to prevent offending and this must always be the starting point. However, other sentencing objectives may well assist in determining the most appropriate way to prevent this youth from offending, namely:

- Punishment
- Protection of the public
- Rehabilitation
- Deterrence to others.

4. Options

- What is the most suitable option to satisfy the level of seriousness – the prevention of further offending – any other objective AND any welfare needs?
- The victim's views (if known) may affect selection, particularly between custody and community penalty. Would custody cause or add to the distress? Many youths do offend against their own families. (R v Hayes 1999 involved robbery of youth's grandmother. She stated that she had forgiven him and found it difficult to cope without him whilst on

remand in custody. Her wishes tipped the balance from custody to a probation order).

- The youth court is motivated now largely by 'restorative justice' – is there anything the court can do to assist the victim?
- How much/how long? If a detention and training order is appropriate check that the 12 – 14 year olds are 'persistent offenders.' Remember that the DTO periods are fixed. The order should be no longer than necessary to meet the penal purpose which the court has in mind (R v Ollerenshaw 1999).

- Check that the sentence is commensurate with seriousness and any interference with private and family life is proportionate.

8.2 Demonstrating a sound grasp of the youth court powers and functions

(see chapter 7 for full discussion).

8.3 Identifying clear sentencing objectives

The principal aim of the youth court is 'to prevent offending.' The objectives of punishment, protection of the public, rehabilitation and deterrence should always be considered alongside the principal aim. The key question must be 'Why is <u>this</u> disposal likely to prevent <u>this</u> youth from further offending?'

8.4 Maintaining balance between formality and informality

Basically this is about drawing the line between the atmosphere of discussion and the atmosphere of direction. This will be achieved through a change of tone and body language. When is the time for participation and involvement by youth and parent? When is the time to listen up to what is going to happen next and of course, to hear the outcome?

There is an increasing trend to encourage far more involvement on the part of parent and youth, even if represented (see 7.32). The cue and the lead of the chairman is essential to create an informal and participative discussion, whilst retaining the authority to move into a formal and directive mode if necessary, and certainly at the point of pronouncement.

The atmosphere of a youth court is seldom portrayed through the media. Youths and parents are likely to expect all of the features of an adult court. Perhaps one of the important early messages to get across is that the court is aiming to prevent further offending rather than punish and the input of parent and youth is essential.

Three useful recurring words – (i) Why? (ii) Support? (iii) The name of the youth.

> Example:
>
> Why did you do this? Why do you think Andrew did this? Why didn't you go to the attendance centre? Why do you think that Andrew broke his curfew?
>
> What support is there at home for Andrew? What support is there for you (parent)?
>
> Open questions to parent and youth.

These questions need frank, open discussion and informality will assist in the dialogue. Some courts ask parents to sit down as soon as they come into court – they are not on trial. All evidence may well be given sitting down. Youths are particularly embarrassed to begin with, without having to stand up as well. It also avoids the issue of 'when do I stand?', 'when do I sit?,' 'am I doing the right thing?'

It is courteous to explain to the solicitor if you wish to speak directly with youth and parent. This is particularly helpful when protracted instructions are being taken in whispers – better to suggest that the parent may as well tell the court themselves what the weekly income and outgoings are!

8.5 Demonstrating an understanding of young people's behaviour

See 7.21 to 7.31

8.6 Communicating appropriately thereby ensuring that young people, their parents and all in court understand so as to encourage their participation in proceedings

See 7.32 – 7.35.

Explanations throughout the course of the proceedings are necessary in plain, simple language. Introductions should be made so that parents and youths are aware of who is who. A parent is more likely to 'open up' if he is aware that the person sitting at the back of the court is a social worker rather than a member of the press.

Jargon must be avoided. A parent may well be sadly misled by reference to a 'member of the YOT (yacht!) meeting with her after court to 'get her on board' to discuss her son's ASSET!'

Open questions are essential to set the ball rolling. A question, 'Do you have anything to say?' has only a one word answer. To a youth who is standing, feeling gauche and vulnerable, the easiest answer is 'no'. Better possibly to sit him down with a desk to lean on and say:

'Now it's your turn. We've heard what the prosecutor has had to say, but we're interested now in what you have to say. So it was 4 o'clock in the morning, what were you doing?' ...

'How do you suggest that we can help you to stop offending? ...

Making assumptions about young offenders is so easy for all of us and it is so much more difficult to ensure that they too have their day in court. If they can be encouraged to take that opportunity, the court experience in itself may well have a dramatic effect. It may provide the occasion for them to see their parent in a positive, responsible and caring light because that is exactly what the court is doing.

For the older youths – it could be a first for them – someone treated them and respected them as a reasonable adult who has made a mistake, instead of a naughty child. It could be the start of growing up and they may never come to court again!

CHAPTER 9
COMPETENCE 9
Family

INTRODUCTION

This chapter sets out to understand and apply the specialist nature and function of the family proceedings court, which began its present life with the Children Act 1989.

SPECIAL LEGISLATION

9.1 The Children Act 1989 ('the Act'/CA 1989)

This Act contains the vast majority of private and public civil law relating to children and is the linchpin of the family court.

9.1.1 Why did it happen?

There was growing dissatisfaction with the confusing, complicated and unco-ordinated nature of the service offered by the courts in resolving family disputes and protecting children. The magistrates, county court and High Court all had family jurisdiction but did not share a common approach or procedures.

Public debate and concern were active in the 1980s on several fronts concerning responsibility towards children and children's rights. There were concerns about the management of child abuse by social workers notably regarding the death of Jasmine Beckford in 1985 and the Cleveland Report in 1987 which criticised the over-zealous intervention of the local authority in cases of actual and suspected child abuse in Cleveland. The Gillick case in 1986, which allowed a 16 year old to make her own decision to take contraceptives, also had a significant impact.

9.1.2 What did it do?

- The welfare of the child became the 'paramount consideration.'
- A presumption of 'no order' sought to minimise unnecessary state intervention.
- Reasons were required for each decision based upon a statutory checklist.

- A recognition that delay in reaching decisions is likely to be harmful to the child by requiring a timetable to be drawn up for case progress.
- It 'joined up' the relevant courts with common procedures, shared principles and the power to transfer cases freely. Most family proceedings start in the magistrates' court and are then allocated to the High Court or County Court if appropriate by the clerk or the court.
- A flexible range of orders became available with provision to make the most suitable order even if it was not the one applied for.
- Unmarried fathers, grandparents and children themselves were given rights to apply for orders.
- Sharing of evidence by filing statements and relevant documents before the hearing.
- The concept of 'parental responsibility' was introduced.
- Orders were described as 'public orders' or 'private orders'.

9.1.3 'Parental responsibility'

This expression sought to change the emphasis from rights *over* children to responsibility *for* children. It includes 'all rights, duties, powers, responsibilities and authority which by law a parent of a child has in relation to the child and his property e.g. education, health treatment (s.3 (1) CA 1989).

There are a wide variety of people who may have parental responsibility under the Act possibly at the same time:

Examples:

- Conferred automatically on the mother of a child, and also on the father if married to the mother.
- Unmarried fathers by agreement with the mother or by order of the court.
- Local authorities on the making of a care order (some limitations e.g. cannot consent to adoption or bring child up in a different religion).
- NSPCC on the making of an emergency protection order.
- Any person who has been granted a residence order.
- A step-parent on the making of an adoption order.

An important feature of 'parental responsibility' is that it carries a right to be involved in any applications concerning the child e.g. as respondent in an application for a care order. Married parents both automatically have parental responsibility but an unmarried father must apply for a formal court order. The court must consider whether an order would be in the best interests of the child and will consider the level of commitment and attachment and the reasons for applying for the order.

9.1.4 Public and private orders

The 'public orders' under the Act involve either the local authority or NSPCC and are care orders, supervision orders, child assessment orders and emergency protection orders. The 'private orders' involve individuals within a family and are residence orders, contact orders, specific issues orders and prohibited steps orders.

9.2 The welfare principle (and Human Rights Act implications)

Section 1 of the Act states that 'when a court determines any question with respect to the upbringing of a child, the child's welfare shall be the court's paramount consideration.' The Human Rights Act effectively gives core rights to the rest of the family as well which are predominantly covered by Article 8 as set out below:

> Art. 8(1) <u>Everyone</u> has the right to respect for his private and family life, his home and his correspondence.
>
> (2) There shall be no interference by a public authority with the exercise of this right except such as is <u>in accordance with the law</u> and is <u>necessary in a democratic society</u> and in the interests of national security, public safety or the economic well-being of the country, for the prevention of disorder or crime, <u>for the protection of health and morals, or for the protection of the rights and freedoms of others.</u>

This is a qualified right and the key words for a family case are underlined for consideration of the '3 questions';

(i) Is the interference legal, clear and accessible? ('in accordance with the law').
(ii) Does it pursue a legitimate aim? ('protection of health, morals, rights and freedoms').
(iii) Is it proportionate? ('necessary in a democratic society').

Whilst the child's rights will have to be balanced with the rights of his parents, Convention case law states that 'where there is a serious conflict between the interest of the child and one of its parents, which can only be resolved to the disadvantage of one of them, the interests of the child under Article 8(2) prevail (Hendricks v. The Netherlands 1983).

In a later case the European Court stated that the removal of a child permanently from his parents should only be applied in exceptional circumstances but could be justified 'if they were motivated by an overriding requirement pertaining to the child's best interest' (Johansen v. Norway 1996).

The difference in thinking means therefore that other family members now have a domestic legal right to respect for their private and family life. However the child is likely to remain firmly at centre stage if there is any question that their health, morals, rights and freedoms are going to be adversely affected by tipping the balance towards the parent. The cases above can be interpreted to retain the child's welfare as a key feature in determining conflicting rights under Article 8.

A second broad issue relates to the principle of 'equality of arms' in family proceedings. Under this principle the court must ensure that legal processes do not place one party at a procedural disadvantage as against the other and this will usually mean full disclosure of any documents.

9.3 The centrality of the interests of the child and avoidance of delay

In any proceedings regarding the upbringing of a child the court must have regard to the general principle that any delay is likely to prejudice the welfare of the child (s.1 (2) CA 1989). Whilst it is clear that delay is generally 'a bad thing' there are aspects of family work which quite properly require delays to be built in. Hasty decisions without careful consideration and reflection could so easily create a roller-coaster ride into orders which may last for years and years and effects which may last for a lifetime.

The Act requires directions to be given and timetables to be created so that proceedings are managed effectively and efficiently (see 9.11).

> Example:
>
> A delay for a full assessment to be completed prior to the making of a full care order is appropriate and to be encouraged. Provided that the court is satisfied that some intervention is ongoing; that safety checks are in place and that there is good reason for the particular length of adjournment then it is likely to be a beneficial line of enquiry and opportunity for all concerned.

Additionally, Article 6 of the Human Rights Act gives the right to a fair hearing ...within a reasonable time. Convention case law recognises that any procedural delay in family cases may result in the practical determination of the case, particularly regarding where a child should live, before it is legally determined.

There has been recent encouragement to consider twin-track planning of care within the family and potential adoption at the same time, rather than exhausting the rehabilitation option first, as this has caused unnecessary delay in the past (see 9.16.2).

9.4 The concept of 'significant harm'

Care orders and supervision orders may only be considered if the court is satisfied that the child is suffering, or is likely to suffer, 'significant harm.' This is sometimes referred to as the 'threshold criteria' and is discussed further at 9.20. The requirement is to prevent families from invasive orders 'unless there is a manifest need' and there is clear evidence to support this.

'Significant harm' is not confined to physical harm. 'Harm' means ill-treatment (including psychological and sexual abuse) or impairment of health (physical and mental) or developmental impairment. In respect of a child who is an habitual truant it would refer to his social, intellectual and educational development.

The comparison of health and development is that which could 'reasonably be expected of a similar child.'

9.5. The role of the clerk

The new Practice Direction provisions apply as issued in October 2000 with the concurrence of the President of the Family Division (see 5.16 to 5.20 for full detail).

Additionally the clerk must keep a note of the substance of the oral evidence given at a hearing or at a directions appointment. The clerk is also required under the rules to 'record .. the reasons for the court's decision and any findings of fact' (r.21 (5) CA 1991). The reasons must be formulated before making the order and the consultation period may well be lengthy. Whilst some magistrates may prefer to write out their own reasons it must be remembered that it is actually the responsibility of the court clerk. The reality is that the production of the reasons becomes a team approach. There is no doubt at all though that legally the clerk must be involved. A lap top computer is a very useful item for the family court retiring room if reasons are to be easily read to the parties in court.

After the decision, the clerk must ensure that a copy of any order made is served as soon as practicable, and also a copy of the reasons if requested for appeal purposes.

Under delegated powers from the Justices Clerk, court clerks may deal with directions hearings in the absence of a magistrate.

PROCEDURE

9.6 Protocol of the family court

Most family courts have a protocol agreed with members of its family court user group which basically sets out 'who will do what and when they will do it.' This may include local arrangements to encourage conciliation in private applications by arranging an early directions and family meeting. Following the meeting, the court or clerk would hear the views of the court welfare officer possibly for an adjournment for arrangements to be tried out, or alternatively for formal directions to be given towards a full court hearing.

9.7 Conduct of the court: non-adversarial approach

Proceedings in public law cases involving children are intended to be non-adversarial. Using the *Concise Oxford Dictionary* definitions, this means that they should not be 'hostile', 'hurtful', 'injurious' 'placed opposite.' Hence the layout of the court should be with all parties evenly placed as 'together' as possible – probably sat at one table facing the bench. 'The outcome in children cases is not intended to be 'win/lose' but 'resolution'.

See also 9.12 for actions to be taken to create and maintain an atmosphere that 'together we will sort out what is going to be best for the children.'

9.8 The welfare checklist

The statutory checklist is designed to assist the court in determining whether an order is necessary and whether one order rather than another will promote the welfare of the child. It must be covered within the court's reasons whenever the proceedings involve care and supervision orders and in disputed private order cases.

The welfare checklist is as follows:

(i) The ascertainable wishes and feelings of the child concerned (in the light of his age and understanding);
(ii) His physical, emotional and educational needs;
(iii) The likely effect on him of any change in his circumstances;
(iv) His age, sex, background and any characteristics of his which the court considers relevant;
(v) Any harm which he has suffered or is at risk of suffering;

(vi) How capable each of his parents, and any other person in relation to whom the court considers the question to be relevant, is of meeting his needs;

(vii) The range of powers available to the court under the Children Act 1989 in the proceedings in question.

(i) The ascertainable wishes and feelings of the child concerned.

The court will consider the age and maturity of the child. The older a child is, the greater weight can usually be attached to the views given, particularly if they are 'sensible, mature and intelligent.' It has been held that the instructions of a boy of 15 should have been expressed by his solicitor rather than the instructions of his guardian ad litem (see 9.14).

So far as very young children are concerned the court would simply have to say 'too young to form or express a view.' The court should recognise that the child is likely to be influenced, consciously or not, particularly by any party he may be living with at the time. He may also be afraid to voice his own opinion for fear of hurting one of his parents. Even if he does have strong wishes they may not be in his own interests. There is no provision for magistrates to interview children, but judges occasionally do use their power to speak directly.

(ii) The child's physical, emotional and educational needs.

The fact that a parent has material prosperity or offers pleasant surroundings carries very little weight in a dispute as to where a child should live. This will become relevant though if the alternative accommodation offered is considered to be undesirable – dirty, cramped, etc.

More important than accommodation is the day-to-day care. It would be rare to find any parent who is entirely without criticism and it is easy to hear about endless minor failings. The real concerns are about children who are left hungry, dirty or unsupervised on more than the one brief occasion.

In considering emotional needs the court must place weight on the closeness of ties with parents and siblings and the trauma of breaking those ties. The court is reluctant to split up brothers and sisters. There is no general rule that a mother should have the children living with her rather than the father, but in practice she has the advantage with younger children, particularly if she is at home to care for them during the day.

So far as education is concerned this may be significant in respect of older children who face disruption at key stages such as GCSE examination year.

(iii) The likely effect on the child of a change in circumstances

In private cases, with all other aspects being equal, the court will always attach weight to maintaining the status quo particularly if it has existed for a lengthy period.

(iv) The child's age, sex, background and any relevant characteristics

In 1992 the Court of Appeal held that there was a rebuttable (i.e.challengeable) presumption that the welfare of a tiny baby was best served by being with its mother. A 15 year old, by comparison, would generally be considered sufficiently mature to make up his own mind as to where he would like to live (Re W (A Minor)(Residence Order)). The sex of a child is relevant particularly for girls going through puberty – a female carer has an advantage.

Background can cover a multitude of factors such as race, religious upbringing, culture, family environment and so on. Although a child's religious and cultural heritage is a relevant factor when considering a child's welfare, it is merely one factor in the balance. A residence order was made in favour of Catholic foster parents in respect of a child, of an orthodox rabbi and his wife. Efforts had been made unsuccessful to secure a placement with a Jewish family and the Catholic family had come to regard the child as their own (Re P (a child)(residence order: restriction order) 1999).

Relevant characteristics could cover disability, illness, sporting or intellectual factors.

(v) Any harm which the child has suffered or is at risk of suffering

This covers psychological trauma as well as physical injury.

(vi) How capable are the parents and any other relevant person of meeting the child's needs?

Relevant factors will include any question of ill-treatment in the past; illness or criminal offending which may be harmful to the physical or mental state of the child. Extreme religious views or sexual proclivities may be relevant if the court considers that they may be harmful to the child. However they may be dealt with by way of attaching conditions e.g. that blood transfusions must be allowed, that father must wear male-orientated clothes during contact.

'Other relevant person' may include new partners, siblings, grandparents and child minders.

The parental bond is a priority. Where a care plan proposes that a child should be placed under a care order with his father, rather than grandparents, the issue for the court is not where would the child get a better home, but whether it is demonstrated that the welfare of the child positively demands the displacement of the parental right (Re D (a Minor)(Natural parent; presumption of care) 1999).

(vii) The range of powers available to the court

This is an important point. The court may choose to make an appropriate order which nobody has applied for, e.g. grant a residence order to a grandparent who has attended as a witness but states that she would be willing to look after her grandchild. If the court believes however that a care or supervision order is more appropriate than a residence order, the case must be adjourned for the local authority to investigate the circumstances.

9.9 The role of the chairman

Many functions apply but predominantly to control, facilitate and communicate effectively with everyone in court. The chairman will undoubtedly set the tone. There is far more flexibility in a family court and far more discretion about how the court is going to be run.

People's feelings have to be controlled so that they can think clearly and act appropriately. The proceedings have to be facilitated for each case so that it will run smoothly and fairly. The communication must be kept open, calm and relevant both in court <u>and</u> in the retiring room. Not an easy task! Wingers may find it helpful to read through competence 10 – family chairmanship.

9.10 The role of the wingers

Again, many functions, which can perhaps be summarised by the following list:

- To digest the details of the case by reading the papers and identify key issues before the case even begins.
- To share concerns with the chairman so that they may be covered during the proceedings.
- To listen carefully and remain dispassionate throughout distressing evidence.
- To prompt and assist the chairman in a manner which is acceptable to the particular chairman.
- In the retiring room, to make a positive contribution in progressing through the facts and reasons to a decision.

9.11 Directions hearings/appointments

Direction hearings or appointments as they are sometimes called are basically preliminary hearings at which the court (or Justices' Clerk or delegated clerk) may give directions for the subsequent conduct of the proceedings. The intention is to ensure that the hearings will be conducted in the most efficient and cost-effective manner. They can take place at the court's own motion or as a result of a request by one of the parties when the party must specify the direction which is sought. The period of notice for such hearings is usually 2 days, but in urgent cases a request for directions can be made orally and without notice if leave is given.

The principal purpose is to identify what is in dispute and whether there is any chance of any agreement.

The matters which can be dealt with by directions include the following:

- Timetable of proceedings – must draw up in respect of care/supervision and 'section 8' (see 9.21) applications
- Varying time limits
- Service of documents
- Joining of parties
- Preparation of welfare reports and a direction that the court welfare officer responsible for preparing the report shall attend the final hearing to assist the court and to give oral evidence if necessary
- Submission of evidence, including experts' reports
- Guardian ad litem (Children's Guardian) to co-ordinate a conference between the expert witnesses to identify areas of agreement and dispute
- Bundles of documents to be agreed in advance
- Appointment of guardian ad litem/solicitor
- Attendance of child
- Transfer of case to another court
- Consolidation with other proceedings.

When a party is not represented it is essential to stress the importance of filing their statement. An explanation is necessary to explain that it is not intended to 'give the game away' but to make sure that all the arguments and facts are 'on the table' and that he too will have the benefit of reading the statement by the other side.

When a case has to be adjourned because directions have not been complied with the court should consider an order for costs. It should not simply exclude the evidence and go ahead.

9.12 Full hearings (Evidence and procedure)

The court must not begin a case in the absence of a respondent unless he has had reasonable notice of the hearing or the circumstances justify the case proceeding.

The hearing effectively begins by the filing of written statements of the oral evidence which each party intends to rely on together with copies of any relevant documents. A party in family proceedings may not put forward evidence which has not been disclosed in advance to the other parties except with the leave of the court. This creates an atmosphere of 'no surprises' and enables effective preparation by each party.

Before the hearing, the justices must read the documents which have been filed with the justices' clerk. When papers can be sent in advance this will obviously save time and reduces the pressure of reading on the day when the court is waiting. More importantly the families involved do not have the responsibility to set the scene in court by giving long and distressing evidence. That is done already and large parts of the evidence can usually be agreed e.g. the nature of the neglect; the accepted explanations; the home situation and the history of the interim care order. The court and the witnesses can concentrate then on the areas of uncertainty and dispute. It is reasonable for the court to identify the issues which it has identified and limit the evidence accordingly e.g. whether mother is realistically going to co-operate with the care plan or not.

Reading in advance enables the court to place the verbal evidence into a big picture straightaway. It can recognise immediately what is relevant evidence on oath e.g. evidence of mother's various interactions with the local authority.

As stated above, the aim is to create and maintain a non-adversarial atmosphere – as calm as possible in the face of high emotions. This is a difficult task and the court is allowed to regulate its own proceedings far more than in a criminal court.

Unless the court directs otherwise the evidence will usually be given in the following order:

1. Applicant;
2. Any party with parental responsibility for the child;
3. Other respondents (if any);
4. Guardian ad litem (Children's Guardian);
5. The child, if he is a party and there is no guardian.

A family court must be prepared to assert greater control over the conduct of proceedings. This may involve using its discretion to limit the length of opening and closing oral submissions; the time allowed for the examination and cross-examination of witnesses and reading aloud from documents and authorities (Practice Note (Civil Litigation: Case Management)). As soon as a party switches off because of impatience on the one hand or boredom on the other, there is a danger that something important can be missed. Breaks, limits and checking are essential.

The parties and their legal advisers must use their best endeavours:

- To confine issues and the evidence called to what is reasonably considered to be essential for the proper presentation of the case;
- To reduce or eliminate issues for expert evidence;
- In advance of the hearing to agree which are the issues or the main issues.

(Practice Note (Civil Litigation: Case Management)).

The standard of proof is on the balance of probabilities but the more serious the allegation e.g. sexual abuse by a parent, the more convincing must be the evidence to tip the balance. The concept of 'no case to answer' has no place in family proceedings.

In some contested cases where stark factual issues need to be determined, e.g. allegation of sexual abuse, the court may consider proceeding in 2 stages. First, to determine whether or not there has been sexual abuse in order to satisfy the threshold criteria of significant harm for the making of an order and then if appropriate to move on to the wider welfare issue in order to consider options.

Hearsay evidence is admissible when given in connection with the upbringing, maintenance or welfare of a child e.g. 'the child-minder says that she is always late in picking up the children'. The weight given to such evidence is however a matter for the court. Hearsay is specifically allowed in the statements of children and statements submitted by a guardian or local authority (The Children (Admissibility of Hearsay Evidence) Order 1990).

Children's evidence may be given through videotape unless the other side issue a witness summons.

Before completing its determination of the case the court must proceed through the recommended structured decision-making process as set out at 9.38.

After the final hearing the court must make its decision as soon as practicable. When making an order or refusing an application the court must state any findings of fact and the reasons for the court's decision.

RELEVANT COURT SERVICES

9.13 Social Services role and practice in child protection measures

Under the Children Act 1989 the local authority has many obligations which include the following:

- 'To safeguard and promote the welfare of children within their area who are in need; and so far as is consistent with that duty, to promote the upbringing of such children by their families, by providing a range and level of services appropriate to the children's needs.'
- To provide accommodation for any child if there is no person with parental responsibility for the child or if the carer is prevented from providing suitable accommodation or care or if the child is abandoned.
- To take reasonable steps to prevent children suffering from ill-treatment or neglect.
- To investigate and take action to safeguard a child if they have reasonable cause to suspect that a child in their area is suffering or is likely to suffer significant harm. The various court order options are considered at 9.18/20.
- To make provisions for services for 'children in need' who are living with their families e.g. provide home help, arrange recreational activities, assistance to enable child and family to have a holiday.
- Take steps to enable a child who is living apart from his family to live with his family or have contact if necessary to safeguard or promote his welfare.
- So far as children who are looked after by the local authority are concerned there are various obligations, including the 'endeavour to promote contact with parents and any relative, friend or other person connected with him'.
- To make a care plan for all children who are subject to care orders made by the court.

Following the case of Re C and others in 2000, the Family Division has provided guidance for social workers where there is a history of social work intervention which is accompanied by a failure of the family to co-operate:

1. Every social work file should have as a top document a running chronology of significant events.

2. Lack of parental co-operation must be seen as a reason to investigate in greater depth, not to close a file.
3. Referrals by professionals, e.g. teachers and health visitors, should be given great weight and investigated thoroughly.
4. Line managers should never make a decision to take no action without having full knowledge of the file and consulting with professionals who know the family.
5. Children who were part of a sibling group should not be considered in isolation but in the context of the family history.
6. To avoid drift, work with families had to be time limited so that an effective timetable could be laid down within which changes need to be achieved.

9.14 Role of the Guardian ad litem (Children's Guardian from 1.4.01) Introduction of CAFCASS

9.14.1 CAFCASS

Whilst the court role of the Guardian ad litem and Court Welfare Officer is to continue for the immediate future in almost identical terms, it is important to be aware of the changes which took place on 1st April 2001 and the expectations for the future.

The new Children and Family Court Advisory and Support Service (CAFCASS), created by the Criminal Justice and Court Services Act 2000 as a non-departmental public body, was established on 1st April 2001. The new service has one headquarters in London and 10 areas which mirror the new English government regions and Wales. Each 'area' is headed by an area manager.

The guardian ad litem panels and probation committees ceased on 1st April and both are replaced by CAFCASS, so far as family proceedings resources are concerned. The new title for the Guardian ad Litem is Children's Guardian. A welfare officer appointed to prepare a welfare report under the Children Act has a title change, to Children and Family reporter.

The new service therefore brings together the Family Court Welfare Service and the Guardian ad litem Panels. The practitioners involved in the transfer will carry out their existing functions and cases for the immediate future.

The statutory functions of the service are as follows:

(a) safeguard and promote the welfare of children,
(b) give advice to any court about any application made to it in such proceedings,
(c) make provision for the children to be represented in such proceedings,
(d) provide information, advice and other support for the children and their families,
(e) make provision for the performance of any functions conferred on its officers.

The service may authorise officers to conduct litigation in relation to any proceedings in any court and to exercise a right of audience. He may be cross-examined to the same extent as any witness but not merely because he is conducting litigation.

The integrated service intends to provide a comprehensive and flexible resource to the court and ultimately the skills of existing guardians and court welfare officers will be shared and developed within the service. As a new body, there will clearly be a developmental period to build up the joint teams and cultures to achieve a harmonised service.

9.14.2 Children's Guardian

Guardians are social workers or probation officers who have experience of working with children. They are appointed by the court to look after individual children's needs during care proceedings.

A guardian must be considered and appointed as soon as practicable in any relevant proceedings. 'Relevant proceedings' are any cases involving a care order, supervision order or emergency protection order. The appointment must be made unless the justices' clerk or court considered that it is not necessary to safeguard the interests of the child e.g. child is a competent 16 year old and a supervision order does not seek to change the status quo in any way.

This decision to appoint can be taken at any point during the proceedings even though there is no application for such an appointment – issues of concern may arise subsequently e.g. court considers that a full care order would be more appropriate than a supervision order.

Essentially the guardian is under a duty to safeguard the interests of the child. The rules set out the following specific duties:

- Attend directions appointments and hearings and advise the clerk or court on the following:

  - ➢ Level of child's understanding of the court process including submission to medical examinations and assessments.
  - ➢ Wishes of child regarding the proceedings, including whether he wishes to attend.
  - ➢ Appropriate court and timing of case.
  - ➢ Options available and the respective suitability of each and what order should finally be made.
  - ➢ Any other matter on which the court or clerk seeks his advice.

- Appoint a solicitor to represent the child unless already appointed and instruct him, unless the child is mature enough to instruct a solicitor directly. The guardian therefore normally sits next to the child's solicitor in court. Separate representation is possible if guardian and mature child have different views.
- Notify any party who the guardian believes should be joined as a party e.g. grandparent, of their right to apply.
- Serve and accept service of documents on behalf of the child.
- Access local authority records.
- Contact or interview such persons as he thinks appropriate or as the court directs.
- Obtain any necessary professional assistance.
- At least 7 days before the hearing file a written report advising on the interests of the child

The guardian's independence must be ensured when the local manager allocates the guardian to a particular case and equally it is important that the court does not compromise the independence by placing any restriction on carrying out the duties e.g. by asking that a distraught sibling is not interviewed. The role ceases at the close of the proceedings.

9.15 Role of legal representatives in family proceedings

In proceedings involving a care order, supervision order or emergency protection order a solicitor must be appointed by the guardian, or if no guardian is appointed, then a solicitor may be appointed by the court. Instructions are given by the guardian unless the child is instructing directly or wishes to give instructions which conflict with the guardian e.g. child of 15 is likely to have sufficient understanding to instruct directly if he so wishes. The guardian will continue to proceed with the other duties if the child is instructing directly.

The proceedings are informal and the various advocates will usually sit next to their client rather than in front of them. The reality is that the legal representatives also play an active role in striving to reach agreement between the parties.

9.16 Fostering and adoption procedures

9.16.1 Fostering

Fostering arrangements are made directly between the foster parent(s) and the fostering agency or local authority and the court plays no part in making any orders of any description to cover this relationship. The reality is that a large proportion of children placed in local authority care will be placed with foster parents either on a short term or long term basis and family panel magistrates should therefore have some awareness of the role.

Following an application the prospective foster parent(s) receive visits from a Fostering and Adoption officer who will prepare a report. This is usually considered by a Fostering Panel or possibly a local authority director who is responsible for selection, registration, matching and de-registration if necessary. Courses and training are offered to demonstrate and practice the skills involved in fostering. Financial allowances are made e.g. £88.80p per week for a child aged 11-12, in March 2000. Additionally there are fee-paid fostering schemes which essentially create a self-employed full-time job e.g. to make written assessments on children in care; to look after children who are on remand for criminal offences and a weekly wage is paid in respect of each child involved. The local authority must have agreed processes for approval, de-registration and support which will involve an assigned social worker.

The foster parent does not acquire parental rights and is simply given day-to-day care and control at the local authority's discretion.

9.16.2 Adoption

An adoption order gives parental responsibility for the child to the adopter(s) and the original parents usually cease to have any responsibilities, including any requirement to maintain the child. The child becomes part of the adoptive family and any legal relationship with the natural parents is severed. The child receives a new birth certificate and is described as a child of the adoptive parent(s).

(i) Applicants.

An application may not be made by more than one person unless they are a married couple (+ age/domicile requirements). An individual applicant must be aged over 21. The applicant(s) may choose to keep their identity confidential and they may apply for a serial number to be assigned.

(ii) Residence of the child with the applicants.

Where the applicant is a parent, step-parent or relative of the child, or he is placed by an adoption agency, the child must be at least 19 weeks old at the time of the order and he must have lived with them for the previous 13 weeks. Basically a newborn baby adoption can take place when the baby is 5 months old.

In any other case e.g. adoption follows a fostering arrangement with the local authority, the child must be at least 12 months old and have lived with the applicants for the previous 12 months.

(iii) Application to the court.

Straightforward applications are dealt with increasingly by the magistrates' court and transferred to the county court if complications arise. A detailed application must be completed and the local authority must be given 3 months notice to investigate suitability and circumstances, unless the child is placed by an adoption agency.

(iv) Parental consent.

The legitimate parents must consent to the order or the court must dispense with consent on one of the following grounds:

- Cannot be found or is incapable of giving agreement.
- Is withholding his consent unreasonably.
- Has persistently failed without reasonable excuse to discharge the parental duties in relation to the child.
- Has persistently ill-treated the child.
- Has seriously ill-treated the child and rehabilitation within the household is unlikely.

Convention case law has held that natural parents must be properly involved in the decision making process and that full account must be taken of their views (McMichael v. UK 1995). The European Court has held that an adoption placement amounted to a breach of the Convention because the child was placed without the knowledge or consent of his father (Keegan v. Ireland). This will depend upon the relationship and level of contact between natural father and child and adoptive father and child (Soderback v. Sweden 1999).

(v) Preparations for the hearing.

When the child is not placed by an adoption agency or is not the child of one of the applicants, there must be a medical report made within 3 months prior to the application on the health of the child and each applicant.

Once the application is received, notification will be given to the local authority if necessary and to all interested parties including the parents and any person making maintenance payments.

When the order is agreed by both parents, a reporting officer from the local authority's adoption panel will make enquiries to ensure that the consent is freely given and understood and the consent will then be obtained in writing.

When the order is not agreed or if the welfare of the child so requires, the court will appoint a guardian to investigate the case. The guardian will consider any report submitted by the local authority or adoption agency, any requests to dispense with consent and any other matters which appear to be relevant. The guardian will advise whether the child should attend and will submit a report for the assistance of the court in determining whether or not to make the order. The report is confidential to the court, but parties must be informed if there are any adverse comments and allowed to address the court on the relevant points.

(vi) The hearing.

The court must have regard to all circumstances of the case, first consideration being to safeguard and promote the welfare of the child throughout his childhood. The court must so far as practicable ascertain the wishes and feelings of the child and give due consideration having regard to his age and understanding. The child will attend together with the applicant(s) unless it appears to the court that there are special considerations rendering attendance unnecessary. One spouse need not attend if the applicants are a married couple provided that he has made a declaration before a magistrate or other specified person. Any person on whom notice has been served may attend court e.g. person liable to make maintenance payments.

The court may make a 'section 8' order if considered appropriate e.g. make a residence order instead of an adoption order.

On making an adoption order, the court may attach terms or conditions e.g. that the child should be brought up as a Muslim, that he should have contact with a natural parent and/or sibling.

In normal circumstances it is desirable that there should be a complete break on the making of an adoption order, but each case must be considered on its facts. The court should not, except in the most exceptional circumstances, impose a term or condition regarding contact with members of the child's natural family unless the adopting parent agrees. The question of contact should not be re-opened after the adoption unless there is some fundamental change in circumstances.

An interim order may be made for up to 2 years as a probationary period and the order can include terms. In exceptional circumstances the court may make a supervision or care order instead.

(vii) Freeing for adoption.

An adoption agency may apply for a child to be freed for adoption either with the consent of the parent or after their consent has been dispensed with. Parental responsibility is transferred at this stage to the adoption agency rather than the prospective adopters. The issue of parental responsibility is therefore resolved and any subsequent adoption can be planned with certainty, without any delay when the time comes for any adoption to go ahead and without any need for a reporting officer to be appointed.

A parent may make a declaration that he does not wish to be involved in any further question regarding the child's adoption. In the absence of such a declaration, the parent must be informed after 12 months if the child has not been placed for adoption. In this event, the parent may apply for the freeing order to be revoked.

(viii) Other aspects of adoption.

Recent guidance has been given by Mrs Justice Bracewell that if a local authority consider the options for a care plan are either rehabilitation with the family, or adoption outside the family, the authority should pursue its enquiries on a twin-track approach. Traditionally, local authorities have tended to exhaust the possibility of rehabilitation before beginning to address permanency outside the family. This has caused lengthy delays. The court should be proactive at early direction hearings to enquire whether twin-track planning is suitable and then give appropriate directions (Re D and K (Minors) (Care plan:Twin-track planning) 1999).

Adoption proceedings are highly confidential. When the child is 18 he may apply to the Registrar-General for access to the court records.

POWERS OF THE FAMILY COURT IN PUBLIC LAW/PRIVATE LAW

9.17 The No Order principle and 'agreed orders'

'Where a court is considering whether or not to make one or more orders ...it shall not make the order or any of the orders unless it considers that doing so would be better for the child than making no order at all' (s.1(5) CA 1989).

This is part of the general principle that wherever possible the courts should not interfere with the arrangements made by parents in respect of their children unless it is necessary in the interests of the children to do so. Sometimes the court process may be necessary to bring matters to a head, but workable agreements are frequently made 'on the day' with the assistance of solicitors, court welfare officers and the court itself. The investment is likely to be greater if the parties have agreed their own arrangements rather than having them imposed by the court on the inevitable basis of leaning more towards one party than the other.

Very often the bench will read through the court papers only to hear that 'they've agreed'. This is not the end of the matter for the court and certainly should never be seen as a rubber stamp of 'no order' or an 'agreed order.' The court has to consider that balance of whether to make no order at all or to make an agreed order, and in both cases to make sure that the arrangements in place are practical, understood and in the best interests of the child.

Whilst flexibility is preferred, it is important to recognise that the parties have come to court because there are particular difficulties in operating a flexible arrangement, often because of stalemates in communication between the parties. This can create enormous tension in making detailed arrangements for picking up children, dropping them off and deciding upon what is acceptable for them to do during contact. Even in the most functional of families this is difficult enough – add in, temperamental children, anxious parents and changes in plan because of a wet afternoon.

What have the problems been? The court needs to know, either through the court welfare officer or the solicitors. There is little point in building up emotions to a court hearing and then falling into difficulties and having to start the process all over again. The problems need to be sensibly resolved – today if possible.

Late pick ups? – suggest informally or build into the agreement that telephone calls really must be made. Venues? – suggest that ideas are shared the night before or at pick-up and some confirmation is given about where they are going. Illness? – again telephone calls perhaps to postpone though rather than to cancel.

Sometimes an order will be necessary e.g. parental responsibility (and all that goes with it) may only be given to a grandmother if there is an actual residence order. To make 'no order' in such a case would deprive grandmother of the 'bag of rights' such as consent to medical treatment.

An order must still be drawn up if the final decision is 'no order.'

9.18 Child Assessment Orders and Emergency Protection Orders (EPO)

A Child Assessment Order is available to cover the situation where the court is satisfied that the applicant has reasonable cause to suspect that the child may be at risk of significant harm and his parents refuse to co-operate with the assessment process. The application must be made at a full hearing in which the parties are able to participate. The court may allow up to 7 days for the assessment to be made and the parent must produce the child to the person named e.g. paediatric expert at local hospital. In fact such orders are seldom sought.

When there are serious concerns and there is a need to either remove or detain a child, the relevant order is the Emergency Protection Order (EPO). This may be an *ex parte* application i.e. made without notice to the parents.

Article 6 gives the right to a fair hearing and the concept normally involves all parties being present. However the parents' rights must be balanced with the need to protect the child by holding an emergency *ex parte* hearing. A breach is unlikely provided that a full inter parties hearing follows shortly afterwards. Under Article 6 reasons must be given.

Article 8 gives the right to respect for private and family life. An *ex parte* application to remove a child certainly involves interference with family life. It is a qualified right and the 3 questions must be asked, principally, 'Is this action proportionate to the facts heard?'

9.18.1 What is an EPO?

- It authorises the removal of the child at any time to accommodation provided by the applicant e.g. to foster parents or prevents removal e.g. from hospital.
- Maximum period of 8 days + one extension of up to 7 days.

- No discharge application before expiry of 72 hours.

- Applicant acquires parental responsibility.

- Directions may be given e.g. contact, medical assessment. The applicant must allow the child to have reasonable contact with parents/any other person with parental responsibility/person living with at the time/ contact order person and anyone acting on their behalf.

- The applicant has a duty to return the child to his parent if it appears that it is safe for the child to be returned e.g. immediately after a satisfactory medical examination has taken place.

9.18.2 Exclusion provisions in an EPO

This provision was made by the Family Law Act 1996 and principally allows the court to exclude suspected abusers from the child's home and enable the child to remain, rather than being removed and increasing the child's distress. The exclusion requirement may be added to the EPO in the following circumstances:

Reasonable cause to believe that if a 'relevant person' e.g. mother's partner is excluded then,

- The child would not be likely to suffer from significant harm, <u>or</u>
- The inquiries would cease to be frustrated and access to the child would be allowed

<u>and</u>

- Another person living in the house is able and willing to give the child the reasonable care and consents to the exclusion requirement e.g. mother, grandmother.

The exclusion requirement may require the person to leave the home; to prohibit his entering the home and a provision excluding him from a defined area around the home. The court may attach a power of arrest for all or part of the order in respect of the exclusion requirement(s). The exclusion requirement will cease to have effect after 24 hours of the applicant removing the child to another address.

A non-molestation order may also be made if an exclusion requirement is included in the Emergency Protection Order.

9.18.3 Criteria

A court may make an EPO if it is satisfied that on the application of a local authority or 'any person' that:

There is reasonable cause to believe that the child is likely to suffer significant harm if he is not moved to accommodation provided by the applicant e.g. to foster parents, or if does not remain in the place where he is e.g. in hospital.

There is also provision for making an EPO if the local authority or NSPCC have reasonable cause to suspect that a child is suffering or likely to suffer significant harm and their enquiries are being frustrated because access to the child is being refused.

9.19/9.20 Care Orders and Supervision Orders

The two orders are considered together because the criteria are the same and the court may grant either order on any application. Very often the court will have to decide which order is the more appropriate between the two.

9.19.1 What is a Care Order?

- The child is placed in the care of his local authority until his 18th birthday unless the order is discharged earlier.
- The local authority obtains parental responsibility. Parents however do not lose their parental responsibility but the local authority may determine the extent as necessary in order to safeguard or promote the child's welfare. Most dramatically the local authority may decide where the child is to live and this may involve removing the child from living with his parents at any time during the order.
- The normal presumption of enabling a child to live with his parents becomes a mere power to do so. Placement with parents will obviously be the first option for consideration and review.
- The local authority acquire duties towards the child, principally to safeguard the welfare of the child and more specific duties e.g. to provide accommodation and maintenance.
- The order discharges all existing private orders e.g. residence, contact.
- There is a presumption that the child will have reasonable contact with parent/guardian/person who looked after child under residence order. However the court may make a specific contact order either at the time or subsequently (see below).

- There is no power to attach any conditions e.g. to place child with parents, for guardian to continue to be involved, for a review in 6 months time. The local authority must have full discretion once the order is made.

- It places restrictions on change of name and removal from jurisdiction.

Article 8, the qualified right to respect for private and family life will certainly engage when making a care order. Removal of a child from his family is a serious interference with family life. The '3 questions' which come with qualified rights must be considered and dealt with in the reasons. Is the restriction on family life by making an order –

(i) Legal, clear and accessible? A care order may be made under the Children Act.
(ii) Does it pursue a legitimate aim? e.g. to protect the health and morals of the child.
(iii) Is it proportionate? Would a lower level of interference deal with the concerns of the particular case e.g. by a supervision order instead.

9.19.2 What is a Supervision Order?

- Child is placed under the supervision of his local authority or of a probation officer for a maximum period of 12 months (may subsequently be extended up to 3 years).

- It does not grant parental responsibility to the supervisor.

- The supervisor must 'advise, assist and befriend' the child and take steps as reasonably necessary to give effect to the order and consider variation/discharge. Note that there is no supervision of the parent as such.

- Conditions may not be imposed other than a requirement to comply with the directions of the supervisor or requirements which have the consent of a responsible person.

- Requirements cannot be directly enforced. The option is to apply for a care order if serious concerns arise.

- A warrant may be issued authorising a constable to assist the supervisor to gain entry into the child's home.

9.19.3 Criteria for care and supervision orders ('must know' information!)

The application may be made by the local authority or the NSPCC. The court must be satisfied that:

(a) The child concerned is suffering or is likely to suffer <u>significant harm</u>; and
(b) The harm or likelihood of harm is attributable to –

- **The care given to the child, or likely to be given to him if the order were not made, not being what it would be <u>reasonable to expect a parent to give</u> him; or**
- **The child's being beyond parental control.**
  (s.31(2) Children Act 1989).

In a recent case the judge found that there were non-accidental injuries which amounted to significant harm, but was unable to determine whether the injuries were caused whilst in the care of mother, against whom the application was made, or the child minder, and he dismissed the application. It was decided by the Court of Appeal that it was not necessary to require the harm to be proved due to a failure of care by one or more identified individuals before the court can make an order. It is sufficient that the harm was attributable to an absence of proper care to the objective standard laid down (Lancashire County Council v. A 1999).

9.19.4 Assessing the evidence

There are a few technicalities in processing the above criteria, particularly in terms of definitions. It is worth repeating the concept of significant harm.

'Significant harm' = ill-treatment (includes psychological and sexual abuse), or impairment of health (physical and mental), or developmental impairment (includes physical, intellectual, emotional, social or behavioural development).

The harm, or likelihood of harm must be caused by the care given to the child, or likely to be given to him if the order were not made, 'not being what it would be reasonable to expect a parent to give him' <u>or</u> by the child being beyond the parent's control (s.31(2) CA 1985). What is reasonable care? This will vary with the age of the child e.g. regular feeds and changes of nappy for a baby, through to providing meals, clothes and a reasonable curfew for a young teenager. The consistent feature at all ages for 'reasonable care' must be some demonstration of care and affection.

The standard required is that of <u>a</u> reasonable parent with <u>this</u> particular child. The characteristics and needs of the child should therefore be considered carefully. The test is a 'reasonable' parent rather than a 'superhuman paragon!'

When the decision is based on a likelihood of harm in the future it is obviously far more difficult. The court does not have a crystal ball, but must never be tempted to act on mere suspicions and be tempted to 'think safety' before the criteria are even satisfied. The danger is to feel doubtful about the evidence and satisfy this by making a supervision order rather than a care order. Both orders require the threshold criteria to be properly satisfied first.

What is the basis of the belief? There must be an element of 'gravity' to any feared harm in the future. The possibility must be 'one that cannot sensibly be ignored having regard to the nature and gravity of the feared harm in the particular case.'

The first stage of the proceedings is to determine whether or not the 'significant harm' test is satisfied. If so, the court then moves on to consider whether an order is required. The standard of proof is that of the balance of probability. There is no different standard in cases involving sexual abuse, but the more serious the allegation the more cogent is the evidence required (In Re H (minors) (Sexual Abuse: Standard of Proof) 1996).

The local authority must produce to the court a care plan which sets out what is intended to happen to the child – where he will live and who he will have contact with etc. The court cannot direct a particular type of placement or direct that particular services be provided for the child. The court must therefore scrutinise the care plan carefully and if it does not agree then it may make a contact order (see (iv)) in addition to the care order or may even refuse to make a care order at all.

9.19.5 Parental contact with children in care

This issue may well arise during the course of an application for care order. Alternatively it may be the cause of a later application if the local authority feel that it is necessary to refuse or terminate contact arrangements. The application may be made by the local authority, the child or parent/guardian/person looking after the child under a residence order or any other person with leave.

The court may authorise the authority to refuse contact; make a contact order possibly with conditions or make no order. The long-term plans of the local authority will of course be relevant and if adoption is the aim there is less likelihood that contact will be in the child's best interests than if the intention is to re-integrate the child with the parent. However it must be stressed that this is by no means a clear-cut case. Contact does successfully take place within adoption and long-term fostering. Considerations may include whether this particular child will feel a sense of loss which contact may reduce; whether a seal of approval by his mother will enable him to commit to another family; whether he will lose his personal identity without some family connection.

One consideration may be to make the contact for a limited period with another hearing fixed to review the progress of arrangements and make a long-term decision. The contact order can be for whatever period the court feels appropriate and with whatever conditions e.g. 14 days to meet with the child under supervision to say farewells; 2 hours weekly contact to be arranged by the local authority during the period of the care order.

Interestingly, the local authority effectively retain discretion to re-commence contact even if the court make an order for 'no contact.'

Convention case law has emphasised that in principle a parent has the right of access to their child unless there are serious concerns (W v. UK 1987). Additionally any restrictions must be justified e.g. local authority placing children so far away that access is impractical would engage the right, but the co-operation of parents and efforts made by the authority will be relevant to any breach proceedings (Olsson v. Sweden 1988, Riemme v. Sweden 1992).

9.19.6 Care Order/Supervision Order – decision checklist

Before either order is made it is important to go through a structured process in order to cover all the legal requirements.

1. What are the agreed facts?
2. What are the disputed facts? What are the findings on those facts?
3. To what extent were the parties and witnesses believed or disbelieved?
4. Information relied upon. Authorities cited.
5. Is the threshold criteria satisfied? i.e. significant harm/reasonable parent test.

<u>If so</u>

6. Welfare checklist – judgement or findings of fact under each head.
7. Is it better for the child to make an order or is 'no order' appropriate?
8. Consider options and suitability of each order – including contact.
9. Decision.

9.19.7 Discharge of Care and Supervision orders

Both care orders and supervision orders may be discharged prior to the child's 18th birthday. A care order will cease automatically if an adoption order or residence order is made. The orders may also be discharged on the application of the person with parental responsibility, the child or the local authority. The court must consider the welfare checklist in making the decision. It is possible to discharge a care order but substitute it by a supervision order.

9.19.8 Interim Supervision and Care Orders

The reality is that very few cases can be resolved at the first hearing. More time is needed for information to be gathered and in the meantime the court must ensure that the child is appropriately cared for. To this end the court may make interim orders until all the relevant material is before the court to make a final decision.

The power to make an interim order arises where the proceedings are adjourned on an application for a care or supervision order or if the court requests the local authority to investigate the child's circumstances on applications for other orders. The court must be satisfied that there are *'reasonable grounds for believing'* that the criteria are met. Obviously it may not be possible to prove that the child is definitely suffering serious harm or 'is likely to' at this point in the proceedings.

The initial order may last for up to 8 weeks and thereafter may be extended for up to 4 weeks at a time. Directions may be given in respect of medical or psychiatric examination or other assessment e.g. testing to determine whether or not children are HIV positive; that no medical or psychiatric examination shall take place. The court is obliged to draw up a timetable in the meantime and the interim order dates can often be tied into the various dates for actions to be taken.

The following matters were identified for consideration in all cases involving interim orders in the case of Hampshire County Council v. S (1993).

(a) The court should bear in mind that it will usually be required to establish no more than a holding position after weighing all relevant risks.

(b) The court must make sure that the final hearing takes place at the earliest possible date, by transferring laterally to another court if necessary.

(c) The court should rarely make findings as to disputed facts in an interim hearing.

(d) The greater the extent to which the interim order deviates from a previous order or status quo, the more acute is the need for an early hearing. The preferred course should be to leave the child where he is with a direction for safeguards and the earliest possible hearing date.

(e) When the court considers making an interim order which will lead to a substantial change in the child's position the court should consider permitting limited oral evidence to be heard and challenged by way of cross-examination. However the evidence must be limited to the issues which are essential at the interim stage.

(f) If possible, the court should have before it the written evidence of the guardian. If there are substantial issues between the parties the guardian should also be at court to give oral evidence and a party who opposes the guardian's recommendations should have the opportunity to question the guardian.

(g) The mandatory rules must be complied with e.g. to read all documents which have been filed before the hearing, findings of fact to be given and reasons.

(h) If the justices are delayed in the preparation of their written findings of fact or reasons they should adjourn the making of the order or giving of the decision until the following day or the earliest possible court date. One of the bench can be allocated to present the reasons and the orders of the court where necessary.

(i) When granting an interim order the justices should state their findings and reasons concisely, and summarise briefly the essential factual issues between the parties.

An exclusion requirement may be attached to an interim care order and this may carry a power of arrest in breach (see 9.18).

9.19.9 Care and Supervision orders at the instigation of the court

When the court is considering an application for a private order e.g. residence, the court may direct the local authority to investigate the circumstances of the child if concerns exist. An adjournment will normally be required and an interim order may be necessary whilst the report is compiled. In the meantime the local authority may apply for a care or supervision order. Alternatively they may report back to the court with information as to any advice or assistance which has been given together with reasons why an application has not been made for an order.

9.19.10 Education Supervision Order (ESO)

This order has no connection whatsoever with the threshold criteria. It is purely and simply about education.

An ESO may be made on the application of the local education authority if the court is satisfied that the child is of compulsory school age and is not being properly educated. 'Properly educated' means 'full-time education suitable to his age, ability, aptitude and any special educational needs he may have'. The supervisor's responsibility is to advise, assist and befriend and give directions to the child and his parents to ensure that he is properly educated. The initial order has effect for one year and may be extended thereafter for up to 3 years. A level 3 fine may be imposed for breach.

9.19.11 Secure Accommodation Order

This is an order which allows the local authority to place a child who is 'being looked after' by them into secure accommodation. The court must consider the following criteria:

- That he has a history of absconding and is likely to abscond from any other description of accommodation, and
- If he absconds, he is likely to suffer significant harm or
- If he is kept in any other description of accommodation he is likely to injure himself or other persons (s.25 CA 1989).

The maximum initial period of authorisation by the court is for 3 months but the order must be for no longer than necessary and reasons must be given as to the period selected. A guardian must be appointed unless there are exceptional circumstances. The court must be satisfied that there is no alternative option. There must be a clear record of the facts as found by the court and sworn evidence is required unless the matter proceeds by way of agreement.

The order clearly involves a restriction of liberty and Article 5 is therefore engaged. The Article does allow a restriction on liberty for the purpose of 'educational supervision'. In the case of Re K, 2000, the President of the Family Division confirmed that the section was not incompatible with the Human Rights Act. It was emphasised that 'educational supervision' embraced far more than simply classroom teaching and extended to any aspects of parental rights by the local authority and liberty could be restricted for this purpose under the Article.

9.21 Section 8 orders (private orders)

The expression 'section 8' order applies to the following and any order varying or discharging them:

(a) Residence order.
(b) Contact order.
(c) Prohibited steps order.
(d) Specific issues orders.

Each order is discussed in detail below, but the procedures are common to all 'section 8' orders and are considered first.

The important feature to remember is that an application may well be made for one order e.g. residence but the court may ultimately make a different order e.g. care order + contact order if this is in the best interests of the child.

9.21.1 Pre-hearing

The court must draw up a timetable with a view to determining the issue without delay and give directions to ensure that the timetable is adhered to. Many courts arrange for a court welfare officer or conciliation officer to attend the directions appointment and a family meeting is held at this stage to identify whether conciliation may be productive. If so, the case may be adjourned for further conciliation/mediation meetings or for agreed arrangements to be tried out. Alternatively the case will usually be timed and adjourned for a final hearing and welfare reports will be ordered.

Copies of written statements of the substance of the oral evidence and any relevant documents must be filed and served on the parties as directed prior to the hearing. So far as 'section 8' proceedings are concerned the rules state that no document other than as required must be served and no statement must be made other than as required without the leave of the court. This aims to prevent information being set down in writing which may only serve to inflame an already volatile situation. The emphasis must remain on the child's welfare and the role of the adults as carers rather than in their relationship with each other. If the matter does proceed to a contested hearing then the court will allow further evidence to be filed e.g. witness statements from child minder and general practitioner.

9.21.2 Court Welfare Officer's role (re-named as Children and Family Reporter from 1.4.01) and the welfare report.

See 9.14 for commentary on CAFCASS and the new management structure and title for Court Welfare Officers.

The court may call for a welfare report when considering 'any question with respect to a child'. The report may be in writing or oral as the court requires. Preparation will normally take 10 weeks after the papers have been received by the reporting officer, but there are local variations and each case should be considered individually in any event.

The report will deal with all matters on the welfare checklist and any specific matters raised by the court. CAFCASS is expected to encourage a tighter direction from the court as to what exactly the court is looking for, and where the priorities lie. Lengthy histories may be irrelevant in some cases, whilst the views of competent children may be particularly important.

The reporting officer will be able to see copies of all the statements and will see both parties preferably in their own homes and with and without the children present. If the children are old enough the officer will also see the children on their own. He may also contact the child's school, other relatives, any social workers who have been involved with the family, the family doctor, etc. The report is considerably longer and more detailed than a pre-sentence report and National Standards require a 'specific, reasoned recommendation where appropriate.'

Hearsay evidence is acceptable in the report but the court will attach to it whatever weight it thinks fit. It may be necessary to cross-examine the officer if for example it is said that he has not reported conversations accurately or if he has made a recommendation which the party wishes to challenge.

The report must be filed at least 14 days before the hearing or as directed and copies will be served on the parties and guardian if appointed. The court may order in exceptional circumstances that parts of the report should not be disclosed if satisfied that the information is reliable and that real harm to the child would ensue from disclosure. After the filing of the report the court or clerk may direct that the officer attends. This may be to enable questioning about reported conversations which are disputed or more usually to challenge the recommendation.

It is wrong for the court to reject the content of the report without hearing from the officer. When the court is contemplating rejecting the recommendation the officer should be given the opportunity to consider the justices' misgivings or anxieties. Similarly the court must be open about any aspects which they feel have not been fully explored or reported upon.

9.21.3 Conditions/Directions

The orders may contain directions about how they are to be carried into effect and impose conditions which must be complied with for specified periods or for the duration of the order.

9.21.4 Duration of 'section 8' orders

There is no provision for interim 'section 8' orders as such but the court may make orders of any duration e.g. 14 days whilst gathering information to make long-term orders or order until the next stage in the proceedings. In such circumstances the normal approach is to maintain the status quo unless there are strong reasons against this.

As a general rule 'section 8' orders will continue until discharged by the court or otherwise until the child is 16 unless there are exceptional circumstances when the order may extend to 18. Residence and contact orders will also cease to have effect if the parents live together for a continuous period of 6 months or if a care order is made.

9.21.5 Enforcement of 'section 8' orders

The person with the order may enforce it by proving that the order has been disobeyed and seeking punishment by way of a sum up to £50 for every day of default (up to £5,000) or committal to prison for up to 2 months or remedy of the default (s.63 Magistrates' Courts Act 1980).

Convention case law has placed public authorities (which includes the court) under an obligation to promote contact. In Hokkanen v. Finland 1996 the father had a contact order in his favour against the child's grandparents. They refused to comply. It was held that the local authority had not done enough to enforce his contact order and the non-enforcement of these rights was a breach of Article 8. This is authority for the court to take a robust stance to enforce the right of the applicant.

The court must try to discover why the order has not been complied with and endeavour to make a variation which is acceptable to both parents if possible – breach proceedings are to be regarded as a weapon of last resort.

An alternative provision enables the court to authorise an officer of the court or a constable to enter and search premises and take charge of the child and deliver him to the person who holds the court order. (s.34 Family Law Act 1986).

The orders may subsequently be varied or discharged.

9.21.6 Residence order

This is an order which settles who the child lives with. When the person is not a parent or guardian they will automatically acquire parental responsibility with the residence order e.g. grandmother leaves court with a residence order and the right to make decisions about day-to-day arrangements for the child. When the person is an unmarried father the court must specifically make a parental responsibility order alongside the residence order. The parental rights in such circumstances do not extend to giving consent to adoption. The court cannot add conditions as to specified addresses.

The usual order will be with a sole residence. However if there is a 'positive benefit', it may be made in favour of 2 or more persons who do not live together. The order may simply be for a joint/shared residence order or it may be split and specify the periods during which the child is to live in the different households e.g. to live with father from Friday until Sunday and with mother from Sunday until Friday.

There is no presumption of law that a child of any given age is better off with one parent or another and it is wrong to start with any proposition that little girls naturally go with their mothers (Re A (a minor)(residence order) 1998). The overriding factor is that the child's welfare is the paramount consideration.

9.21.7 Restrictions when a residence order is in force:

1. No change of surname and
2. No removal of the child from the United Kingdom for more than one month

without the written consent of every person with parental responsibility or with the leave of the court.

A local authority may not apply for a residence order nor have one made in its favour but a party may apply for a residence order to be made in respect of a child in care. If successful, the care order will be discharged.

9.22 Contact orders

The order requires the person with whom the child is living to allow the child to visit or stay with the named person or to have contact with them.

The order is usually for 'reasonable' contact but may be for 'defined' contact if there is no measure of agreement.

Contact may take various forms from weekend stays to mere telephone contact and correspondence. There is a wealth of case law which provides some basic guidelines as to contact.

Contact – basic guidelines:

1. Contact should not be refused between parent and child unless absolutely necessary in the child's best interest.
2. The child's right is to know both parents unless there are cogent reasons why this should be denied.
3. Wherever possible a child should get to know his estranged parent.
4. It is a normal assumption that a child will benefit from continued contact with a natural parent.
5. To deprive a parent of contact is to deprive a child of an important contribution to his emotional and material growing up.
6. The payment of maintenance cannot 'buy' a parent the right to contact.

Sometimes the implacable hostility of the mother towards the father means that the child might be at serious risk of major emotional harm if the mother is compelled to accept a degree of contact with the father against her will (Re D (A Minor) (Contact: Mother's Hostility) 1993). This must be distinguished from the almost inevitable upsets which will arise when parents have separated and they have found it necessary to come to court for an order. In this situation the court must look to the longer term. The child's wishes will have more significance depending upon their age, e.g. boys of 12 and 9 did not want to have contact with transsexual father and no contact was ordered.

It is not a ground for denying contact that the child is very young and has no knowledge of his biological father. It is important that a child should be able to gently assimilate the truth about his parentage and it may be appropriate to make an order for indirect contact.

Where a parent is applying for contact with a child of mixed race, the court should have regard to the child's origins and deal with any concerns about the child's confusion about racial identity.

Some limitations may be reasonable, particularly if the court is not allowing physical contact e.g. father is allowed to 'telephone child no more than once per week', otherwise nominal contact orders can become more intrusive than physical contact arrangements.

The court cannot order a mother to read out the contents of letters to the child. She is allowed to censor if she wishes. Similarly the court cannot order a mother to send progress reports to the father – this is going beyond a contact order.

Access/Contact centres are now available in most localities and can provide a neutral meeting place with basic children's facilities available. The centres are also useful for re-introducing parents into a child's life in an informal setting where other children and experienced support staff are available to help the process for all concerned. Such orders will usually be defined contact orders e.g. 'from 2pm to 3pm each Saturday at the contact centre at ...'

The existence of a blood tie is highly significant. The long term must be considered as children are likely to seek their natural parent in any event. On the other hand relationships with father figures should not be endorsed into court orders unless the court really feels that the welfare of the child requires ongoing contact. This may be affected by the existence of a new father figure and the effect of the new family dynamics.

Regular staying contact may be dealt with by either a contact order or alternatively a 'joint' residence order. The major difference is that the residence order would bring parental responsibility with it but a contact order does not.

An order for 'no contact' falls within the definition of a contact order.

The European Court has repeatedly stated that the mutual enjoyment of parent and child of each other's company constitutes a fundamental element of family life and a parent normally has a right of access to his child. A balancing exercise between parent and child must be undertaken but as a qualified right the child's interests may take precedence if there are concerns about health/morals and the child's 'rights and freedoms'.

9.23 Prohibited steps orders

The order directs that a specific aspect of parental responsibility cannot be exercised without the consent of the court e.g. prohibiting a parent from removing the child from the jurisdiction, prohibiting a parent from arranging or permitting the child to be circumcised without the permission of the High Court. It can only relate to an action which is within the power of a parent and does not bind the child or give the court control over the decisions which the child is entitled to take for himself.

The order cannot be used basically as an ejection order by prohibiting a father from entering the home as this becomes a back door method of making a residence order and/or contact order in favour of the other party. When the court wishes to prevent contact it should make a 'no contact' order rather than a prohibited steps order.

The order cannot be made in respect of a child who is subject to a care order. Few prohibited steps orders are made.

9.24 Specific issue orders

The order enables a person (anyone, including the child with leave) to bring a particular question relating to the exercise of parental responsibility to be determined by the court. Specific issues include which school the child should attend, changing the child's surname, consent to medical treatment, approval for blood transfusion where the parents are Jehovah's witnesses. The local authority may also apply for instance for an order for sterilisation and/or abortion, in relation to a child in care. Such matters should be considered for transfer to the High Court including the local authority seeking approval for blood transfusion to a child whose parents were Jehovah's witnesses.

'All options' are open to the court on any application.

Examples of 'section 8' applications

1. Facts:
Father applies for residence order. He has not seen the children for the 3 months since he left the family home.
Mother applies for residence order to keep the children with her.
Outcome:
Case adjourned for 3 months for the preparation of welfare reports.
In the interim a residence order is made to mother in order to maintain the status quo and a reasonable contact order is made with father in order to reinstate him into the children's lives.

2. Facts:
Mother applies for a specific issues order to return the child and a prohibited steps order to prevent further removal as father has snatched the child after school.
Outcome:
The court grant a residence order which carries a condition against removal of the child by father and also make a 'no contact' order in respect of the father. The substantive orders to age16 cover all that is required in the child's interests.

3. Facts:
Grandmother is concerned about care given to grandchild and seeks a residence order for the child to live with her.
Outcome:
The court has serious concerns and adjourns the case for the local authority to make investigations and in the meantime makes an interim care order.

9.25 Parties to the proceedings

9.25.1 Care proceedings.

Application may be made by the local authority or 'an authorised person', currently only the NSPCC.

The respondents must be:

- Every person whom the applicant believes to have parental responsibility at the time of the application or prior to a care order i.e. married parents, person with a residence order, unmarried father with a parental responsibility order.
- The child.
- Any other person must apply for leave to be joined.

In care proceedings a father should receive notice of the proceedings and he may then apply to be joined as a party. The onus on any other type of person is to show that there is some justifiable reason why he should be joined. In the case of a father, he should be permitted to join the proceeding unless there is some justifiable reason for not joining him as a party (Re K (care proceedings: joinder of father 1999)).

9.25.2 Residence/Contact proceedings.

Application may be made as of right by the parent/guardian/person with a residence order + some other categories defined in the rules.
Any other person, including the child must apply for leave. A child's application for leave to apply must be made in the High Court.

The respondents are as for care proceedings except the child is not a respondent.

9.25.3 Factors to take into consideration in granting leave.

- Nature of the proposed application.
- Applicant's connection with the child.
- Any risk of the application disrupting the child's life to such an extent that he would be harmed by it.

- If the child is looked after by the local authority – the plan for the future and the wishes and feelings of the child's parents.
- The likely outcome of the hearing if leave is granted.
- If the applicant is the child then the application should be transferred to the High Court.

9.26 Cases between spouses

Private orders regarding children – residence (9.21), contact (9.22), prohibited steps (9.23), specific issue (9.24).
Maintenance provision (9.27).
Occupation orders (9.28).
Non-molestation orders (9.28).

9.27 Maintenance

Maintenance assessment in the magistrates' court is now a very small part of the day-to-day work for the following reasons:

1. The implementation of the Child Support Act in 1993 which basically transferred the assessment of child maintenance to the Child Support Agency except in the case of agreed orders payable to a carer who is not in receipt of state benefits.
2. Change in culture in that more women are now financially independent of their partners.
3. Divorce may proceed after just one year of marriage and assets can be divided relatively quickly.

The court business is largely concerned with the approval of agreed orders, dealing with variations of the 'old' orders, enforcement and making a handful of new matrimonial orders. The latter is excluded as its complexity and length cannot be justified given the very small number of cases. The clerk's advice on the day in the particular scenario is essential as grounds must be proved and statutory assessment criteria and appropriate formula must be applied.

9.27.1 Agreed orders

's.6 order' Domestic Proceedings and Magistrates' Courts Act 1978 (DPMCA 1978)

Either party may apply for the order – payer or payee. The agreement may include periodical payments and unlimited lump sums to the spouse and/or children of the family. The court must be satisfied that there is genuine agreement and that 'there is no reason to think it would contrary to the interests of justice to make the order.'

The court must feel that the order makes a proper contribution to the needs of the children. It is helpful to have the DSS rates available for children as a starting point e.g. March 2001 job-seekers allowance rate for one dependent child up to the age of 11 is £30.20; £15.95 for a 2nd child. When both parties have income then clearly the starting point must be divided between the two of them – how does the balance fall? Clearly this is merely a subsistence level figure and the family may well be able to support a higher standard of living which should be maintained so far as possible.

When the respondent does not attend he must supply written consent and details of his financial resources.

The court may grant or refuse the application and/or suggest an alternative for agreement. The latter course should be approached with caution. There is a far greater commitment to agreed orders and if one of the parties is not happy with the court's suggestions they can simply decline and the case is discharged without order. The alternative then is to apply for a matrimonial maintenance order.

The order may begin from the date of the application i.e. backdate from the hearing. It will cease on the death of either party; a payee-spouse's remarriage; children attaining age of 17 (birthday after compulsory school age limit) unless the welfare of the child requires further extension.

's.7 order' (DPMCA 1978)

Very rare. This arises when the parties have been living apart for at least 3 months and periodical payments have been made to the spouse and/or child. An application may be made for an order which does not exceed the aggregate amount paid in the 3 months e.g. £100 per month paid – order for £80 per month.

The court may grant or refuse and treat the application as a domestic maintenance application and give full consideration to each party's means and the statutory criteria.

9.27.2 Variation/revival/suspension/revocation

Existing orders may be varied, revived, suspended and revoked. The court must so far as it appears just to do so, give effect to any agreement which has been reached between the parties and all the circumstances of the case, first consideration being given to the welfare of any child under 18. The circumstances to be considered include any change in any of the original matters before the court and a list of statutory considerations which will be supplied by the clerk. However, the law does not actually require a change of circumstances as such. There will always be the over-optimistic agreed order and the orders which are made solely on the complainant's evidence which are better reduced to a realistic level than not paid at all.

It may be appropriate to reduce an order to a purely nominal order such as 5p per year simply to keep the order alive if circumstances should change e.g. payer wins the lottery. It is absolutely essential to explain why nominal orders are made. They are not about the court making a derisory and insulting order which is possibly the perception of the payee. They are about saying that there is no finance to support an order but the court is keen to leave the door open and make it clear that the legal basis of the order remains.

The variation may be varied from a future date e.g. 1st July when son ceases full-time education and begins work. An order in respect of a child may be revived e.g. when child begins full-time further education after a period of working.

Suspension may be relevant for instance if a child is going to live with a spouse for a 6 month trial period. It is easier for all concerned if the order is suspended rather than revoked. Similarly suspension may be agreed if a party has temporary financial difficulties such as inability to work for a fixed period of time.

Many applications to vary will also contain a request to remit arrears which have accrued in the meantime and the court will also effectively be dealing with an enforcement situation at the same time.

> Example:
>
> Application to reduce order to a nominal amount as the payer is unable to continue in full-time employment due to disability and to remit all arrears which have accrued since disability began on .....(3 months ago). Child Support Agency confirm that they do not wish to intervene and make an assessment.
>
> Outcome – order reduced to 5p per annum; previous 3 months arrears remitted but balance of arrears for the previous 3 months payable at £4 per week.

9.27.3 Maintenance enforcement

A summons or warrant may be granted to enforce maintenance arrears. The means enquiry and enforcement options are the same as for fines except that there is no facility for deduction of benefits (see chapter 12). The similarity extends to the fact that the matter may appear before a public crime court. The court may determine that the proceedings should be treated as family proceedings so that there is some privacy for the benefit of the defaulter and the payee.

As with a fine defaulter the court should explore at the outset why payments have not been made. If the answer is that the payer has suffered a substantial reduction in income it is more appropriate to advise him to apply for a variation of the order along with an application to remit arrears. A date should preferably be arranged for the variation hearing before he leaves the court so that the arrears can be adjourned to a fixed date for determination. Remission cannot take place without notification to the payee unless it is unnecessary or impracticable e.g. address is unknown or order is payable to DSS. This is to allow an opportunity for written or verbal representations to be made.

The starting point for remission of arrears is that arrears which are more than 12 months old should not normally be enforced, unless there are special circumstances. This may arise for instance if a payee has persistently sought to enforce but the payer has prevaricated with the court and deliberately avoided execution of the warrant and does have the means to pay. Reasons must be given if stale arrears are to be enforced, based upon evidence e.g. that defaulter was working at particular times and was able to pay, or that he was not working when work was available to him (R v. Cardiff Magistrates ep Czech 1999).

If the court is satisfied that the defaulter has either wilfully refused to pay or culpably neglected to pay and an attachment of earning order is inappropriate then the court may order a committal to prison and suspend if appropriate. Referral to the duty solicitor should be made before making a committal order.

> The periods are 7 days – up to £200; 14 days - £201 to £500; 28 days - £501 to £1000 with a maximum of 6 weeks for amounts over £1,000.

When a suspended committal falls to be activated a defaulter is sent an '8 day notice' which invites him to give written reasons why the order should not be put into effect. When a response is given the issue becomes a discretion for the court. The implications of a custodial sentence upon any future relationship with any children involved is possibly a factor to consider along with the fact that the arrears are not wiped out by serving the period in default. Such arrears are likely however to be remitted in subsequent proceedings.

9.28 Domestic violence/ personal protection/exclusion from home.

- 1 woman in 4 experiences domestic violence at some stage in her life and it is estimated that between 1 in 8 and 1 in 10 have experienced domestic violence in the past year (British Crime Survey, 1998).
- Every week 2 women are killed by their current or former partners (Homicide Statistics, 1998).
- Domestic violence includes violence by women on men and is likely to be grossly unreported.

This jurisdiction falls under the Family Law Act 1996. It is particularly important to recognise that the High Court and county court have jurisdiction in the same matters and transfers are possible whenever a case is complex or may be dealt with more conveniently in another court. Under this Act it is clear that the family court must not deal with any applications which involve disputes as to any legal rights in property unless it is unnecessary to resolve the particular application.

9.28.1 Non-molestation orders

- What is molestation?

There is no definition in the Act. Previous legislation referred to threats and violence, but case law states that 'molestation may take place without the threat or use of violence and still be serious and inimical to mental and physical health.' The order therefore contains a prohibition on behaviour which is wider than threats and acts of violence e.g. serious pestering and harassment.

- Who may apply?

'Associated persons' = spouses, divorced couples, cohabitants and former cohabitants, a wide range of relatives, 3rd party representatives, children under 16 with the leave of the High Court and the court of its own motion when dealing with an application in family proceedings.

- Criteria for grant

The court shall have regard to all the circumstances including the need to secure the health, safety and well-being of the applicant and any relevant child (as defined, but basically any child who is reasonably expected to live with either party).

- Content of the order

To prohibit the respondent from molesting a named associated person and relevant child. The order may be in general terms but should include relevant specifics so that it is both understandable and enforceable.

> Example:
>
> The respondent is forbidden to contact the applicant in any way and in particular must not speak to her, telephone her, send text messages, e-mail or letters to her and must not enter within 100 yards of 1 Long Street (respondent's home) and the Black Bull public house (respondent's place of work).

9.28.2 Occupation orders

These orders deal with rights of occupation or exclude a person from all or part of a building. The law is complex and the clerk should be asked to give a synopsis of the requirements in respect of the particular parties before the court as differences arise in terms of scope and duration depending upon the party's qualifications. Whenever there is a dispute about proprietary rights the court must consider transferring the case to the county court or High Court.

The court must consider the 'balance of harm' between the parties and any children involved. A respondent who is threatened with exclusion is likely to suffer some hardship but his wife and children may be likely to suffer significant harm if there is evidence of abuse by him and the order will be justified. Total exclusion is a serious action and the court should consider whether a molestation order or exclusion to rooms within the house would be sufficient.

Matters relating to non-molestation orders and occupation orders

9.28.3 Ex parte orders

Both orders may be made on an ex parte basis without notification to the respondent, where the court considers that it is 'just and convenient to do so.' In making the decision to proceed ex parte the court must consider all the circumstances of the case and also the matters set out below:

(a) any risk of significant harm to the applicant or a relevant child attributable to conduct of the respondent if the order is not made immediately;
(b) whether it is likely that the applicant will be deterred or prevented from pursuing the application if an order is not made immediately; and
(c) whether there is reason to believe that the respondent is aware of the proceedings but is deliberately evading service and that the applicant or a relevant child will be seriously prejudiced by the delay involved in effecting service of proceedings.

Ex parte occupation orders should only be granted in exceptional circumstances because of their draconian nature (Chalmers v. Johns 1999).

9.28.4 Undertakings

Where the court has power to make either order it may instead accept an undertaking that the respondent will either do or not do specific acts. The undertaking is enforceable as if it were an order of the court. However the major difference is that a power of arrest may not be attached.

9.28.5 Power of arrest

The court is obliged to attach a power of arrest in all cases where it appears to the court that the respondent has used or threatened violence against the applicant or a relevant child unless it is satisfied that in all the circumstances they are adequately protected without one.

A discretion is given to attach a power to ex parte applications if the respondent has used or threatened violence and there is a risk of significant harm attributable to the conduct of the respondent if the power of arrest is not attached immediately. The respondent must be produced before a court within 24 hours of arrest.

When a power of arrest is not attached the applicant may apply for a warrant by attending court and giving evidence on oath that the respondent has failed to comply with the order.

If the breach action is adjourned and the respondent is given bail it will be civil bail, with or without conditions.

9.28.6 Sanction for breach

Upon hearing a breach application the court will determine the case on the balance of probabilities. The court may order the respondent:

(a) to pay a sum not exceeding £50 for every day he is in breach up to £1,000, or a sum not exceeding £5,000; or
(b) to be committed to custody for a period not exceeding 2 months or until he has remedied his default.

The committal may be suspended upon condition of obedience to the order. However serious breaches should be punished immediately.

9.28.7 Discharge/variation

Either party may apply for discharge or variation of the order.

AWARENESS

Socio – Psychological issues

Whole textbooks have been written on these issues. The content below provides the essential aspects of information which may prompt further reading if so desired.

9.29 Child development

Evidence of 'failing to thrive' and 'failing to reach milestones' will frequently be given particularly in public law cases as indicators of 'harm', but may also be relevant in arguments put forward in private law cases.

9.29.1 Some relevant development milestones:

- 0 – 12 months

Child shows marked preference for primary care giver e.g. mother. This does not mean that a child of that age has chosen not to relate to his father!

- 12 months – 18 months

Bears weight on legs and starts to walk. Engages in play with objects. Shows distress when separated from care giver e.g. mother. This is normal behaviour and cannot carry a negative inference on its own against a father who is seeking contact with his child. On the other hand it may be worthy of comment that a child is not showing any preference for the primary carer and is going to strangers for comfort.

- 24 months – 30 months

Has daytime control of bowel and bladder. Is able to feed himself with a spoon. Can climb stairs. Fine motor skills develop e.g. able to pick up small objects. Struggles to accept dependence/control of adult occasionally and starts to express own feelings with temper outbursts if frustration is not managed. Some kicking and banging is not, on its own, a sign of a deranged child at this age!

- 30 months – 36 months

Begins to develop ability to identify other humans as 'people' and empathy begins e.g. feels sorry if someone is hurt.

- 36 months – 48 months

Child is ready for relationships outside the family/support network. Starts to make friendships and shows preferences for others. Able to dress himself with help.

9.29.2 The centile charts

These are often used in evidence where there are concerns about physical development. Basically they demonstrate by a graph the line of the height and weight expected of a child of a particular age. The weight chart begins with the birth-weight and then shows the line of expected weight gain up to say 24 months. Similarly the increase in height can be demonstrated. There is 'a norm' for 50% of children – the 50th centile. When a child is referred to as 'being on/in the 3rd centile', his weight and height will fall into the lowest 1/3 of height/weight measures for children of his age.

Being in the lowest group is not in itself a concern for various reasons, principally that genetically he may be destined to be of small stature and slight build. More importantly it is significant to note whether the child has maintained the anticipated growth rate for a child of that weight/height or whether it is 'falling below the line' drawn for the 3rd centile.

Concern must also arise when there is a sudden or gradual drop in position on the centile chart with no obvious explanations e.g. he is born on the 60th centile and then moves down to the bottom of the chart for no identifiable health reason.

When presented with centile charts it is important to identify the significance of variations at relevant times rather than simply registering that a child is smaller and thinner than 'a normal child' as this in itself is of no significance.

9.30 Patterns of parenting

History can repeat itself and this is often the case when considering patterns of parenting. Parents generally copy the pattern of their own parents/care givers and deprivation is often repeated in future generations. The 'cycle of deprivation' refers to the likelihood of the children of the poor growing up in an impoverished framework where they have little access to consistent education and good health care.

A poorly educated, socially isolated adult who does not have access to positive family/community support is likely to struggle to provide adequate emotional, practical and social support to their own children.

It is important to recognise the links between social achievement, psychological adjustment and employment opportunities and how this intertwines with good parenting skills and self-respect.

Where can intervention break the cycle? This may well arise at the point when children unfortunately have to be taken into care. There is some cynicism about 'parent-craft' classes and the realistic prospect of 'making a good parent', perhaps because it is recognised that the task is likely to involve a massive change for the parents involved. When it is successful, and it can be, the winners are not only the present family but most likely the next generation as well.

9.31 Cultural parenting and the importance of race

The local authority are under a duty to consider the racial group to which a child belongs when making any arrangements for the child's care. When placing a child with foster parents they must secure that where possible the foster parents are of the same religion as the child or that they give an undertaking that the child will be brought up in the same religious persuasion.

There are some racial/cultural issues which may be of interest in relation to admissions to public care, reported in 'Child Care Now' (Rowe *et al*) 1989:

- Black children were over-represented in admission to care rates although the extent to which this was happening varied considerably.
- Asian children were under-represented in all age groups.
- African and African-Caribbean children were over-represented particularly in the pre-school and the 5-10 age group.

The most outstanding feature about minority children in public care is the grossly disproportionate number of those of mixed race parentage. Bebbington and Miles calculated that children of mixed parentage were 2½ times more likely to enter public care as white children.

Young children of mixed parentage are also more likely to have multiple admissions. Their re-admission rate was more than twice that of young white children in the 'Child Care Now' sample.

The very small number of Asian children who need care outside of their family network is worthy of comment. It may be the strength of the family and community support which makes public care less necessary, but it could be that the child care services are not offered in a way which is acceptable to Asian parents. This observation may be relevant when hearing evidence about lack of co-operation by Asian parents with the authorities. It would seem that there is a cultural issue and this should be weighed in the balance.

9.32 Social problems in the family

Deprivation is closely associated with entering public care. In a study in 1989 by Bebbington and Miles of 2,500 children admitted into care the research found the following factors existed before admission:

- Only 1/4 were living with both parents
- Almost 3/4 of their families were in receipt of income support
- Only 1 in 5 lived in owner-occupied housing
- Over 1/2 lived in poor neighbourhoods

The social problems of lack of available social support; environmental problems; family stress and breakdown combine to lead to many children being taken into care, whether that be voluntary care or under a court order.

Interestingly in 1989 a report concluded that young offenders were in fact less likely to come from severely deprived households and more often than not come from two parent families (Farmer and Parker 1989).

9.33 Issues in child abuse

What is child abuse? There are 4 main types of abuse though a child may experience more than one kind of abuse at any one time. The following definitions and statistics are set out in the NSPCC publication 'A guide to understanding child abuse.'

1. Physical abuse – when parents (or responsible adults) deliberately inflict injuries on a child or, knowingly, do not prevent them. It includes

hitting, shaking, squeezing, burning or biting. It also includes excessive force when feeding, changing or handling a child. Giving a child poisonous substances, inappropriate drugs or alcohol and attempting to suffocate or drown a child.

2. Emotional abuse – when parents or adults continuously fail to show their child love or affection, or when they taunt or shout at a child, causing him or her to lose confidence and self-esteem, and to become nervous or withdrawn.
3. Neglect – when parents fail to meet their child's essential needs, such as adequate food, clothing, warmth and medical care. Leaving children who are too young to look after themselves alone or without proper supervision.
4. Sexual abuse – when an adult forces a child to take part in a sexual activity, using the child to satisfy his or her own sexual desires. This can involve sexual intercourse, fondling, masturbation, oral sex, anal sex, or exposing children to pornographic videos, books, magazines or other material.
5. At least one child dies each week in this country as a result of cruelty. More than 35,000 children are at risk of abuse and have to be protected by the authorities. There are at least 11,000 adults in this country who have been convicted of sex offences against children.

ABILITY TO

9.34 Listen closely

How does a witness or advocate know that you are listening? What actions can convey this? Leaning forward, nodding, eye contact, making notes, repeating back, questioning. One difficult area in family court is to make it clear that you are checking information in the statements or reports, often whilst someone is speaking, rather than simply 'reading something.' This can be conveyed by maintaining some eye contact and then very deliberately marking the relevant points.

The evidence may take a long time and may be given very slowly. When you find that your concentration is wandering and it is becoming difficult to listen, consider whether it may also be appropriate for the witness to be given a break and take a short retirement at a timely point in the evidence.

The best check of listening is to check out whether key points have been picked up or not.

9.35 Comprehend long reports/material

Family court reports are far longer than pre-sentence reports and the information is far more complex. Family histories alone may take several pages, before the case history begins and then the current circumstances follow on. As stated above it may well be helpful for you to dip into certain parts during the evidence and personal annotations, highlighting and even 'post-it' markers may be useful.

Before the case begins you may wish to note the names and relationships of key players so that references to first names can be readily understood. Similarly the ages of relevant children should also be noted conspicuously so that actions can be judged in an appropriate context. Finally, it is important to build a mental picture of what is alleged and what is proposed.

One of the main purposes of reading the papers before the case begins is to enable the court to identify the points of interest and tell the parties the issues on which it wishes to be addressed (Practice Note (Civil Litigation: Case Management)). This can save a lot of time but more importantly it can focus the emotional energy into relevant evidence and avoid needless recitation of unhappy facts.

9.36 Maintain a dispassionate understanding of sometimes complex and fraught issues

No tears. No lump in the throat. Calm.
No anger. No horror. Calm.
No impatience. No pain. Calm.
No decision until all the facts are impartially heard in full.

9.37 Contribute actively to formulation of bench decisions

It is very easy in the retiring room to let a single person take control particularly in drawing up reasons. Reasons must never be seen predominantly as a grammatical exercise or an effort of flowing prose. They are not the property of the person writing them. Every magistrate should be contributing to the discussion by answering a single recurring one word question – why?

Reasons are required so that the court eventually arrives at a carefully thought out decision and so that a judge dealing with an appeal can understand the basis for the magistrates' decision. They are not required to try and persuade the parties or soften the blow and the reality is that the parties will not hear everything and may never read everything. The solicitors may read them in order to decide whether to appeal. A judge on appeal will read them. They are the audience for reasons. This does not prevent the chairman from explaining or commenting to the parties.

The magistrates who do not have the pen in their hand must be assertive and take an active part. As stated earlier a lap top computer in the retiring room has the advantage that the reasons are legible, can be changed and copies can quickly be ran off for a final check through by all of the bench before returning to court. If you are not sure what has been written, then you are not sure what the reasoning is and cannot genuinely be a part of the decision-making process.

9.38 Prepare reasons for decisions/Structured approach to decision making

After the hearing the court must make its decision as soon as practicable. Before the order is made or refused the clerk must record the names of the magistrates and in consultation with the justices, the reasons for the court's decision and any findings of fact, before making the order. Reasons are not simply required for final decisions. They must also be given for interim orders, requests for leave, withdrawal of applications, refusing an application to adjourn, decisions as to disclosure of medical reports and making or refusing to make directions on a contentious matter after hearing full argument.

The court cannot announce its decision and then defer stating reasons and findings of fact to a later date even if the parties agree to such a course of action.

The Divisional Court has given guidance on how the requirement to record reasons for a decision in children's cases should be complied with (R (J) v Oxfordshire County Council 1992). The headings are given along with a very brief outline of the <u>type</u> of information which would fall under each heading.

1. Facts not in dispute e.g. *child's age, parents and nature of injuries.*

2. Disputed facts e.g. *whether the injury was caused accidentally by falling or deliberately.*

3. Facts found proved e.g. *that injury was caused by a deliberate blow to the leg by a belt.*

4. The extent to which the parties and witnesses were believed or disbelieved and the information on which the court relied in reaching its decision e.g. *medical report gives only one possible explanation and mother's explanation is considered to be implausible.*

5. Authorities cited by the parties or referred by the court *(Acceptance that Article 8 is engaged. It is a qualified right. Consideration must be given to the '3 questions' and will be answered at the conclusion of the*

reasons. (I) Is the restriction legal, clear and accessible? (ii) Does it pursue a legitimate aim? (iii) Is it proportionate?)

6. Whether a welfare report has been considered. *Yes, with recommendation of a full care order.*

7. The judgement or findings of fact in relation to each of the heads under the welfare checklist (see 9.8.)

   (i) The ascertainable wishes and feelings of the child concerned – *age 9 and states that he wishes to stay with grandmother.*
   (ii) Physical, emotional and educational needs – *attends local school regularly, mixes with other children well and meets educational milestones.*
   (iii) Likely effect on him of any change in his circumstances – *no change is proposed.*
   (iv) Age, sex, background and any characteristics of his which the court considers relevant – *grandmother is also African-Caribbean and can provide for child's cultural needs.*
   (v) Any harm suffered or at risk of suffering – *has recovered from injury caused by mother and all contact with mother is supervised by grandmother.*
   (vi) Capability of each parent and any other relevant person – *mother is incapable at the present time. Grandmother is 52, healthy and an experienced carer.*
   (vii) Range of powers available – *public and private orders or 'no order.'*

8. Reasons for taking a different course to guardian or reporting officer *e.g. residence order with grandmother made instead of placement with grandmother under care order plan. Grandmother has had actual care for 6 months and there are no reported concerns whatsoever and she is anxious to become independent of the local authority. Supervised contact with mother on terms ...*

9. Article 8. Answers to the qualified right questions (set out at 5) which emerge from the findings.

10. Decision, including reasons why an order is made or 'no order' is made.

If the parties agree on certain issues the parties should be invited to agree the basis of the facts on which the court is invited to proceed. This must be acknowledged by either a signature of the parties or their legal representative *e.g. that mother has neglected the child due to her ill health; accepts the content of the guardian's report; accepts that the threshold criteria are satisfied; accepts that a care order is appropriate; accepts that the intervention under Article 8 is lawful, legitimate and proportionate and will comply with the care plan to reinstate the child with her when her medical treatment is complete.*

9.39 Help maintain an appropriate level of informality

The essence of the family court is to strive towards 'sorting matters out' rather than creating a 'win/lose' situation particularly when children are involved. Although the parties are generally 'applicant' and 'respondent' it is rarely helpful to attach such labels in court.

It is particularly important to find out how people wish to be addressed e.g. Miss/Mrs/Miss as the name is likely to be used a lot more than in a criminal case and can help to keep parties engaged and maintain some informality.

The magistrates are taking on an investigative role which necessarily involves questioning. This can take the form of an intimidating cross-examination which is designed to 'get to the bottom of things' rather like a criminal trial. Coupled with emotional instability this approach can very quickly trigger feelings of hostility and rage. Evidence becomes disorientated and unpleasant remarks are made. Most seriously such an approach can cause long-term damage to the relationships of the parties and their children when words are spoken in anger and remembered.

Questioning may more helpfully take the form of an interested and sensitive enquiry which is clearly designed to 'sort matters out.' As feelings begin to run high, a break may be helpful for everyone.

Similarly the court can generate a calmer response by asking all parties to give their evidence sitting down. This is another example of creating an atmosphere of '<u>we</u> are <u>all</u> sorting this out together' rather than 'now it is your turn and we'll see what you have to say about all this.'

The informality extends to trying to reach agreements and allowing parties the time and space, possibly on the day of the hearing to talk together and try to resolve issues with the assistance of court officers. The reality is that the parties in a family case are often going through a traumatic and chaotic period in their lives and instructions can be inconsistent, variable and difficult to organise until the day of the case. Periods in the retiring room are not 'wasted time' if progress is at last focused and everyone involved in the case are at last together in one building with a very clear ultimatum that today is the day for a decision.

During the proceedings the parties should feel that they can jot down any questions or speak very briefly with their representative as matters arise.

This means giving them a table to spread out documents, some notepaper and easy physical access to their solicitor.

However, at the end of the day when the decision is reached, the parties need the true formality of the court with its dignity and authority. It is always a serious matter. This is the final decision and nobody's life is going to be quite the same again.

CHAPTER 10
COMPETENCE 10
Family Chairmanship

This chapter deals with the practical application by the chairman, of the powers, principles and procedures of the family proceedings court as detailed in chapter 9.

10.1 Dealing competently with adjournments; cases involving an unrepresented party and acceptable agreements.

10.1.1 Adjournments

In the adult and youth courts it is reasonable to work on the basis of a 'presumption of progress' and to question and push for action on the day in court. In the family court this may be counterproductive. Periods for reflection, for 'trying out arrangements', for reports and then further reports may be necessary and cannot be hurried. The outcome of a family court order may last for a lifetime. The important issues at the point of any adjournment are to:

- Carefully manage the proceedings and
- Avoid unnecessary and possibly harmful delays.

Careful management means careful questioning to ascertain exactly what is intended, making sure that it is going to happen and then determining when the matter can usefully come before the court again. In the meantime it is important to assess the needs of the child and balance any harm caused by further delay. Relevant questions must be raised so that appropriate directions may be given.

Example:

Application to adjourn the case for 3 months for an expert report to be prepared and in the meantime to extend the interim care order for 28 days by agreement.

> **'Managing' questions.**
> What are the issues to be addressed by the expert?
> What is the relevance?
> Is leave sought for a medical or psychiatric examination? (Necessary if evidence is to be adduced).
> Who is the expert?

Has any work been undertaken already?
Why is 3 months suggested?
Is the expert's availability known for the final hearing to be fixed?
Can the evidence be properly obtained by joint instruction of one expert by all parties?
Can the evidence be adduced by the guardian by co-ordinating 2 experts if necessary?

Welfare and delay questions.
Where is the child living in the meantime?
Is there any intention to change any residence arrangements during the adjournment?
What are the contact arrangements with parents?

10.1.2 Cases involving an unrepresented party

Ideally parties should have the benefit of legal advice in family matters and the court should ensure that the duty solicitor facility is explained, the possibility of legal aid and also the extent of the court's powers if a case is found proved. Of course it is a matter for the individual but any choices and possible outcomes should be explained before the case begins. Some parties do wish to proceed without representation and in these circumstances, the legal adviser may assist as necessary.

The Practice Direction 2000 places duties on the legal adviser to ensure that every case is conducted fairly and to assist unrepresented parties to present their case, 'without appearing to be an advocate for the party concerned'. The Direction also gives the power for him to ask questions of witnesses and the parties in order to clarify the evidence and any issues in the case.

This tends to arise most frequently in cases of maintenance default and arrests following alleged breaches of family court orders and it may be useful to allow the legal adviser a few minutes to discuss the matter with the unrepresented party before commencing the case.

Cross-examination in particular is a complex and difficult task for any lay person, let alone in heavily charged emotional circumstances. It may be easier for the witness to deal with questions phrased through the legal adviser, rather than facing spasmodic questions and the inevitable lengthy statements directly from the other party.

An unrepresented party is less likely to have had the benefit of discussion and advice about his case and his conduct in court. He is therefore more likely to be nervous, angry and emotionally charged. Put bluntly, he may literally 'not do himself justice.' The court must provide ample explanation and direction to calm the situation and ensure that he too has his day in court.

10.1.3 Acceptable agreements

The family court is never a 'rubber stamp' court. Matters have reached the court because agreement has not been possible despite often protracted and painful efforts by one or both parties. Agreement must never be reached because one of the parties capitulates at the prospect of 'having to take the stand' and give their evidence in court. If their case is deserving then it is a poor reflection of justice that someone 'gives up at the final hurdle.' There is also the situation of 'forced compromise' with the chance that the evidence will be discharged angrily, petulantly and inappropriately through family life for a long time to come, rather than in the arena of the court. Better to hear it once and for all in an appropriate environment in such circumstances and reach a judicial decision.

It is therefore essential that the possibility of capitulation rather than agreement is taken away by showing that the court is informal, private, and that space and time are available for this particular case to go ahead as planned.

That said, minds do focus and discussions do reach satisfactory conclusions without the need to 'air the dirty linen'. It is simply about keeping the options open and being sure that there is free choice in the matter and that the agreement is fair and reasonable.

In financial cases the court must consider that the amounts are not 'contrary to the interests of justice', and that any maintenance for children is 'a proper contribution towards the financial needs of the child.'

In private order cases the court will normally ask whether there is any prospect of any agreement, possibly using the services of the Court Welfare Officer or a local mediation service at the first directions appointment. Even a measure of agreement is a start, and an adjournment to try out arrangements may be useful before a full welfare report and final hearing are arranged. There is the prospect of psychological pride, family unity and commitment in reaching a 'no order' or 'consent' order situation albeit with the help of the court process.

10.2. Following a structured approach and using the welfare checklist effectively where applicable (see 9.38 for recommended headings)

As a chairman this involves the assertive task of stopping your wingers in their tracks from walking into the retiring room and saying 'Well I think this child needs a full care order.' Not easy, particularly if you wholeheartedly agree.

Whilst the technical approach is to work through the facts and checklist, the reality is probably to alert wingers to the possible orders and make it clear that there really is some purpose in analysing the facts, the child's long-term welfare and the options.

Options exist until the decision-making process is complete. Yes, it is looking like a full care order but do you have all of the facts to make that decision today? Do you feel that mother has some genuine concerns about the proposed contact arrangements and they should be enshrined in a contact order on the court's initiative? Might it just be reasonable to make a supervision order instead? Could a residence order be made for the child to carry on living with his aunt?

Individual practices vary as to who will record the reasons. The chairman may wish to do this in order to keep some control but it must be emphasised that the requirement under the rules is as follows:

'..the justices clerk shall record in writing ...in consultation with the justice(s), the reasons for the court's decision and any findings of fact.' (Rule 21(5) Family Proceedings Rules (Children Act 1989) Rules 1991).

10.3 to 10.6 Range of orders - knowledge, identification, requirements and appropriateness

Full details of each order are considered in chapter 9, but a summary follows:

(1) Public children orders.

About 80% of public cases are dealt with in the magistrates' court.

- Child assessment order (9.18) – requires production of the child to an individual named in the order to make an assessment of the child and to comply with any directions. Maximum period of 7 days (not necessarily immediately).
- Emergency protection order (9.18) – authorises or prevents removal of child and may be made ex parte. Exclusion provisions may be included. Maximum of 8 days + extension up to 7 days.
- Care order (9.19) – Significant harm/reasonable parent threshold test. Child placed in care of local authority until aged 18. Parental responsibility to local authority.
- Supervision order (9.19) – Significant harm/reasonable parent threshold test. Supervision for 12 months + extension up to 3 years.
- Interim care/supervision order (9.19) – 'Reasonable grounds for believing' that threshold test is satisfied. Maximum of 8 weeks extended by up to 4 weeks at a time.

- Parental contact with child in care (9.19) – 'Reasonable contact' presumption but court may make formal order or refuse contact.
- Education supervision order (9.19) – No 'threshold' test. To ensure that child is 'properly educated.' Maximum period of 1 year with extension to 3 years. Level 3 fine for breach.

For completeness there are 2 relatively new orders which are used very rarely:

- Child safety order – Local authority application in respect of a child under 10 who has behaved in a manner which would have been 'criminal' if aged over 10. Supervision with requirements for 3 months + extension to 12 months.
- Parenting order – When a child safety order is made and the court feel that a parenting order would be desirable to prevent any repetition of the behaviour. Order applies to parent(s) to comply with requirements for up to 12 months e.g. to ensure that child is always supervised by an adult when not at school and also to attend parentcraft sessions up to once per week for up to 3 months. See 7.14 for fuller discussion.

(2) Private children orders (Section 8 orders)

About 30% of private cases are dealt with in the magistrates' court.
Usually to age 16. Enforceable by fine/imprisonment.

- Contact order (9.22) – requires person with whom child is living to allow the child to have contact with another person. 'Reasonable' or defined.
- Residence order (9.21) – an order which settles who the child should live with. Sole or split orders.
- Prohibited steps order (9.23) – directs that a specific aspect of parental responsibility cannot be exercised without the consent of the court.
- Specific issues order (9.24) – determination of a particular aspect of parental responsibility by the court.

(3) Domestic violence orders (9.28)

May be made ex parte and carry power of arrest.
Enforceable by fine/imprisonment.

- Non-molestation order – prohibits the respondent from molesting a named 'associated person' and relevant children. May be made 'until further order.'
- Occupation order – deals with rights of occupation or excludes a person from all or part of a building. Criteria, duration and content will depend upon the qualifications of the applicant. Balance of harm test between the parties and the children involved.

(4) Adoption (9.16)

The child becomes a full member of the adoptive family and any legal relationship with the natural parents is severed. Parental responsibility passes in full to the adopter(s) although a natural parent may exceptionally retain contact.

10.7 Announcing full reasons for the decision of the bench
10.8 Ensuring that the parties understand

These competences may usefully be considered together. The rules require the reasons to be recorded in writing before the order is made or the application is refused. They also require that when making the order or refusing the application one of the justices shall 'state the reasons for the court's decision.'

Announcing the reasons can be done in various ways. On the one hand it can simply amount to reading the reasons out in a monotone as if it is a chore of public speaking or a challenge in translating someone else's writing! Alternatively it can amount to an unfolding process which will point towards and conclude with a decision. In the second scenario there are pauses, eye contact, and a recognition that this is important to the individuals concerned and this is the best explanation of the decision that they will ever have.

Understanding is vital. A decision to make a full care order requires a straightforward and clear explanation on the lines of 'the local authority now have the responsibility to do what is best for the children, including deciding where they are going to live.' Where does the parent fit in? Is that the end of the road or not? Again, some explanation that they still have responsibility as a parent and that the court hopes that there will be co-operation with the care plan e.g.' that you will continue to build up your relationship by contact visits.'

When the order is complex e.g. defined contact, it may be helpful to tell the parties what the court has in mind first of all in simple, straightforward terms. It may be at this point that one of the parties will raise a query e.g. 'How long do I have to wait in McDonalds for his dad to come before we can leave? Surely we don't have to wait for the full 2 hours. He'll only come if he feels like it'. Further negotiation and clarification may follow.

It may then be useful to check understanding after the decision has been made. This need not be framed as a test, but rather on the lines of 'This has been complicated for me to explain and I'd like to check with you whether I've been clear enough about the times in particular.'

10.9 Agreeing the correct order of proceedings and allowing flexibility where appropriate

The chairman has far greater flexibility and control of who will speak when and how long they will be given. There is a starting point plan as follows:

1. The applicant
2. Any party with parental responsibility
3. Other respondents
4. The guardian ad litem
5. The child if he is a party.

The order may be varied. This will usually be discussed at the previous direction hearing and the order of speeches may be settled then by identifying a logical progression of information from what is agreed, through to the disputed matters and in order to enable expert witnesses to listen and comment as appropriate.

In the absence of any previous direction it is worth checking with the parties before the case begins whether they are content for the usual order to be followed. If so, the parties can be told by the chairman who is who in court and who will speak when. This assists in showing that the chairman is in control and avoids any impression of a 'free for all' except for the respondent who will usually be last. To advise that he will speak later but will have the benefit of hearing first what the application is all about may reduce his anxiety.

The chairman may intervene at any stage to suggest that a witness may be taken out of the usual order. This may be on the grounds of convenience e.g. a doctor's limited availability to attend court when his evidence may be interposed at a particular time. Alternatively it may be to enable the court to deal with the evidence in a structured manner by hearing about one issue at a time such as whether the threshold criteria is satisfied before moving on to the need for an order.

The chairman may also intervene to limit the length of opening and closing submissions by indicating what the court would seek to be addressed upon, rather than listening to a repetition of what has just been read or heard. Lengthy cross-examination may be similarly cut down by summarising what the bench understand about a particular matter and suggesting that questions be confined to identified relevant issues, namely ... It is essential that parties do not switch off through anger, frustration or boredom. The information flow must remain relevant throughout.

10.10 Ensuring observation of the rules of evidence as applicable

There are a few basic rules of evidence/procedure which are peculiar to the family court and they are summarised below:

1. All filed documents must be read by the magistrates before the case begins.
2. Normally oral evidence may only be given if a written statement has been served on the parties and the court. The court must otherwise give leave for the oral evidence to be given.
3. Normally a child cannot be physically or medically examined or assessed for the purpose of expert evidence without the leave of the court.
4. The burden of proof rests on the applicant to prove the matter on the balance of probabilities.
5. The possibility of 'risk' of significant harm in care proceedings must be based on facts rather than suspicions.
6. The standard of proof does not change with the nature of the allegation, but the more serious the allegation is, the more convincing the evidence must be to tip the balance.
7. In public law cases nobody is excused from giving evidence or answering any questions on the ground that it might incriminate him or his spouse e.g. admits to a criminal assault, as the evidence will not be admissible against the person concerned in a criminal trial.
8. Evidence concerning the upbringing, maintenance and welfare of a child is admissible even if it is hearsay evidence e.g. social worker can give evidence based on another person's notes. The court will obviously attach more weight to first-hand evidence.
9. The court may accept a witness as an expert and may then hear evidence based on his opinion rather than simply fact.

See 9.12 for a full discussion of evidence and procedure.

DEALING DIRECTLY AND APPROPRIATELY WITH CHILDREN AND FAMILY MEMBERS AND THEIR ADVOCATES

10.11 Using simple language without jargon

We would all like to think that we do not use jargon. The reality is that court jargon gradually becomes part of our day-to-day language and it becomes difficult to spot the jargon and translate it as necessary. Suggestions of 'simple language' will vary from one person to the next.

Examples.

Adjourn	= 'put off' today because/so that ....
'Interim' order	= 'temporary' order for the next 28 days.
Care order	= giving the local authority the responsibility to do what is best for John and that includes deciding where he should live.....
Residence order	= deciding who John is going to live with.

10.12 Maintaining eye contact (where appropriate)

Eye contact is extremely helpful to gauge whether a party or witness is engaged with the chairman or not and whether there are indications of understanding or not. It is accepted in case law that it is unnecessary to hold eye contact for prolonged periods and it may indeed be 'disquieting' to do so.

Assumptions may be made that 'looking the bench in the eye' may indicate honesty and veracity, but care should be taken in interpreting the response to eye contact in this way. In some South Asian societies it is considered by women that eye contact with a man is brazen and immodest. Additionally, along with African and Caribbean cultures, it may be considered appropriate to look away from a person in authority to indicate deference and respect.

10.13 Ensuring young people and all in court understand (see 10.8)

Explanations throughout the course of the proceedings are necessary in plain, simple language. Introductions as to who's who is very important. This includes anyone who is sitting in court e.g. new panel members who are observing, trainee social worker. Parties are expected to give very personal information to the court and it is essential that they know who is listening.

Only the following people are allowed to be present during the hearing – the officers of the court; parties, representatives and 'other persons directly connected with the case'; bona fide press and those specifically permitted by the court if they have 'adequate grounds' for attendance.

The press can report details of the parties, the grounds of the application, submissions on points of law and the decision of the court. However there is an important exclusion. No material may be published which would lead to the identification of a child in any proceedings in which powers under the Children Act may be exercised. The court also has power to exclude the press during the taking of indecent evidence.

In adoption proceedings only court officers, parties, representatives and those 'directly connected with the case' must be present.

In order to ensure understanding of instructions and requests it is possible to use the informality of the proceedings to advantage. Far more two-way conversations with officers and representatives is expected in comparison to the formality and bustle of a crime court. It is quite in order to make requests of the local authority and guardian in open court; seek views and clarify issues.

10.14 Speaking clearly and concisely

It is very easy to drop volume and speak more quickly when the proceedings are informal. Additionally there is likely to be far more involvement by the chairman during the proceedings and more is going to be said. The tone is intentionally less authoritative during the proceedings. It is helpful therefore to check that everyone is catching what you are saying and that the volume stays at an 'easy listening' rather than 'hard to hear' level.

One of the tasks of the chairman is to make sure that the hearing is not unnecessarily prolonged and that everyone is kept tightly within relevant issues. This applies to the chairman's contributions as well!

10.15 Preparing what is to be said, after appropriate consultation with colleagues

The responsibility for recording the reasons and findings of fact lies upon the clerk. The chairman must ensure that the clerk does not effectively (and unintentionally) take over the chairman's job. It is for the chairman to lead the decision-making process and make sure that everyone is playing an active part. It is for the chairman to be satisfied that what is written down represents the true feelings of the majority of the bench.

The chairman may well feel that something more needs to be said to the parties or to any of the court officers. Additional explanations may be necessary. Whilst the reasons are required by law this does not prevent the chairman from adding a summary in simple language or giving advice or comment as in any other proceedings. As elsewhere the 'add-ons' need to be approved by colleagues.

10.16 Avoiding patronising tone

The relevant definition of 'patronise' in this context is to 'treat condescendingly'. To condescend is to 'be gracious enough though showing one's feeling of dignity or superiority.'
(Concise Oxford Dictionary).

In terms of most family cases there is little scope for superiority. Nobody has committed a criminal offence and there is no basis on which anyone can be 'looked down upon.' Broadly speaking the parties are people who have done their very best. They would far prefer to be at home with a healthy and loving family around them than having to turn to the court for something that inevitably is going to be second best.

The suggested recurrent theme for the family court is one of 'let's work this out together', rather than 'we are going to judge how you and your family will lead your lives from now on.'

10.17 Using precedents appropriately

Suggested pronouncements are available from various sources and are helpful to ensure that all aspects have been covered. There has always been debate about whether it is appropriate for pronouncements to be 'read.' Provided that there is eye contact at relevant points, a chairman may feel more confident, and delivery may therefore be of a higher calibre if a pronouncement is read. There are 3 issues worth considering before reading from a standard pronouncement:

1. Personalise as much as possible. As any sales representative is well aware – get hold of the names – keep saying them and you have more chance of your audience been hooked, e.g. 'Mr. Smith, you must pay off the arrears for John at ...or else .... Do you understand, Mr. Smith?'
2. On the same basis, use the word 'you' and 'your' at every opportunity, e.g. '<u>your</u> responsibility to meet John on time ... it was <u>your</u> suggestion, so we expect <u>you</u> to keep to <u>your</u> times.'
3. Understand the content so that you are able to clarify personally or alternatively calmly deflect questions to the clerk.

10.18 Being attentive and being seen to be attentive

Magistrates should be seen to be paying attention and it is irrelevant that every word has been heard and understood, if the magistrate is giving the impression of being uninterested. Injustice has been held to have occurred where a witness did not receive the undivided attention of one member of the bench, because the magistrate had been reading a bench guide during some of the evidence.

How can attentiveness be demonstrated positively? Expressions such as 'I see', 'and then what happened?'. Behaviour such as a gentle nodding from time to time (not nodding off!); making a note of what is being said; repeating back information, e.g. 'so you say that ...'

As a chairman it is important to take responsibility for wingers and check that they are engaged in the case. This may involve a suggestion that a break should be taken for the benefit of everyone involved in a lengthy case.

10.19 Asking appropriate, relevant and understandable questions

Sometimes it is helpful to explain why a question is being asked. The most common difficulty arises when a financial order is being made or enforced and the court asks about the income of the payer's partner. The answer is frequently 'I have no idea.' It may be different if an explanation is given. Something on the lines that the partner's income most certainly will not be used to pay the maintenance order. However the information is needed so that the court can get a feel for how much of the household expenses are actually falling on the respondent personally. Without that information, assumptions may be made which are incorrect e.g. that a 'working' partner will effectively be financing half of all outgoings.

10.20 Enabling wingers to ask questions where appropriate

Local practices vary. Some courts take the view that the proceedings are informal and there is a flexibility to allow wingers to question directly with the chairman's consent rather than having to whisper questions through the chair. Others take the view that the parties should focus on one person, the chairman, and he should take all speaking roles to avoid any confusion or feeling of 'what's coming next <u>and</u> where is it coming from?'

The practice should be agreed before the bench go into court. How are questions going to be raised? Personally or by nudging/telling or jotting down on a piece of paper and pushing across the bench.

The chairman may also wish to retain some discretion as to what questions may properly be put and perhaps when they should be put. There may well be some disagreement as to relevancy e.g. a winger may wish to ask about the content of the children's meals whilst the chairman may consider that there is no issue about this aspect of care and it may create unnecessary hostility. When difficulties arise, the chairman must ensure that explanation is given or consult the clerk for a view on relevancy.

10.21 Demonstrating a positive manner

Does your body language say 'we're going to help to sort matters out today – let's get to grips with it' or does it say 'oh no, not another family case.' The chairman must lead by example to get the best out of the bench <u>and</u> the parties.

10.22 Ensuring courtesy to all court users

This is a little more complicated than in the crime court because the chairman has greater powers to regulate proceedings. The skill lies in 'how it is done'.

> Example:
>
> In curtailing a repetitive cross-examination.
>
> 'I think we have heard enough about this.'
> 'I'd be interested to know where these questions are leading us.'
> 'How much longer are you going to be?'
> Exaggerated sighs and rolling of the eyes.
>
> = 'SHUT UP!'
>
> An alternative might be 'You have helpfully provided us with/gleaned by your questions sufficient information about ....thank you, and we are ready to move on.'

There needs to be some recognition of the professional expertise of the social workers and guardians. They bring a massive dimension into the courtroom which must be respected and worked with as a team together with the court. Even the most apparently straightforward requests may actually be more complicated and it is preferable to combine any requests with an opportunity for an opinion to be given. Discussion with the experts before making a decision is far better than backtracking after one-sided imposition.

> Example:
>
> We would like you to interview the children on their own. Do you have any views about our making a direction to that effect?

10.23 Addressing the parties in an appropriate manner

The only person who knows best how they wish to be addressed is the person concerned. It is helpful if the court usher can establish this informally outside the court, if only because the usher will be speaking to them and possibly keeping them informed in any event. When the case is called on the appropriate form of address can be given e.g. Ms. Joan Smith and Mohammed Ali. This saves the court making an initial guess; ignoring any possible titles completely or raising the question after identification. A courteous but relaxed relationship can begin immediately 'Do sit down, Ms Smith and Mohammed Ali.'

10.24 Showing appropriate concern for distressed parties and witnesses

Appropriate concern can only be generated if there is empathy with the person concerned. Can you put yourself into their shoes? Can you see the situation from their point of view? What might a mother see, hear and feel in care proceedings? ...

> 'The evidence isn't going well. It's coming over that I'm not fit to look after my own child. The magistrates must think that I'm a bad parent – a bad person even. I'm about to lose my son to the authorities. I still love his dad but he won't even look at me in court. Where did everything go so wrong? I'm just giving stupid answers to their clever questions. Just as my mother said, 'it's all sewn up between the social workers and the court – you can't change anything.' I've lost him.' Tears of frustration well up.

Then the chairman says 'We can understand that you're distressed but today we all want to work out what is going to be best for John. Not surprisingly we can see that you're upset. You know more about John than anyone else and we need to hear from you. This is important so we'll take a short break so that you can get some strength back. Then we'll finish off the cross-examination and we'll hear what you think should happen.'

That day John went home with his mum and dad. It was against the guardian's recommendation but it was the right decision. They were ever grateful to a good chairman and a competent bench.

CHAPTER 12
COMPETENCE 12
Money orders enforcement

The ability to apply effective enforcement of financial penalties (and other financial orders)

Unless stated otherwise the enforcement of compensation, costs, legal aid contributions and crown court fines are the same as for enforcement of magistrates court fines.

INTRODUCTION

Why is effective money enforcement so important?

- Money order penalties comprise around 96% of the magistrates' court's penalties.
- It is therefore essential in order to maintain credibility and authority.
- Fines are usually the first penalty for an offender. A message that 'the court means business' at this level of offending and penalty can go a long way to preventing further offending.
- There are court budget implications in ensuring that arrears do not accrue.
- In 2000, the Prison Service reported that 1200 people were jailed for not paying motoring fines and 80 were jailed for defaulting on a television licence fee penalty. The 'teeth' are there, bringing a serious need to tread carefully, but not necessarily, slowly!

12.1 Means Enquiries

A structured means enquiry is the linchpin of effective enforcement. The purpose of the enquiry is to reach an order which the particular defaulter will obey – whether by encouragement or threat depending upon the individual's likely response. There are a wide variety of options which aim to deal with individual ability and attitude. The responses to the means enquiry must therefore be used as evidence of character and motivation as well as a list of figures.

A specimen list of questions/possible responses is produced at section 14 following the discussion of the various options and so identifying the significance of the various questions. Essentially the enquiry is aimed at establishing why payment has not been made as ordered, identifying the financial situation of the defaulter and determining the most productive disposal.

A means enquiry must take place before the imposition of custody in default.

The Practice Direction (Justices: Clerk to Court) 2000 emphasises that the role of the clerk is to assist the court in the means enquiry and they must not act in an adversarial or partisan manner. With the agreement of the justices, the clerk may ask questions of the defaulter to elicit information and may advise on the available options. However, it is inappropriate for the clerk to set out to establish wilful refusal or culpable neglect, to offer an opinion on the facts or to urge a particular course of action upon the justices. The spirit of this direction applies equally to the bench and magistrates must not cross the line from objective enquiry into prosecution mode.

12.2 Warrant for arrest

Whilst individual courts use different strategies for default collection, there is one common final step and that is to issue a warrant of arrest in order to conduct a means enquiry with one final common sanction, namely custody in default.

The optional strategies before issuing a warrant include the following:

(1) Making 'enforcement' orders at the point of imposition, namely:
- Money payment supervision orders.
- Attachment of earnings orders with the consent of the defaulter, or
- Fixing a date for a means enquiry if payments are not made as ordered.

(2) Sending a reminder letter which may include an option to either write to the court or attend for administrative discussion or hearing to make a payment plan.

(3) Issue of a distress warrant (see below).

(4) Issue of a warrant for overnight detention.

(5) Issue of a summons to attend default court.

Should the options prove to be unsuccessful, then a warrant of arrest will be issued. A discussion of the various court options follows.

12.3 ATTACHMENT OF EARNINGS (AEO)

- **Legal**

The court may direct that an employer deducts specified sums and pays them to the court. The order may be made in default proceedings without the defaulter's/employer's consent. Both the defendant and the employer must notify the court of any change of employment. An administration charge may also be deducted by the employer. It is an offence for the employer to fail to comply with the order.

- **Practical**

The court must fix a **Normal Deduction Rate,** payable after obligatory deductions e.g. £10 per week.

It must also fix a **Protected Earnings Rate,** below which a deduction will not be made e.g. £140 per week. The protected rate will take account of commitments and responsibilities and should normally cover at least the DSS income support rate, particularly if the defaulter is financially responsible for dependants. Shortfalls may be deducted in subsequent weeks.

Full employment details must be obtained – job title, number, works address and wages office address. The order may subsequently be discharged or transferred to a subsequent employer.

AEO.

YES!

Avoids temptation to spend the money
Large organisations are familiar with debt deductions
Anonymity can be preserved in a large organisation
Likelihood of payment is high if secure employment.

NO!

Knowledge of conviction may put job at risk
Inconvenience of payment may put job at risk
Firm may be too small to cope efficiently with order
Defaulter is on a short-term or temporary contract.

12.4 & 12.5 DISTRESS WARRANTS and ROLE OF BAILIFFS

Legal

A distress warrant may be issued before or after court default proceedings. It may issue forthwith or be postponed upon payment terms e.g. distress warrant postponed upon payment of £5 per week. The warrant authorises entry and removal by the bailiffs of money and goods to the value of the financial penalty + the bailiff's costs. The distress warrant may be issued by a single justice or delegated court officer.

The court must be satisfied that there are likely to be distrainable goods e.g. the defaulter admits that he is the sole owner of a vehicle and it is not subject to any hire purchase arrangement.

The defaulter must be given the opportunity to make representations about the proposed distress warrant e.g. to emphasise that the car is essential for employment.

The bailiffs may only enter property lawfully and they cannot break into property. They may not take clothes, bedding or tools of trade of the defaulter or his family. Six days must pass before any goods are sold and household goods must not be removed until the day of sale. It is an offence for the defaulter to remove or sell goods which have been distrained upon.

The distress warrant will be cancelled upon payment to the bailiffs.

The qualified right to respect for private and family life is engaged and it is important to consider whether it is proportionate to issue a distress warrant. Arguably a small sum for a minor offence may not warrant such an intrusion with the removal of family furniture until other efforts have been made to collect.

Practical

When a postponed distress warrant is issued the defendant should be warned that the warrant will issue upon one missed payment and will result in the bailiffs visiting the defaulter's home and collecting goods/payment of the outstanding amount. When a vehicle is involved, it is helpful to the bailiffs if the registration number is obtained in court. The reality is usually for the vehicle to be clamped by the bailiffs in the driveway until payment is forthcoming.

It should also be pointed out that the defaulter will be liable for the bailiff's expenses in addition to the penalty, even if cash is paid in full to the bailiff.

DISTRESS

YES!

Available goods and no good reason why they should not be taken

No cost to the court

Postponement allows the opportunity to pay as ordered.

NO!

Defaulter does not own sufficient goods
Property is subject to hire purchase or joint ownership
Removal will deprive defaulter of livelihood and means to pay.

12.6 DEDUCTIONS FROM INCOME SUPPORT (ATTACHMENT OF BENEFIT ORDER - ABO)

Legal

The court may apply to the DSS adjudication officer for any default financial penalty to be deducted by weekly amounts from income support and job-seekers allowance. The current deduction rate is £2.70 per week (April 2001). Default is necessary and the order cannot be made at imposition. Only one application may be entertained at one time, albeit it may contain several fines. New fines therefore cannot be 'tagged on' to existing orders – a later application must be made.

Practical

- Check the full name of the actual claimant.
- Obtain date of birth, benefit office and national insurance number in order to expedite the application.
- Check for any existing deductions. The maximum deduction is 3 arrears orders + council tax + child maintenance and no further deductions may be ordered.
- Check that the benefit office and amount are likely to remain static - any change may terminate the attachment.
- Adjourn for a period, usually 4 weeks, for the application to be made, adjudicated upon and notified by DSS to the court and defaulter. The defaulter need not attend on the adjourned date if the attachment is effected.

Whilst payment at the default hearing is always to be encouraged, there is an administrative problem in ordering further payment in the interim period as the attachment will be made in the sum applied for at the time of the court hearing.

ABO

YES!
No additional expense to the defaulter
No effort required of the defaulter
Benefit to administration of bulk transactions
High likelihood of payment.

NO!
Able to pay **substantially** more than fixed deduction rate
Re-assessment of benefit anticipated
Travellers without a fixed address.

12.7/12.8 MONEY PAYMENT SUPERVISION ORDER (MPSO) and ROLES OF THE PROBATION SERVICE

Legal

The order may be made on conviction or subsequently. Whilst consent is not required, it is relevant to the assessment of co-operation. The order may be made in absence, provided that a written notice is issued. The supervisor must be specifically appointed e.g. a civilian enforcement officer or named probation officer.

The supervisor's duty is to 'advise and befriend the defendant with a view to inducing him/her to pay the sum adjudged to be paid and thereby avoid committal to custody, and to give any information required about conduct and means'. A report should be obtained before committal which will briefly outline the efforts to encourage payment and any response.

The order may be discharged at any stage e.g. failure to respond to correspondence or personal visits.

Practical

The order is not a probation order and in busy courts the liaison may be based upon the defaulter taking the initiative and making contact for any advice rather than on home visits. When this is the situation, it should therefore be made clear that the service is essentially the use of a given telephone number, if and only if, a payment cannot be made. It is not usually an order based upon waiting for an appointment to be made but an opportunity for the defaulter to seek advice if necessary.

The court will normally give delegated powers to the money payments supervision officer to vary payment rates and due dates of payment. This may be particularly helpful in situations where the court wishes to avoid unnecessary warrants for missed payments in short-term, problematic situations.

In some courts the task is undertaken by the probation service and in others it is undertaken by the court's civilian enforcement officers. In any event it is helpful to name the supervising probation officer if there is already a probation order in force as the payment of the fine should become part of the probation plan.

MPSO

YES!

Defaulter appears incapable of managing finances
Defaulter needs encouragement and/or discipline
Court foresees genuine temporary difficulties - e.g. hospital stays, rehousing.

NO!

Defaulter able to manage finances - previous payments, sustained catalogue payments
Unlikely to respond - previous breach of community orders.

12.9/12.10 WILFUL REFUSAL/CULPABLE NEGLECT AND COMMITTAL TO PRISON

Legal

The following aspects must be satisfied before a defaulter is committed to prison:

- The defaulter must be present and a means enquiry must be held. Either before or during the enquiry a justice may order a defaulter to furnish a statement of means within a specified period.

- Wilful refusal or culpable neglect must be found. This must be established beyond all reasonable doubt. Wilful refusal means a deliberate defiance of a court order. Culpability, or blameworthiness, requires a purposeful unwillingness rather than sheer inability. A useful test is to ask whether the court feels that this defaulter is actually capable of being culpable? If not, the court may be limited to an attachment of benefit and one day's detention.

- The court must consider or try all other methods of enforcing payment and it must appear to the court that they are inappropriate or unsuccessful.

- The court must be of the opinion that no other method of dealing with the defaulter is appropriate.

- Legal representation must be considered and the court records must be disclosed to the defaulter if sought, with proper facility for the preparation of the defence (Article 6(3)). In the community charge case of Benham v. UK 1996 the applicant was imprisoned for non-payment of community charge. The European Court held that legal aid should have been granted because the proceedings were 'not straightforward'; the test for culpable neglect was hard to understand and the deprivation of liberty was at stake. The proceedings were classified on this basis as 'criminal proceedings' which brings with it the right to legal aid, disclosure and proper facility for the preparation of the defence. In practical terms, it is likely to be a referral to the duty solicitor.

- Imprisonment is a major interference with private and family life and the court must consider whether imprisonment in default is proportionate or not, particularly if the amount outstanding is small and other options have not been carefully considered.

- Reasons must be given, verbally in court, and in writing, for discarding all non-custodial options in respect of all defaulters – extended from the 'under-21s only' to all defaulters by the requirement to give reasons under the Human Rights Act.

* The above restrictions do not apply if the defaulter is already serving a custodial sentence.

Imprisonment may be imposed forthwith on the following scale. If part payments are made then the period is reduced proportionately.

Maxima

To £200	7 days
£201 to £500	14 days
£501 to £1,000	28 days
£1001 to £2,500	45 days

Where there are consecutive terms for a number of fines on one warrant, the total must not exceed the term for the aggregate of the sums due e.g. total of 8 fines of £100 each is £800 = 28 days.

Where separate warrants are issued and consecutive terms are allowed in law, the court should consider the totality and nature of the offences and the extent of the default in determining an appropriate period e.g. 8 fines of £100 each could carry 7 days each = 56 days. However this may be considered over punitive if they are all minor road traffic matters and on a single commitment they would carry only 28 days.

As with any custodial penalty, it is important to determine an appropriate period based upon the particular facts rather than simply imposing the maximum period available.

"The purpose of all enforcement measures is to compel payment and commitment to prison is no exception. If a defaulter actually serves a period of imprisonment, enforcement in his case has failed." (Lord Chancellor's Division Best Practice Guide 1992).

12.11 SUSPENDED COMMITTAL

Legal

If the court 'thinks expedient to do so', it may fix a term of imprisonment and postpone the issue of the warrant on payment terms e.g. pay £5 per week or serve 7 days imprisonment in default.

The terms may subsequently be varied and the commitment may be further postponed if circumstances change.

Following default, the defaulter must be notified in writing of the date and time when the issue of the commitment will be considered by the court. The court must be satisfied that the defaulter is aware of the notice e.g. cannot proceed to commit in absence if the notice is returned in the post.

The date set for consideration must be at least 21 days after the notice is issued. The defaulter is invited to attend or make written representations as to why the commitment should not be issued e.g. employment has ceased and income has reduced substantially. In such circumstances the order may well be varied by reducing the payment amount and re-suspending the commitment.

When the defaulter fails to respond to the notice, the commitment may be issued in the absence of the defaulter for arrest and he may be arrested and taken straight to prison unless the full amount is paid. It is true to say that few defaulters do attend court on notice and most defaulters do not attend default court again after a suspended committal has been issued. There must be a recognition that a suspended committal is therefore a serious order to make.

12.12 REMITTING OF ALL OR PART OF THE SUMS DUE

12.12.1 Remission

The court may remit the whole or any part of a fine it thinks just to do so, 'having regard to a change of circumstances.'

Example:

> Fine was fixed on a net income of £200 pw at level B = £200, but defendant subsequently becomes unemployed and in receipt of £41 pw benefits. It would be appropriate to remit the fine down to £41.

12.12.2 Rectification

The court may also rectify a fine if it has been fixed in the absence of sufficient details of the defendant's financial circumstances, particularly if the fine has been fixed in absence and based upon 'local average net income' and a 'not guilty' plea.

A defaulter may well attend default court and indicate that he was simply unaware of the proceedings. He does not wish to make a statutory declaration as he states that he would plead guilty and wishes to finalise the matter today. He is in receipt of benefits. The figure could then be adjusted to the appropriate net income band with credit for co-operation.

Rectification may also be appropriate if it subsequently transpires that the defendant has multiple outstanding fines. What is a reasonable global figure which can realistically be paid?

It is important to assess whether the sentence has been fixed on the guideline figure, without any aggravating or mitigating features e.g. defendant was earning £300 – a level B fine for a guilty plea would be £200. If it has been pitched higher on the basis of aggravating features, then the reduction to a net income of £60 should carry a higher fine than £40. The court did not give a straight 1/3 credit at sentence and the default court should reflect this at rectification.

12.12.3 Review of compensation orders

The court may discharge or reduce compensation orders on limited statutory grounds. The most frequently used ground is that 'the defendant has suffered a substantial reduction of his means which was unexpected at the time when the order was made and that his means seem unlikely to increase for a considerable period'.

It must be remembered that the maximum period for repayment of a compensation order is 2 years, or exceptionally 3 years, as opposed to the 12 months maximum for a fine. The compensatee must be notified and allowed to make representations at the review hearing as to the proposed discharge or amendment. Representations may be made in writing. It is important to explain the basis of the application clearly to the compensatee and even give some guidance as to the criteria for payment and review of compensation and the right to pursue any balance through the county court.

12.12.4 One day's detention

It is not possible to remit costs, excise penalties, back duty, or crown court fines (except with the consent of the crown court), and the use of 1 day's detention (possibly with immediate release) is often required to 'clear the books' in such cases in 'the interests of justice.'

One day's detention may be served either in court or in a police station until 8pm at the latest. The only criterion is that it is in the 'interests of justice' to impose one day's detention as an alternative to the money order. It can also be used for magistrates' court fines if there is not a change of circumstances to justify remission e.g. defaulter is realistically incapable of paying the fine and he is 'incapable of being culpable' to justify custody.

The task of considering potential remission/rectification/review/1 day's detention may usefully be explored at the outset of the decision-making process so that 'the bill' is effectively fixed before determining how it is going to be paid. Clearly, the amount may affect the suitability of particular options, especially the prospect of effective distress.

12.13 OTHER ORDERS

12.13.1 Attendance Centre Order

Legal

An important sanction particularly for the youth who is made responsible to pay his/her own financial penalty. The court may order a person under 25 to attend an attendance centre for a minimum of 12 hours and a maximum of 24 hours (to 18 years) and 36 hours (to 25 years), in default of paying a financial penalty. The defaulter must be present when the order is made and culpable neglect/wilful refusal must be found. All other options should therefore be considered first.

The centre must be available locally and be reasonably accessible. Part payment will reduce the hours pro-rata.

On failure to attend without reasonable excuse, or on breach of the rules, the defaulter may be brought back before the court in breach proceedings. The options are to (a) allow the order to continue, (b) fine for breach (additionally!) and allow to continue (c) revoke the order and consider other options – possibly custody will be the only remaining option.

The venue and date of first attendance should be notified verbally before leaving the court and by formal order.

ACO

YES!
Substantial restriction on liberty
Not as severe as custody - and cheaper!
Social skills training and discipline may be beneficial.

NO!
Facility is not available in locality or only for males.
Defaulter states that he/she will not attend
Previous breach of community penalties.

12.13.2 Overnight detention

Legal

Power to order overnight detention until 8 a.m. the following day (police may allow earlier release to enable defaulter to attend work). A default hearing is unnecessary.

Practical

This option is used by some courts as a method of collecting small fines under threat of overnight detention, rather than going through the default court process. In reality the police will usually allow a period for the cash to be obtained before arrest.

The longer period may be more appropriate for the punitive scenario mentioned under the one day detention section. Legal representation, perhaps through the duty solicitor, should be offered if this option is being considered in court.

12.13.3 High Court/County Court

Such orders are effectively pursued by the justices' clerk. The court may usefully identify whether there is any possibility of such an order and if so, then retire to consult the clerk. The occurrence of such orders is very low. They are complicated to pursue and the reality is that substantial assets are usually available and the defaulter is either in a position therefore to pay up or be subjected to a distress warrant. The mere threat of applying for a garnishee order, charging order or appointing a receiver may well be sufficient to encourage payment.

- Attachment of debts and garnishee proceedings

Defaulter's own debtors are ordered to pay debts direct to the court if the debts have already been proved. This arises in the situation where a defaulter says that he would pay 'if only his cash-flow was sorted out and he was paid all that he was owed'. Basically the court can join in to take the monetary orders straight from his debtors.

- Charging order

Impose a charge on land or on an interest in land of the defaulter, or on his securities if the property is owned absolutely. He owns his house solely and outright but will not pay the £1000 compensation – a charge for the £1000 can be imposed on the house.

- Appointment of a receiver for land or rent and profits

This could arise if the defaulter is a landlord whose income is essentially rent. The court cannot make an attachment of earnings but this is the second best option – to appoint a receiver for the rents and hand them to the court. It is important to check that there are no 3rd party rights to the rent.

In all three situations the court must consider the potential expense of taking the action and the prospects of recovery of the sum due. A distress warrant should always be tried first.

12.14 SPECIMEN MEANS ENQUIRY

D is a male aged 20 years old. Six months ago he was fined £60 for driving without insurance and ordered to pay costs of £40. He was ordered to pay at the rate of £10 per week. Nothing has been paid.
A warrant has been outstanding for several weeks and he appears before the court in custody. He has declined legal representation.

Chairman - C

Nothing at all has been paid on this fine. Bearing in mind that the court may send you to prison today in default for 7 days, please explain to us why you have not paid.

(Ability and attitude?)

Defaulter - D

I lost my job after the court case because I was disqualified from driving. I've been on job seekers allowance since then and have a lot of debts which I took on when I was working. I've been through a really bad time and the fine just slipped my mind.

C. How much money do you have with you today?

(Can a forthwith order be made?)

D. About £8. – but I need my bus fare to get home and meant to do some shopping

C. Did you take any action at all to sort out the fine?

(Culpability?)

D. No. I kept meaning to pay it. My mum said she would come down and sort it all out but she didn't bother.

C. When did you become aware of the warrant for your arrest?

(Culpability? + warrants often record the efforts and communications made with defaulters)

D. I had a letter a few weeks ago and it said that I had to pay up in full or there would be a warrant. I couldn't pay it all at once. I didn't hear any more until I was arrested this morning.

C. What is the difference in your income?

(Possible remission)

D. From about £90 take home pay down to £33 benefit.

C. Do you have any savings?

(Lump sum payment?)

D. No. Not now.

C. So your income is £33 benefit. Is that all?

(Extras?)

D. Yes.

C. Are any deductions being taken from your benefit to cover debts?

(Explore suitability for deduction of benefit – maximum of 3 deductions)

D. Yes. £8.10 a week for gas, electric and rent arrears. £2.70 for each of them. That's why I only end up with just over £33 a week.

C. Is your income likely to alter in the near future?
D. I'm going to sell raffle tickets at the football ground from next Saturday and I'll get about £10 a week for that.
(Saturday commitment rules out attendance centre order)

C. Tell us now about what you have to pay out each week
(An open question as a starter may produce a longer list than a series of closed questions from the bench and provides a basis for detailed questions if necessary)
D. Board of £15 a week
Catalogue of £3 a week

C. What are you buying?
D. A television

C. When did you take on that payment? (*evidence of culpability*?)
D. Last year when I was working

C. How much is left to pay? (*possible distress if imminent ownership*)
D. About £30

C. Do you pay your catalogue regularly? (*may rule out any need for supervision order*)
D. Yes – or they'll take it back

C. Do you have any other items on hire purchase?
(more likely to reveal items for distress than asking if anything can be sold!)
D. No.

C. So, all of your property belongs to you, does it?
D. Yes, but I'm back now with my mum and all I have are my clothes and telly. I still have to pay off the debts from the flat as well, but they're taken from my benefit.

C. And the car – was that your own car? (*traffic offence + highly distrainable item*)
D. Yes, but I had to sell it to pay off debts. I only got enough to pay off the loan.

C. If you are allowed your liberty today, how would you propose to pay this fine?
(an offer from the defaulter may carry more commitment to pay than one which is imposed – it may also be higher!)

D. £5 a week

DECISION-MAKING PROCESS

1. Is the fine figure appropriate?

Remission of the fine is appropriate because of the change in financial circumstances. A lower net income applies and with credit at band B, this would be a remission from £60 down to £22 fine (£33 income less 1/3 credit) + £40 costs.

2. Consider all options – inappropriate or unsuccessful? Why?

- Distress warrant – *no goods apart from clothes and a television on hire purchase.*
- Attachment of earnings – *unemployed.*
- Attachment of benefit – *maximum deductions already taken.*
- Money payment supervision order – *capable of managing finances if so desires – catalogue payments sustained.*

3. Is there evidence of wilful refusal or culpable neglect?

Yes. Defaulter is capable of being culpable. He understood the obligation and had the money to pay. He was aware that proceedings were being taken for default and chose to avoid paying.

4. Is a community order appropriate?

Attendance centre order is not appropriate as he has a Saturday job and can pay the fine from the income.

5. Is there no other method of dealing with the defaulter?

No. Custody of 7 days.

6. The purpose of committal is to compel payment rather than serve a custodial sentence. Should the opportunity be given for payment by instalments in this case?

Yes. Pay £5 per week or serve 7 days detention.

DECISION

"We are going to help you today. The fine will be reduced from £60 to £22 because your financial circumstances have changed since the order was imposed. The costs of £40 will also have to be paid. That's a total of £62.

Secondly we have considered all options but feel that they would not be appropriate. We cannot issue a distress warrant on your goods because you do not have anything to take. We cannot deduct directly from your wage because you are not working at the moment. We cannot ask for a deduction directly from your benefit because there are already the maximum of 3 deductions for other debts. We do not think it is necessary for a money payment supervision order to be imposed because you are quite capable of paying your catalogue on a regular basis and we believe that you can manage to pay your fine as well. We cannot send you to the attendance centre as you have a Saturday job and we will not deprive you of the income.

We find that there is culpable neglect in this case. You were well aware of the obligation to pay and you have had the money to pay. You will therefore pay £5 per week or serve a period of 7 days detention in a Young Offenders Institution. You will not have to serve the 7 days provided that you pay the £5 every week. The first payment will be made today and every Monday by 4pm.

Failure to pay a single instalment on time means that the commitment may be issued and you will be arrested and taken straight to the Young Offenders Institution. Do you understand?"

12.15 Enforcement of council tax

This enforcement of council tax is a regular activity in court. The process must be followed carefully as there have been many successful challenges in this area.

Pre-court:

- Local authority serve (i) Demand notice (ii) Reminder notice (iii) Final notice.
- Local authority make complaint for a liability order.
- Issue of a summons by a single justice or justices' clerk.
- Date fixed for applications for liability orders to be made.

Court hearing:

The council must satisfy the court that:

- The council tax has been set by resolution of the authority – a certified copy of the resolution.
- A sum has been demanded in accordance with the regulations i.e. appropriate notices served – computer records compiled by the authority are admissible if legally certified as 'evidence compliant' (clerk will check).
- A summons has been served.

Liability order:

A liability order must be issued unless the court is not satisfied on one of the above elements. The order will include costs and gives the local authority the power to take enforcement action e.g. issue distress warrant, attach benefits.

Committal proceedings:

- Local authority must attempt to levy distress before committal.
- When measures are ineffective the local authority may request a means enquiry with a view to commital to prison in default.
- Summons or warrant issued.
- Defaulter must be present.
- The Administrative Court has recently confirmed that 3 years should be the maximum period for payment of council tax arrears i.e. compares to compensation order maximum.
- Legal representation must be considered.
- Court papers must be disclosed if sought.
- Private and confidential facilities must be available for the defence.
- Means enquiry must be conducted.

The court may impose a period of up to 3 months if satisfied that failure to pay was due to wilful refusal or culpable neglect.

- Relevant period to assess culpability begins with the issue of the liability order.
- Consider all options as for a fine defaulter and suggest use of fine default custody maxima as a guideline.
- Give reasons.

Courts powers.

- May issue warrant of commitment.
- May issue suspended warrant of commitment – there will be a further hearing before the actual issue (unlike a fine default commitment).
- Adjourn or dismiss the application.
- Remission – seek representations of local authority before taking this step.

There has been much controversy about the payment of local taxes over the years and enforcement must be conducted efficiently so that there is a clear message that everyone has to pay – either the cash, or the consequences.

Effective enforcement of money orders is important. Most people do pay – often with enormous difficulty. Ensuring that everyone 'pays their dues' is one of the greatest acts of fairness and equality performed by magistrates.

APPENDIX 1

EUROPEAN CONVENTION – DECISION MAKING GUIDE KEY POINTS

STAGE ONE. Is a right or freedom under the Convention engaged?

▼

STAGE TWO. Which Article and what type is it?

Absolute rights. Art. 2 – Right to life. Art. 3 – Prohibition of torture, inhuman and degrading treatment (*subject to 'minimum level of severity'*). Art. 4 – Prohibition of slavery. Art. 7 – Prohibition of punishment without law *i.e. certainty and definition of any obligation is essential e.g. what is 'good behaviour'?*

Limited rights. Art. 4(2) – Prohibition on forced labour. Art. 5 – Right to liberty. Art. 6 – Right to a fair trial (*see next page for the 'bundles of rights')*.

Qualified rights. Art. 8 – Right to respect for private and family life and home. Art. 9 – Freedom of thought, conscience and religion. Art. 10 – Freedom of expression. Art. 11 – Freedom of assembly and association.

▼

STAGE THREE. Has the Convention been breached?

Absolute rights. Yes. No limitations or qualifications! e.g. Art. 7- certainty.

Limited rights. Check the list of limitations, e.g.

Art. 4(2) Forced labour – Limitations: Work done in course of detention or during conditional release; emergencies in the community; normal civic obligations; service of a military character.

Art. 5 Liberty – Limitations: After conviction by competent court; arrest on reasonable suspicion; for non-compliance with court order *e.g. breach of bail, probation;* to prevent committing an offence or 'fleeing' *(i.e. the usual bail exceptions which enable restrictions on liberty by custody or conditions).*

Qualified rights. Arts. 8–11. Check whether the 3 qualifications apply.

1. Is the restriction legal, clear and accessible? e.g. statute. Is it lawful and capable of being understood? Could an individual find out clearly what the law is?
2. Does it pursue a legitimate aim i.e. is it justifiable? e.g. 'prevention of crime and disorder' *with real evidence of that likelihood*; 'protection of rights/ freedoms/morals of others'.
3. Is it proportionate? i.e. no more than is necessary in a democratic society or is it 'a sledgehammer to crack a nut'?

If 'yes' to all 3 questions, then the qualifications apply and there is no breach. e.g. bail condition 'not to associate with X' – Art. 11 is engaged. (1) Lawful = Bail Act (2) Legitimate aim = prevent offending (3) Proportionate?

▼

STAGE FOUR. Identify the source of the breach and take relevant action.

Primary legislation e.g. statute. If it cannot be read compatibly e.g. by adding words, proceed to sentence. The High Court may later make a declaration of incompatibility and fast track statutory change will be set in motion.

Secondary legislation and case law. If it cannot be read compatibly then ignore and apply Convention rights instead (unless legislation is primary-dependent). Apply common-sense actions to maintain rights/freedoms.

▼

STAGE FIVE. Prepare basis for decision using a structured approach and reach a decision.

STRUCTURE FOR JUDGEMENT AND REASONS

BAIL

- ADJOURNMENT – Why can't the case go ahead today? Why is the delay necessary?
  Why this period? (Art. 6)
  What is going to happen in the meantime?
- BAIL – Why is unconditional bail denied? (Art. 5)
  What are the exceptions and reasons found?
  Why are the conditions necessary and proportionate? (Arts. 8 –11)
- CUSTODY – Why is a remand in custody for this period necessary?

VERDICT

- *WHAT NEEDS TO BE PROVED AND BY WHOM?*
- FACTS NOT IN DISPUTE
- FACTS IN DISPUTE
- FINDINGS OF FACT – preferred evidence and why?
- CONVENTION ISSUES AND DETERMINATION e.g. inferences from silence?
- IS CASE PROVED?

SENTENCE

OFFENCE SERIOUSNESS – aggravating/mitigating circumstances etc.
OFFENDER MITIGATION – credit for co-operation etc. Defendant's net income (fines).
OBJECTIVES – what is the bench trying to achieve and why?
OPTIONS - is the final penalty proportionate to seriousness?

ARTICLE 6. RIGHT TO A FAIR TRIAL.

Civil and criminal

- A fair and public hearing *(+ effective participation).*
- Within a reasonable time *(not left in state of uncertainty for too long).*
- By an independent and impartial tribunal.
- Judgement to be pronounced publicly (*basis for decision must be given)* unless limitations apply e.g. would prejudice interests of justice. *Transparency!*

'Criminal' offences

- Presumption of innocence until proved guilty.
- Informed of nature of accusation promptly and in language he understands.
- Defend himself in person or advocate of choice, or free legal advice if interests of justice so require.
- Time *and confidential* facilities to prepare defence.
- Examine live witnesses.
- Obtain attendance of witnesses (+ *disclosure of material for/against).*
- Free assistance of interpreter *(no means test).*

APPENDIX 2
BASIC COMPETENCES - SPECIMEN APPRAISAL FORM

BASIC COMPETENCES FOR ALL MAGISTRATES (Numbers 1 to 4)

KNOWLEDGE COMPETENCES

LEVEL 1.
The standard required for these competences is the ability to give *one* relevant sentence only. Only 3 competences will be selected by the appraiser for comment.

COMPETENCE 1

1 House of Lords, Appeal Court, High Court
2 Civil Division/Crown Court
3 Criminal Division/Crown Court
4 Magistrates' Court
5 Appeals
6 European Court of Justice
8 Home Office, Lord Chancellor's Dept.
9 Police, Prison and Probation
11 Other prosecuting agencies/users
12 Legal profession/paralegals
13 Legislation on which matters brought
14 Community safety legislation
15 General licensing
16 Role of local authorities
17 Other agencies and court users
18-21 Local area
22-26 Local community
27 Magistrates Courts Committee
28 Local Advisory Committee
29 Specialist panels
32 Liaison judge
33 Sitting patterns
34 Bench policies and procedure
36 Magistrates' Association activities
37 Informal activities

COMPETENCE 2

1 Laying an information
2 Issuing a summons
3 Issuing a warrant
4 Community safety
5 TV licences
6 General licences (if listed for all JPs)
7 Prosecution outline
8 Prosecution case
10 Defence case
14 Sequence and purpose of questions
16 Hearsay evidence (an example)
17 Difference in civil/criminal cases
18 Role of police
19 Role of Crown Prosecution Service
20 Role of e.g. health authorities
21 Prosecutor in court
22 Defence lawyer in court
23 Role of witnesses
24 Statutory time limits
25 Court diary
26 Case in court for the first time
31 Police, CPS, probation
32 Court clerk
33 Court office
34 Bench itself
35 Lay magistrate sitting alone
36 Principle of justice delayed
40 Utilities and others
42 Emergency Protection orders
43 Passport endorsements
44 Limits of JPs power

COMPETENCE 3

1 Different cultures and ethnic minority communities
2 National and local population statistics
3 Disadvantaged and vulnerable groups
5 Relevant equality legislation inc. Oaths Act
10 Body language

Please indicate the 3 competences on which an outline was requested. Please make a brief note of the basis of any recommendation for further development or training.

Any level 1 competences which are not ticked in the PDL ....

LEVEL 2.
The standard required for these competences is the ability to give 3 or 4 sentences on each heading and sub-heading. Only 3 headings/sub-headings will be selected by the appraiser for discussion.

COMPETENCE 1

4 Magistrates court – summary jurisdiction
5 Appeals from Magistrates Courts
7 European Convention on Human Rights
11 Crown Prosecution Service
31 Bench Training and Development Committee
35 Training, mentoring, appraisals

COMPETENCE 2

6 General licences (if listed for all JPs)
9 No case to answer criteria
11 Verdict – structured approach
12 Mitigation – inc. record//PSRs/SSRs
13 Sentence decisions:
'Seriousness'
Structured approach agenda
Each option:
- Discharge
- Fine
- Compensation
- Costs
- Attendance centre order
- Community service order
- Combination order
- Curfew order
- Drug treatment and testing order
- Probation order
- Custody
- Exclusion order
- Restraining order
- Binding over order
- Endorsement
- Disqualification (discretionary/obligatory)
- Committal for sentence

15 Tests of evidence/burdens of proof matters
28 Adjournments and effects
29 Remands:
- Grounds and exceptions
- Conditions
- Structured approach
- Breach of conditions
- Failure to surrender

30 Plea before venue:
- Mode of trial/MOT guidelines
- Committal proceedings

36 Delay principles
38 Enforcement of disposals:
- Fine default
- Breach of community options

39 Police applications – search warrants
41 Statutory declarations

COMPETENCE 3

4 Discrimination (direct and indirect) and its impact
6 Fairness, impartiality and equal treatment
7 Own conditioning and personal prejudices
8 Labelling and stereotyping *inc. appropriate language*
9 Language and cultural differences inc. different religions

Please indicate the 3 competences on which detail was requested. Please make a brief note of the basis of any recommendation for further development or training.

Any level 2 competences which are not ticked in the PDL ....

OBSERVABLE COMPETENCES

(to be completed in respect of wingers in the adult court only)

The standard required is to demonstrate by behaviour in court and in the retiring room that there is an understanding of relevant knowledge and skills as described in the textbook. The appraiser will consider the various competences which are demonstrated in the particular court and determine whether the appraisee is competent (C) or requires 'personal development' (D) or 'training support' (T) or 'not observed' (N/O).

COMPETENCE 3 – Think and act judicially	C	D	T	N/O
3.6 The exercise of fairness, impartiality and equal treatment.				
COMPETENCE 4 – Participate on the bench				
4.1 As a note-taker. ***Accurate and relevant notes are seen by the appraiser.*** ❒ ***Notes are used and interpreted in discussion.*** ❒				
4.2 As a referrer of handbooks/guidelines. ***Magistrates' guidelines opened at relevant page.*** ❒ ***Used and interpreted correctly by appraisee.*** ❒ ***Ability to make necessary fine calculations.*** ❒				
4.3 Observing particular people/conduct. *Court awareness demonstrated.*				
4.4 Appropriately draw chairman's attention to evidence and procedure if appropriate.				
4.5 Contribute to structured decision-making process + *awareness of relevant agenda.* ***Bail.*** ❒ ***Sentence.*** ❒ ***Trial.*** ❒				
4.6 Helping identify the issues – *before court, during the court and in the retiring room.* ***Adjournment/delay.*** ❒ ***Seriousness.*** ❒ ***Objectives.*** ❒ ***PBV/MOT.*** ❒ ***Bail – grounds and exceptions.*** ❒ ***Trial.*** ❒				
4.7 Helping keep the focus on the evidence as presented. ***Appropriate challenges to speculation, assumptions, 'gut feelings' and 'what if' discussions***				
4.8 Challenging any views that seem partial or discriminatory.				
4.9 Contributing to discussions with the court clerk as appropriate.				
4.10 Assisting in the formulation of announcements to be made in court *particularly reasons and identification of ancillary issues*				

SUPPORTING INFORMATION FOR COMPETENCES APPRAISED:

COURT APPRAISAL SUMMARY

Any competences requiring some personal development.		
Competence number(s).	Basis.	Agreed action.

Any competences requiring some training support.		
Competence number(s).	Basis.	Any suggestions by appraisee.

Appraiser's summary.

Signed: ....

Appraisee's comments.

Signed ....

APPENDIX 3
FINES CALCULATOR

1. Calculate net weekly income.
   Deduct rent/mortgage (or contribution towards) or 1/2 board, and council tax (if local bench policy).
   Ignore child benefit.
2. Relate to band of offence, using figure from 1 (above).

A = 50% of net weekly income.
B = 100% of net weekly income.
C = 150% of net weekly income.

3. Round down to a figure divisible by 3 and deduct 1/3 for guilty plea if appropriate (see table below – rounded down figure on left – credit figure on right).
4. Assess maximum repayable in 12 months from disposable income. Select most serious offence(s) if maximum is reached; mark remainder as 'no separate penalty' and check that the totality is fair and proportionate.
5. Compensation – repayable in 2 years and exceptionally 3 years. Maximum of £300 may be imposed against uninsured driver convicted of 'bad driving' i.e. causing the accident. Physical injuries – see guidelines. Damage – prove, or agree, and may limit due to means. 'Terror and distress' to victim – consider seriousness of offence and means available. Seek representations. Reasons to be given if not awarded.

£

6	4	**84**	56	**162**	108	**240**	160
9	6	**87**	58	**165**	110	**243**	162
12	8	**90**	60	**168**	112	**246**	164
15	10	**93**	62	**171**	114	**249**	166
18	12	**96**	64	**174**	116	**252**	168
21	14	**99**	66	**177**	118	**255**	170
24	16	**102**	68	**180**	120	**258**	172
27	18	**105**	70	**183**	122	**261**	174
30	20	**108**	72	**186**	124	**264**	176
33	22	**111**	74	**189**	126	**267**	178
36	24	**114**	76	**192**	128	**270**	180
39	26	**117**	78	**195**	130	**273**	182
42	28	**120**	80	**198**	132	**276**	184
45	30	**123**	82	**201**	134	**279**	186
48	32	**126**	84	**204**	136	**282**	188
51	34	**129**	86	**207**	138	**285**	190
54	36	**132**	88	**210**	140	**288**	192
57	38	**135**	90	**213**	142	**291**	194
60	40	**138**	92	**216**	144	**294**	196
63	42	**141**	94	**219**	146	**297**	198
66	44	**144**	96	**222**	148	**300**	200
69	46	**147**	98	**225**	150	**303**	202
72	48	**150**	100	**228**	152	**306**	204
75	50	**153**	102	**231**	154	**309**	206
78	52	**156**	104	**234**	156	**312**	208
81	54	**159**	106	**237**	158	**315**	210

APPENDIX 4
SELF-TEST QUIZ

Adult Basics – Chapters 1 to 4

1. What Human Rights Act question should be asked before making a court order?
2. What are the aims of the new National Probation Service?
3. What is the agenda for a structured approach to (a) bail and (b) sentencing?
4. What are the 5 steps in calculating a fair fine?
5. Name the community orders available to the court.
6. What are the 3 most common exceptions to unconditional bail?
7. What is the maximum period for (a) a first remand in custody, (b) a second remand in custody before conviction?
8. What is the Oxford Dictionary definition of 'prejudice'?

Chairmanship – Chapters 5 and 6

1. What are the duties of the legal adviser under the new Practice Direction?
2. What are the 5 elements of a pronouncement?
3. What are the aspects of a competent pronouncement delivery?
4. What questions may be appropriate when an adjournment is sought?
5. What is the structured approach agenda for drawing up reasons following a trial?

Youth – Chapters 7 and 8

1. What is the principal aim of the youth justice system?
2. What is the statutory duty of the youth court?
3. What is the fixed period for an action plan order?
4. Parents must normally attend court, pay money orders and be bound over for which age group?
5. What is the restriction on making a detention and training order on a 12-14 year old for an offence which is considered to be 'so serious'?
6. An offence carrying 14 years imprisonment qualifies for a secure remand, but a 2nd limb must also be satisfied. What is it?

Family – Chapters 9 and 10

1. What is the statutory 'paramount consideration'?
2. What is the usual order of evidence in children's proceedings?
3. What is CAFCASS?
4. What are the time limits for (a) a care order, (b) a supervision order?
5. What are the 'threshold criteria'?
6. What is the maximum penalty for breach of a 'section 8' (private order), non-molestation order and occupation order?

Default – Chapter 12

1. What enforcement orders may be made at imposition?
2. How many debt deductions may be ordered from job-seeker's allowance?
3. What is the duty of a money payment order supervisor?
4. May a compensation order be remitted?
5. What are the legal requirements before ordering imprisonment in default?

APPENDIX 5
ANSWERS

Basics – Chapters 1 to 4

1. Is the interference with rights and freedoms (i.e. the court order) proportionate?
2. Protect the public, reduce re-offending and provide for proper punishment of offenders.
3. Bail – ABC – Adjournment (why? how long?): Bail (why not unconditional bail? Identify exceptions/reasons? Consider possible conditions?): Custody.
   Sentencing – 4'O' – Offence; Offender; Objectives; Options.
4. Guideline band; Net income; Aggravating/mitigating features; Credit for guilty plea; Outgoings and 12 month limit check.
5. Attendance centre order; Community punishment order; Community rehabilitation order; Community punishment and rehabilitation order; Curfew order; Drug Treatment and Testing Order.
6. Fail to surrender; Commit further offences on bail; Interfere with witnesses/obstruct the course of justice.
7. (a) 8 days (b) 28 days
8. Preconceived opinion.

Chairmanship – Chapters 5 and 6

1. Provide justices with advice; assist in formulation of reasons and recording of reasons; ask questions of witnesses and parties; ensure every case is conducted fairly; assist unrepresented parties; ask questions of defaulter.
2. (i) Reasons. (ii) Detail. (iii) Explanation. (iv) Warning. (v) Check understanding.
3. Volume is loud enough for everyone in court to hear easily; Steady pace throughout; Pauses between each piece of information; Changes of tone; make personal to this defendant.
4. What is the reason for the adjournment? What was the anticipated action today? How many previous listings? What steps have been taken to resolve the difficulty? Can it be resolved today/differently? If not, what is realistic minimal period for adjournment?
5. What are the elements of the offence charged? What is the burden of proof and where does it fall? Agreed facts? Facts in dispute? Exclude any inadmissible? Findings of fact and preferred evidence?

Youth – Chapters 7 and 8

1. To prevent offending.
2. To have regard to the welfare of the child/young person.
3. 3 months.
4. 10-15 year olds.
5. Must be a persistent offender. Time limits – 4,6,8,10,12,18,24 months.
6. Court is of the opinion that only remanding to secure accommodation would be adequate to protect the public from serious harm from the defendant.

Family – Chapters 9 and 10

1. The welfare of the child.
2. The applicant; Any party with parental responsibility for the child; Other respondents; The guardian; The child if he is a party and there is no guardian.

3. Children and Family Court Advisory and Support Service (integrated new service which brings together the Family Court Welfare Service and Guardian Ad Litem panels).
4. (a) care order -18th birthday (b) supervision order – 12 months + may extend to 3 years.
5. (a) that the child concerned is suffering, or is likely to suffer, significant harm; and
   (b) that the harm or likelihood of harm is attributable to –
      (i) the care given to the child, or likely to be given to him if the order were not made, not being what it would be reasonable to expect a parent to give him; or
      (ii) the child's being beyond parental control.
6. (a) Pay £50 per day of breach up to £1,000, or a sum up to £5,000, or
   (b) Commit to custody until default is remedied, or for period up to 2 months.

Default – Chapter 12

1. Money payment supervision order, attachment of earnings order, fix review date.
2. 3. (April 2001 = £2.70p per deduction).
3. To advise, assist and befriend with a view to inducing payment + report.
4. Cannot remit, but may review/discharge if unforeseen, substantial and long-term reduction in means. Compensatee's views must be sought.
5. Means enquiry; Wilful refusal/culpable neglect found; Considered or tried all other methods and consider to be inappropriate or unsuccessful; Reasons given for discarding each non-custodial option.

BIBLIOGRAPHY

Ashcroft, P. et al. (1999) *Human Rights and the Courts: Bringing Justice Home.* Winchester: Waterside Press.

Audit Commission Update (1998) *Misspent Youth '98.* Abingdon: Audit Commission Publications.

Bing, I. (1999) *Criminal Proceedings and Sentencing in the Magistrates' Court.* 5th ed. London: Sweet and Maxwell.

Black, J., Bridge, J., and Bond, T. (1998) *A Practical Approach to Family Law.* 5th ed. London: Blackstone Press Limited.

Card, R., and Ward, R. (1998) *The Crime and Disorder Act 1998: A Practitioner's Guide.* Bristol: Jordans.

Draycott, A.T. and Carr, A.P. (1999) *Stone's Justices' Manual 1999.* 131st ed. 3 vols. London: Butterworth & Co. and Shaw & Sons.

Durham Board of Studies (1999) *Magistrates' Handbook: Personal Development Log Support Notes.* Durham: Durham Board of Studies.

Elliot, C. and Quinn, F. (1998) *English Legal System.* 2nd ed. London: Longman.

Gordon, W., Cuddy, P., and Black, J. (1999) *Introduction to Youth Justice: Incorporating An Introduction to the Youth Court.* Winchester: Waterside Press.

Home Office (1997) *No More Excuses – A New Approach to Tackling Youth Crime in England and Wales (Cm. 3809).* London: Home Office.

Home Office (1998) *Youth Justice: the Statutory Principal Aim of Preventing Offending by Children and Young People.* London: Home Office.

Home Office (1999) *Statistics on Race and the Criminal Justice System: A Home Office Publication under s.95 of the Criminal Justice Act 1991.* London: Home Office Research and Statistics Directorate.

Honey, P. (1998) *Improve Your People Skills.* London: Institute of Personnel Management.

Judicial Studies Board (1999) *Race and the Courts: A Short Practical Guide for Judges.* London: Judicial Studies Board.

Justices' Clerks' Society (2000) *Fair Treatment Pack. London: Justices' Clerks' Society.* Winchester: Waterside Press.

Judicial Studies Board (1998) *Magistrates Bench Handbook: A Manual for Lay Magistrates.* London: Judicial Studies Board.

Laken, E., Bazell, C., and Gordon, W. (1997) *Introduction to the Family Proceedings Court.* Winchester: Waterside Press.

Leng, R., Taylor, R., and Wasik, M. (1998) *Blackstone's Guide to the Crime and Disorder Act 1998.* London: Blackstone Press Limited.

Moore, T.G. ed. (1999) *Anthony and Berryman's Magistrates' Court Guide 2000.* London: Butterworths.

NACRO Race and Criminal Justice Unit (1998) *Equal Treatment Training for Lay Magistrates: Training Materials.* London: Judicial Studies Board.

Royal College of Physicians (1995) *Alcohol and Young People.* London: British Paediatric Association.

Starmer, K. (1999) *European Human Rights Law: the Human Rights Act 1998 and the European Convention on Human Rights.* London: Legal Action Group.

Youth Justice Board (2000) *Youth Justice: Working Together: Practitioners' Course Workbook.* London: Youth Justice Board.

INDEX
Youth Court index follows separately

YOUTH COURT INDEX